THE RELEVANCE OF KEYNESIAN ECONOMIC POLICIES TODAY

Also by Philip Arestis

MONEY AND BANKING: Issues for the 21st Century (*editor*)
POST-KEYNESIAN ECONOMIC THEORY (*editor with T. Skouras*)
ON MONEY, METHOD AND KEYNES (*editor with Victoria Chick and Sheila Dow*)
MONEY, PRICING, DISTRIBUTION AND INVESTMENT
THE BIOGRAPHICAL DICTIONARY OF DISSENTING ECONOMICS (*co-edited with Malcolm Sawyer*)

Also by Malcolm Sawyer

ECONOMICS OF INDUSTRIES AND FIRMS: Theories, Evidence and Policy
THEORIES OF THE FIRM
MACROECONOMICS IN QUESTION
BUSINESS, PRICING AND INFLATION
THE ECONOMICS OF MICHAL KALECKI
THE CHALLENGES OF RADICAL POLITICAL ECONOMY
UNEMPLOYMENT, IMPERFECT COMPETITION AND MACROECONOMICS
THE BIOGRAPHICAL DICTIONARY OF DISSENTING ECONOMICS (*co-edited with Philip Arestis*)

The Relevance of Keynesian Economic Policies Today

Edited by

Philip Arestis
Professor of Economics
University of East London

and

Malcolm Sawyer
Professor of Economics
University of Leeds

First published in Great Britain 1997 by
MACMILLAN PRESS LTD
Houndmills, Basingstoke, Hampshire RG21 6XS and London
Companies and representatives throughout the world

A catalogue record for this book is available from the British Library.

ISBN 0–333–66831–6

First published in the United States of America 1997 by
ST. MARTIN'S PRESS, INC.,
Scholarly and Reference Division,
175 Fifth Avenue, New York, N.Y. 10010

ISBN 0–312–16552–8

Library of Congress Cataloging-in-Publication Data
The relevance of Keynesian economic policies today / edited by Philip Arestis and Malcolm Sawyer.
p. cm.
Includes bibliographical references and index.
ISBN 0–312–16552–8
1. Keynesian economics. 2. Economic policy. I. Arestis, Philip, 1941– . II. Sawyer, Malcolm C.
HB99.7.R454 1997
330.15'6—dc20 96–32987
CIP

This book is printed on paper suitable for recycling and made from fully managed and sustained forest sources.

10 9 8 7 6 5 4 3 2
06 05 04 03 02 01 00 99 98 97

Printed in Great Britain by
The Ipswich Book Company Ltd
Ipswich, Suffolk

Contents

Notes on the Contributors

Bruno Amable is a Research Scholar at the Institute National de la Recherche Agronomique (INRA) and a Research Associate with CEPREMAP. He also teaches at the University of Paris XIII. His research interests include growth, institutions and the macroeconomic implications of technological change. He has published in journals and books.

Philip Arestis is Professor of Economics and the Head of Department of Economics, University of East London. He has also taught at the Universities of Surrey and Cambridge (Department of Extra-Mural Studies) and Greenwich University (where he was Head of Economics Division). He was editor of the *British Review of Economic Issues* and joint editor of the *Thames Papers in Political Economy*, and is joint editor of the recently launched *International Papers in Political Economy*. He has been on the editorial board of a number of journals and is a member of the Council of the Royal Economic Society. His publications include his edited *Post-Keynesian Monetary Economics: New Approaches to Financial Modelling* (1988), his co-authored *Introducing Macroeconomics Modelling: An Econometric Study of the United Kingdom* (1982), his co-edited *Post Keynesian Economic Theory: A Challenge to Neo-Classical Economics* (1984), *The Biographical Dictionary of Dissenting Economists* (1992) and *The Elgar Companion to Radical Political Economy* (1993); also his recent book entitled *The Post-Keynesian Approach to Economics: An Alternative Analysis of Economic Theory and Policy* (1992) and his *Money, Pricing, Distribution and Economic Integration* (1997). He has published widely in journals and books in post Keynesian economics, macroeconomics, monetary economics and applied econometrics.

Paul Davidson is currently the occupant of the Holly Chair of Excellence in Political Economy at the University of Tennessee. He is the Editor of the *Journal of Post Keynesian Economics*. He has also been a Visiting Professor at the University of Nice and Latapsis Research Institute, France; Professor of Economics and Associate Director of the Bureau of Economic Research, Rutgers University; Professor, International Summer School, Centro di Studi Economici Avanzati, Italy; Visiting Professor, University of Strasbourg, France; Visiting Professor, Institute for Advanced Studies,

Vienna; Senior Visitor, Cambridge University, UK; Associate Professor of Economics, University of Pennsylvania; Visiting Lecturer, University of Bristol, UK; Assistant Director, Economics Division, Continental Oil Company. Davidson has been consultant to Resources for the Future; Energy Policy Project (Ford Foundation); Canadian Department of Consumer and Corporate Affairs; a member of the Brookings Economic Panel; and Senior Visitor, Bank of England. Davidson has written, edited, or co-authored many books including: *Theories of Aggregate Income Distribution* (1960); *Aggregate Supply and Demand Analysis* (1964); *The Demand And Supply of Outdoor Recreation* (1969); *Money and the Real World* (1972, 1978); *International Money and the Real World* (1982); *Economics for a Civilized Society* (1988, 1996); *Post Keynesian Macroeconomic Theory; A Foundation for Successful Economic Policy in the Twenty-first Century*, (1994). He has authored over 120 professional articles appearing in journals such as *American Economic Review, Economic Journal, Econometrica, Review of Economics and Statistics, Canadian Journal of Economics, Brookings Economics Papers, Economie Appliquée, Chemical Engineering Process, Economic Inquiry, Land Economics and Highly Research Record.*

Johan Deprez is Lecturer in Economics at the California State University. He has also taught at Alabama State University, Texas Tech University, the University of Manitoba, and the University of Tennessee–Knoxville. He has published on a variety of topics in the post Keynesian analysis of macroeconomics, monetary economics, and international economics. These include 'Rediscovering the Missing Visionary of the Middle Way: A Review of Skidelsky on Keynes', *Journal of Post Keynesian Economics*, Spring 1995; 'The Macrodynamics of Advanced Market Economies: The Post Keynesian Perspective of Alfred Eichner', *Social Science Quarterly*, September 1991; 'Vertical Integration and the Problem of Fixed Capital', *Journal of Post Keynesian Economics*, Fall, 1990; and 'The User Cost of Fixed Capital in Keynes' Theory of Investment', in Paul Davidson (ed.), *Can the Free Market Pick Winners? What Determines Investment* (1993). He is currently editing, with John T. Harvey, *Foundations of International Economics: A Post Keynesian Analysis.*

Amitava Krishna Dutt is Professor and Chair of the Department of Economics, University of Notre Dame, USA. He is the author of *Growth, Distribution and Uneven Development* (1990), co-author of *Keynes's Third Alternative?* (1990), co-editor of *New Directions in Development Economics* (1992), co-editor of *States, Markets and Development* (1994), and editor of *New Directions in Analytical Political Economy* (1994) and author of numerous papers on growth and distribution theory, post Keynesian economics, and development and international economics.

Gary A. Dymski is Associate Professor of Economics at the University of California, Riverside. He has also taught at the University of Southern California and at the Bangladesh Institute for Development Studies. He has written numerous articles on banking and monetary theory, urban and financial policy, post Keynesian economics, racial inequality and discrimination, and exploitation. He is a co-author of the study *Taking it to the Bank: Poverty, Race, and Credit in Los Angeles*. He also co-edited the book *Transforming the U.S. Financial System: Equity and Efficiency for the 21st Century* (1993), with Gerry Epstein and Robert Pollin, and co-edited the book *New Directions in Monetary Macroeconomics: Essays in the Tradition of Hyman P. Minsky* (1994) with Robert Pollin. Gary is a Research Associate of the Economic Policy Institute, and a member of the editorial boards of *the International Review of Applied Economics* and *Geoforum*.

E. V. K. FitzGerald is Director of Financial Studies, Queen Elizabeth House, University of Oxford, and a Professorial Fellow of St Antony's College, Oxford. He has also taught at the Universities of Cambridge, Texas (Austin), the Institute of Social Studies (The Hague) and the Universidad Complutense (Madrid). He has been editor of the *Journal of Development Studies*, and is on the editorial board of the *JDS*, *Oxford Development Studies*, *International Papers in Political Economy* and *Economia Critica*. His recent books include *The Macroeconomics of Development Finance: A Kaleckian Analysis of the Semi-Industrialized Economy* (1993). His research currently focuses on a Keynesian approach to the behaviour of international capital markets and their macroeconomic consequences for small open economies.

James K. Galbraith is Professor at the Lyndon B. Johnson School of Public Affairs and at the Department of Government, University of Texas, at Austin, where he teaches economics and a variety of other subjects, and serves as Director of the PhD program in the public policy. He holds degrees from Harvard (AB *magna cum laude*, 1974) and Yale (PhD in Economics, 1981). He studied economics as a Marshall Scholar at King's College, Cambridge, in 1974–5, and then served in several positions on the staff of the US Congress, including Executive Director of the Joint Economic Committee in 1981–2. He was a guest scholar at the Brookings

Institution in 1985. Galbraith is presently writing a book on wage structures and economic inequality, under a grant from the Twentieth Century Fund. He is co-author with William Darity Jr of *Macroeconomics* (1994). He is also the author of *Balancing Acts: Technology, Finance and the American Future* (1989), and co-author with Robert L. Heilbroner of *The Economic Problem* (9th edn, 1991). He contributes frequently to *The American Prospect, Challenge*, the *Texas Observer*, and a variety of professional journals.

Harald Hagemann has the Chair for Economic Theory at the University of Hohenheim in Stuttgart, Germany. He has been Professor of Economics at the University of Bremen (1982–8), Visiting Professor of Economic Theory and Political Economy at the Free University of Berlin (1980–1) and Assistant Professor at the University of Kiel (1977–80) where he got his PhD in Economics in 1977. He was a Fulbright Visiting Professor at the Graduate Faculty of the New School for Social Research in New York in 1986, Visiting Professor at the University of Cambridge in 1989–90 where he also became a Life Member of Clare Hall; he was also an Erasmus Visiting Professor at the University of Bologue in 1996. His main areas of research are macroeconomic theory and policy, technological change and employment, and the history of economic thought. Harald Hagemann is managing editor of *Structural Change and Economic Dynamics*, a member of the editorial board of the *European Journal of the History of Economic Thought* and of the advisory board of other international journals. He has recently been elected as a member of the Executive Committee and the Treasurer of the European Society of the History of Economic Thought.

Laurence Harris is Professor of Economics and Dean of Research at the School of Oriental and African Studies, University of London. He has previously taught at the London School of Economics, Birkbeck College, The Open University, The University of California, Berkeley, University College Irvine, University College Riverside, and the University of Zimbabwe. Books he has written, co-authored or edited include *Monetary Theory* (1981), *Rereading Capital* (1981), *City of Capital* (1983), *Dictionary of Marxist Thought* (1983), *The Peculiarities of the British Economy* (1986), *New Perspectives on the Financial System* (1988), and his articles cover financial economics and macroeconomics as well as other subjects. He has contributed to economic policy analysis in several countries, especially South Africa, Mozambique and their neighbours. Currently his research is on international capital markets and public finance.

Anthony Laramie is Associate Professor of Economics and Chair of the Economics Department at Merrimack College (Massachusetts). He was a Resident Research Scholar at the Jerome Levy Economics Institute of Bard College. Many of the ideas for his contribution were developed while he was at the Levy Institute. He has written numerous articles on the macroeconomic effects and incidence of taxation which have been published in various books and journals.

Douglas Mair is Professor of Economics and Head of the Department of Economics at Heriot-Watt University, Edinburgh. He is a Vice President of Section F (Economics) of the British Association for the Advancement of Science and a member of the Council of the Scottish Economic Society. He has co-authored *Structure and Growth of the Scottish Economy* (1970) and edited or co-edited *The Scottish Contribution to Modern Economic Thought* (1990) and *A Modern Guide to Economic Thought* (1991). He has an entry in *The Elgar Companion to Radical Political Economy* and has published on Kaleckian tax incidence theory in *Government and Policy*, the *Cambridge Journal of Economics, Review of Political Economy, Journal of Post Keynesian Economics* and the *International Review of Applied Economics*.

Jonathan Michie is a Fellow and Director of Studies in Economics at Robinson College, and University Lecturer in Economics at the Judge Institute of Management Studies, University of Cambridge. He previously worked in Brussels as an Expert to the European Commission. He holds Visiting Professorships at Queen's University, Belfast, and the University of the Witwatersrand, South Africa. He has published several books and articles on globalisation and economic policy, including *Managing the Global Economy* (1995) and *Creating Industrial Capacity* (1996). He is on the editorial boards of the *Cambridge Journal of Economics*, the *International Review of Applied Economics* and *New Economy*.

Pascal Petit is a CNRS Research Officer, affiliated to CEPREMAP, a Parisian centre for economic research sponsored by the French Commissariat du Plan. He also teaches at the Universities of Paris VII and Paris XIII. His main research fields have been on technological change, productivity and employment. His works on structural changes and economic growth focused on the sectoral dimensions of the growth patterns of OECD economies, in a post Keynesian and neo-institutionalist perspective. Recent research include works on changing patterns of internationalisation of modern economies. His publications include *Slow Growth and the Service*

Economy (1986), *The Economies of Industrial Modernization* (1992) (in collaboration with C. Antonelli and G. Tahar) along with articles on the economics of technological change, the productivity slowdown and the dynamics of services.

Robert Pollin teaches economics at the University of California, Riverside, and is Research Associate at the Economic Policy Institute in Washington, DC. He is editor of *The Macroeconomics of Savings, Finance and Investment* (1997), co-editor of *New Perspectives in Monetary Macroeconomics: Explorations in the Tradition of Hyman P. Minsky* (1994) and *Transforming the U.S. Financial System: Equity and Efficiency for the 21st Century* (1993). He has been a member of the Capital Formation Subcouncil of the Competitiveness Policy Council of the US government, and a consultant to the Joint Economic Committee of the US Congress and the United Nations Development Program. He recently directed a study for the City of Los Angeles on a proposal to establish a 'Living Wage' for workers employed by firms holding contracts with the city. He also recently co-directed a research project on globalisation and progressive economic policy for the Economic Policy Institute. He is on the editorial boards of *Dollars and Sense* magazine and the *International Review of Applied Economics*.

Malcom Sawyer is Professor of Economics and Head of the Economics Division at the University of Leeds, and was formerly Professor of Economics at the University of York. He is the author of several books, including *Macroeconomics in Question* (1982), *The Economics of Michał Kalecki* (1982, 1985), *The Challenge of Radical Political Economy* (1989) and *Unemployment, Imperfect Competition and Macroeconomics* (1995). He is the managing director of the *International Review of Applied Economics*, joint editor of the recently launched *International Papers in Political Economy*, and editor of the series *New Directions in Modern Economics*. He has recently co-edited *The Biographical Dictionary of Dissenting Economists* (1992) and *The Elgar Companion to Radical Political Economy* (1993). He has published widely in journals and books in the areas of industrial economics, macroeconomics and political economy. His current research interests include the theory of industrial policy and the conceptualisation of competition and markets in economic theory, the causes and cures for unemployment, as well as continuing to work on post Keynesian macroeconomics.

List of Abbreviations

AD	aggregate demand
AS	aggregate supply
CCA	capital consumption adjustment
CEOs	Chief Executive Officers
COLAs	cost of living adjustments
CRA	Community Reinvestment Act
HOS	Heckscher–Ohlin–Samuleson
IEs	industrial economies
IP	industrial policy
IVA	inventory valuation adjustment
FDI	foreign direct investment
LDCs	less-developed countries
NAIRU	non-accelerating inflation rate of unemployment
NBER	National Bureau of Economic Research
NICs	newly-industrialised countries
OLS	ordinary least squares
PKK	Post Keynesian/Kaleckian
PSBR	public sector borrowing requirement
RoW	rest of the world
S&L	Savings and Loan
SICs	semi-industrialised countries
SMEs	small to medium-sized enterprises

Introduction

The possibility of the pursuit of national Keynesian policies, often identified as the management of aggregate demand in a domestic economy setting, has been increasingly doubted to such an extent that the use of such policies in the pursuit of full employment appears to be off most political agendas. There can be debates on the degree to which Keynesian policies contributed to the post-war 'golden age', which drew to a close in the early 1970s; this era now stands out as one of low employment and relative rapid growth, at least for Western European economies.

Keynesian policies have been deemed no longer relevant for two reasons: the level of employment is constrained by the 'natural' rate of unemployment (or more generally by the NAIRU, the non-accelerating inflation rate of unemployment) and by globalisation, particularly of financial markets, which is seen to have made fiscal and monetary policies difficult to implement and less effective in their impact. These lines of argument, whilst contested by many, have generated a degree of fatalism whereby high levels of unemployment have to be accepted because 'market forces' permit nothing else.

With these thoughts in mind, a conference was held at the University of East London on 19 May 1995. The purpose of the conference, at which the papers included in this volume were first presented, was to scrutinise the issues just raised and consider what would constitute Keynesian policies; and, more importantly, to consider how far they would be relevant for the twenty-first century. The Keynesian policy message of the necessity of adequate aggregate demand to sustain full employment is not negated by observations on supply-side constraints, by possible inflationary implications and globalisation. It is rather that national demand management is not sufficient, and policies at the national level must be designed to overcome the supply-side and inflationary constraints and introduce policies at the international level that would help to construct an international order supportive of high levels of aggregate demand. The authors of the chapters in this book were asked to address the question of the relevance of Keynesian policies from different perspectives: European, American, global and developing countries. It will be evident that the authors do not share a common view on what would constitute Keynesian policies, although no-one identifies those policies solely with demand management. Keynesian policies could be seen to involve measures to strengthen the supply side of economies along with the promotion of investment and a reduction of uncertainty.

We begin with the European scene in Chapter 1, where Douglas Mair and Tony Laramie discuss the macroeconomic effects of taxation in a federal Europe. They argue that the signing of the Maastrict Treaty in 1992 created a dilemma for fiscal policy at both a theoretical and a policy level. The conflict between the increasingly important stabilising role for fiscal policy post-Maastricht and the pursuit of fiscal harmonisation requires a re-examination of the theoretical framework within which policy discussion should take place. Orthodox tax incidence theory cannot adequately analyse the macroeconomic effects of taxation, and the chapter proposes an alternative post-Keynesian approach based on the tax and business cycle theories of Kalecki. To illustrate the applicability of a Kaleckian approach to taxation in a federal system, a model of tax incidence is developed which integrates microeconomic and macroeconomic elements. The macroeconomic effects of state and local taxation within the federal constitution of the USA are examined. It is shown that it is necessary to study the structure of state and local taxation in the USA, the structure of state government receipts, the expenditure functions of state governments, the state government budget stance and the nature of intergovernmental relations in order to identify macroeconomic effects. The US evidence is offered as an example of the potential of the model employed for the purposes of this chapter for a federal Europe.

In Chapter 2, 'New Scale and Scope for Industrial Policies in the 1990s', Bruno Amable and Pascal Petit postulate that changes in the economic and political environment should lead us to appraise the influence that industrial policies can have in the shaping of contemporary macroeconomic policies. This is an important issue to investigate because the view is often taken that industrial policies are only minor complements to macroeconomic policies. This remark assumes more significance because macroeconomic policies appear to lose momentum and industrial policies are looked at from a new perspective. This perspective is first considered in the context of the post-war debate on standard and radical Keynesianism. The main trends in the fields of public interventions up to the 1980s are recalled. It helps to stress the changes which took place in the environment of the 1980s and 1990s, especially those relating to the forms of competition prevailing in product markets. These forms give rise to new opportunities to reshape industrial policies, especially because macroeconomic policies are losing momentum as mentioned above. Despite their renewed legitimacy and efficiency, the question of the macroeconomic impact of these co-ordinated industrial policies remains open, depending on the scale that central and local authorities are willing to give to these new schemes. A further consideration is to point to certain societal changes, along with the political will necessary to support the magnitude of successful industrial policies.

Chapter 3 is a short contribution which is a comment on the first two chapters. Johan Deprez, in 'Industrial Policies and the Macroeconomic Effects of Taxation: Some Comments', finds agreement with both chapters and feels that modern Keynesian policy has much to offer in these two areas beyond what is generally presumed. Expectations formation is pointed to as one area that both these chapters should have incorporated into their arguments more explicitly. Similarly, regional consideration and 'location competition' are held to be important considerations. The role of finance is pointed to as a fundamental Keynesian consideration that needs to be addressed in effectively formulating industrial and taxation policies.

Robert Pollin, in Chapter 4, builds from two explicit policy ideas that Keynes introduced in the *General Theory*: that of a 'somewhat comprehensive socialisation of investment', and that of 'euthanasia of the rentier'. This chapter argues that, to a significant degree, the stagnation of the contemporary US economy can be attributed to the nature of its capital-market-based, or 'exit-led', financial system, which promotes short-termism, speculation and financial fragility, as well as excessive political power for the rentier class. In combination, these factors diminish government's capacity to implement policies that promote egalitarian growth and full employment successfully. In making these points, Pollin contrasts the US financial system with the bank-based or 'voice-led' systems, such as those in Japan, France or South Korea. A series of policy proposals which would address these problems are then sketched out. These problems include regulatory policies which would 'level the playing field upward' among all financial intermediaries, and credit allocation policies that give preference to projects with high social rates of return. The proposals also aim to increase substantially the degree of democratic accountability within the financial system.

Gary Dymski continues with developments in the USA and, in Chapter 5, 'Economic Polarisation and US Policy Activism', he takes issue with the view expressed by mainstream economists that the increased inequality associated with globalisation is the cause of the US 'employment miracle'. The argument is based on the premise that technical change and liberalisation policies pursued by many countries produced flows of goods and services which increased the demand for more skilled labour and decreased that for less-skilled labour. It is argued here that, on the contrary, any such benefits are short lived. Increased income inequality 'caused' by globalisation has been associated with adverse macroeconomic effects which have been ignored by mainstream economists. Inequality has heightened social – and especially racial and gender – polarisation; and the reactions of globally mobile corporations to this polarisation have reduced both access to capital and the size of the fiscal and monetary policy multipliers. Macroeconomic policy to stimulate the level of aggregate demand remains crucial in achieving a more prosperous, less unequal society, but needs to include measures to enhance access to human and financial capital. Restoring the viability of Keynesian policies by reducing instability associated with globalisation will help, but a great deal more is needed, and the chapter makes the point that such viability is also predicted, amongst other things, on racial and gender inequality being eliminated.

In Chapter 6, Harald Hagemann examines the relevant characteristics of the development of Organisation for Economic Co-operation and Development (OECD) countries and the differences between the performance of North American and European economies in recent years. Emphasis is put on output, productivity growth, employment and real wage experiences. The chapter discusses Verdoorn's Law (the question of how real phenomena are linked to monetary ones) and, in particular, the financial constraints on full employment policies. Hagemann identifies a number of difficulties with the policy proposals embedded in the Pollin and Dymski analyses, and he suggests a menu of policies which include: Keynesian-type policies to raise per capita demand; the promotion of research and development for new processes and products; shortening the annual working time; and improving public infrastructure in human capital.

Chapter 7 turns to policy questions in the context of an open economy. Paul Davidson explains why, in an open economy context, Keynes-type demand management policies appear to have lost their ability to create jobs domestically. The new classical 'counter-revolution' and New Keynesian 'counter-counter-revolution' to Keynes's *General Theory*, by encouraging liberalisation of foreign exchange markets and global financial markets, provided the intellectual justification required by the 'New Right' for reducing to a bare minimum the size of the government. The belief in NAIRU, with its implication that full employment inevitably leads to accelerating inflation, implies that unemployment is inevitable and is a cost worth enduring to avoid inflation. Keynesian demand management policies are then seen as neither effective nor needed. Within this intellectual framework, an independent central bank monetary policy is provided as the answer to achieving economic growth without inflation. Flexible exchange rates, free trade and the law of comparative advantage are further requirements to the road to prosperity. The chapter rejects these policies by pointing to the dismal world-wide unemployment record, and to the persistent European double-digit unemployment rates. Remedies are suggested to resurrect Keynes demand-type management policies to stimulate expansion without experiencing balance of payment problems or domestic inflation. A reformed international monetary system is at the heart of these policies.

James Galbraith in Chapter 8 remains within the international context but he concentrates an 'Uneven Development and the Destabilisation of the North: A Keynesian View'. He begins by reminding us that faltering performance in the developed countries continues along lines unrelated to North-South trade. Mainstream writers have argued that these matters are internal problems for the developed countries and emanate from peculiarities in the evolution of technology. Although these views have been challenged, no satisfactory answer has emerged. Galbraith poses the questions of whether Keynesian theory can illuminate the rising North-South trade in manufacturing, the industrial relocation from North to South, the increasing wage inequality and unemployment in the North, and the consequent breakdown of Northern labour movements as effective political forces. He argues that these questions can be answered positively, and that the main relevance of Keynesian theory today may lie in its capacity to capture the dynamics of the North-South relationship, and the influence of Northern macroeconomic policy and Northern business cycles on industrial trading patterns. The literature desperately needs to fill an important gap here, which requires a distinctively Keynesian perspective, one that would be able to tie historical trade and industrial developments to policy. Galbraith makes a start on this issue by bringing together the Weintraub–Davidson *Z-D* analysis and the putty-clay, vintage capital structure in an open economy context, along with North-South wage differentials.

Jonathan Michie, in Chapter 9, considers the relevance of Keynesian economics in the late twentieth century. In doing so, Michie poses two questions: first, to what extent do 'Keynes's insights' help in analysing the world economy; and, second, to what extent does the integration of national economies and globalisation affect the implementation and efficacy of Keynesian economic policies? The chapters on which he comments have tackled these two questions: James Galbraith has considered the relevance of Keynesian concepts in analysing the global economy of today, and Paul Davidson has discussed Keynesian policies in the context of changes in the world economy. Michie concludes by suggesting that Keynesian policies are relevant today, but of equal importance are the changes that have taken place in the world economy, which impose additional limits to the power of national governments to pursue policies.

Amitava Dutt examines, in Chapter 10, the relevance of Keynesian policies – interpreted as those policies implied by Keynes's theoretical analysis of unemployment developed in the *General Theory* – for a subset of developing economies, which are called semi-industrial countries. The recent economic experience of these countries is very disappointing both in terms of policies adopted and of economic performance. The World Bank and the International Monetary Fund (IMF), with the blessing of a significant number of academic economists, have insisted on these countries slashing their government budgets and monetary growth, comprehensive privatisation of state enterprises, and dismantling of government controls on the private sector, especially financial controls. Consequently, Keynesian policies in the shape of using fiscal and monetary instruments for economic expansion, and policies like 'socialisation of investment', have no place on the menu of policies of this category of countries. This chapter draws on recent contributions in development economics to argue that on theoretical grounds Keynesian policies are relevant for semi-industrialised countries even when they are constrained by capital shortages, stagnant agricultural sectors and foreign exchange availability. It then discusses the recent development experience of India to illustrate the empirical relevance of some of these theoretical issues. The chapter concludes that, on both theoretical and empirical grounds, Keynesian policies are relevant and necessary for semi-industrialised countries.

In Chapter 11, entitled 'International Markets and Open Economy Macroeconomics: A Keynesian View', E. V. K. FitzGerald is also concerned with the developing world. The recent apparent resolution of the 'debt' crisis and the end of the Cold War could have provided the impetus of developing countries to have become the main beneficiaries in the new economic world order. Allegedly, free trade and integration of capital markets implied a truly 'global' economy which could have allowed rising incomes in developing countries based on rapid export growth and foreign investment. That optimism, though, proved premature. Chronic instability in global financial markets exposed the lack of regulatory institutions and the risks this entailed. FitzGerald sketches a Keynesian response to the gap between the reality of international capital markets and the 'standard paradigm' of economic theory that underpins the policy model offered to poor countries in relation to their participation in the world economy and their national macroeconomic management. Recent work on imperfect markets implies a substantial modification of this standard paradigm to allow for non-price clearing but this does not appear to have integrated with new trade theories, while the implications of systemic volatility and credit rationing behaviour have not been theorised. The chapter suggests that a return of Keynes's original approach to investor uncertainty and global demand might not only help to integrate international macroeconomic theory in a plausible manner, but also contribute to the formulation of more desirable policy positions.

Laurence Harris, in the final chapter, discusses the contributions by Dutt and FitzGerald. He argues that Keynesian theory is, for several reasons, a weak basis for development policy. Developing countries are characterised by diversity which makes it rather futile to seek a universal theoretical framework for these countries. There are two additional problems identified in this chapter: the disarticulation characteristic of these countries and the lack of economic sovereignty in the sense necessary for Keynesian policies. This chapter suggests that these are fundamental obstacles to the construction of a coherent Keynesian development theory. Harris observes that these obstacles are arguably applicable to any theory of policy, but for reasons of space he concentrates on Keynesian policies alone.

It will be apparent from this review of the chapters in this book that economic policies which can be described as Keynesian extend well beyond the traditional demand management policies. Clearly the authors who have contributed to this volume have taken different aspects of Keynesian policies and were asked to think about them in different contexts. Whilst the authors would not fully agree with one another or with us (and no attempt has been made to come to any common position), there would be agreement that *laissez-faire* policies will not bring about full employment and economic prosperity, and that a range of government intervention is required. The ability of governments to intervene successfully, especially in the macroecnomic area, has been reduced (as compared with say the Bretton Woods era), but this may be seen more as an argument for internationally co-ordinated interventions, policies to reduce the power of financial markets and a focus on supply-side as well as demand-side policies.

Both the studies themselves and the discussants' comments (which are also included here) have been published in volume 10, no. 1 (the January 1996 issue) of the *International Review of Applied Economics*. The authors were invited to revise their contributions for the purposes of this volume. Some have taken the opportunity and revised their papers substantially. We are grateful to the publishers of the *International Review of Applied Economics*, Carfax Publishing Company, for allowing us to bring out the papers and comments in a book form. Financial support for the conference by the University of East London, the Post-Keynesian Economics Study Group and the *International Review of Applied Economics* is gratefully acknowledged. Special thanks must go to the contributors for their willingness to respond to our comments and suggestions when revising their contributions with forbearance and good humour. Thanks are also extended to June

Daniels and Christine Nisbet of the Department of Economics, University of East London, and to Eleanor Lynn of the School of Business and Economic Studies, University of Leeds, for their generous secretarial assistance. Finally, Tim Farmiloe and his staff, as always, have provided much support throughout the period it took to prepare this book.

1 The Macroeconomic Effects of Taxation in a Federal Europe

Douglas Mair and Anthony J. Laramie

INTRODUCTION

The signing at Maastricht on 7 February 1992 of the Treaty on European Union (hereafter the Treaty) has brought back into focus the importance of fiscal policy as a means of achieving the convergence conditions necessary for successful achievement of the Treaty's objectives. Two sets of factors will determine the success or failure of fiscal policy post-Maastricht: (i) the seriousness of the commitment of the governments of the member states to the implementation of the fiscal policies necessary to achieve the objectives of the Treaty; and, (ii) the robustness of the theoretical reference model used to analyse the relationships between the convergence targets and the fiscal variables (Roberti and Visaggio 1994).

A number of commentators, such as Eichengreen (1990, 1992a, 1992b, 1993, 1994), Bayoumi and Eichengreen (1994), Buiter, Corsetti and Robini (1993), Sala-i-Martin and Sachs (1992), have all investigated aspects of fiscal policy in a post-Maastricht context, in several cases using US experience to illustrate the fiscal issues which arise. Implicitly, these studies have used conventional mainstream theories of public finance as their paradigm.

In this chapter, our principal objective is to argue the case for Post-Keynesian/Kaleckian (PKK) theory in the debate over the role of fiscal policy in a post-Maastricht European Union (EU). We outline a PKK macroeconomic theory of tax incidence in which the micro and macro elements which determine the incidence of taxes are fully integrated, and show how it can be used to identify the incidence and macroeconomic effects of state and local taxes within the federal constitution of the USA. We offer the US evidence as an example of the potential of a PKK model for the EU in exploring the macroeconomic effects of fiscal policy at member-state level within a federal context.

THE MAASTRICHT CONVERGENCE CRITERIA

Article 109j of the Treaty establishes four convergence criteria for the adoption of a single currency and admission to Economic and Monetary Union (EMU). These criteria relate to (i) price stability; (ii) exchange rate stability; (iii) convergence of long-term nominal interest rates; and (iv) sustainability of a country's public finance situation. Briefly, the criteria are specified as follows.

Price Stability

This shall mean that a member state has a price performance that is sustainable and an average rate of inflation, observed over a period of one year before examination for suitability for admission to EMU, that does not exceed that of at most the three best performing member states in terms of price stability by more than $1\frac{1}{2}$ percentage points.

Exchange Rate Stability

This shall mean that a member state has respected the normal fluctuation margins provided for the Exchange Rate Mechanism of the European Monetary System (EMS) without severe tensions for at least two years before examination. In particular, the member state should not have devalued its currency's bilateral central rate against any other member state currency on its own initiative for the same period.

Long-term Nominal Interest Rate Convergence

This shall mean that, observed over a period of a year before examination, a member state has an average nominal long-term interest rate that does not exceed that of at most the three best performing member states in terms of price stability by more than 2 percentage points.

Sustainability of Public Finance Situation

There are two quantitative requirements in terms of the budgetary discipline for membership in terms of, first, the budget deficit and, second, nominal gross public debt.

1. In terms of the budget deficit requirement, a member state should have ensured that the ratio of the planned or actual deficit to gross domestic product (GDP) at market prices does not exceed the target of 3 per cent.

2. In terms of the public debt requirement, the member state should have ensured that the ratio of public debt to GDP does not exceed the target of 60 per cent.

Two further constraints which the Treaty imposes on member states are:

Prohibition of Monetary Financing

The central bank of a member state shall be prohibited from purchasing debt instruments directly from the central (federal) government.

Indirect Tax Harmonisation

The provisions for harmonisation of legislation concerning most indirect taxes will be adopted to the extent that such harmonisation is necessary to ensure the establishment and the functioning of the internal market within the time limit laid down in the Treaty.

CONFLICTS IN THE MAASTRICHT TREATY

The conditions summarised above are an attempt by the authors of the Treaty to reconcile two conflicting issues. On the one hand, the creation of the European System of Central Banks and the introduction of a single European currency will result in a loss of monetary autonomy which needs to be compensated by greater fiscal flexibility (Kenen 1969; Eichengreen 1993). With the loss of independent monetary policy, the ability of a member state to take stabilising fiscal action becomes all the more important. On the other hand, the whole thrust of Community fiscal policy since the earliest days of the EEC has been to move towards fiscal harmonisation and to restrain fiscal policy in order to facilitate attainment of EMU.

The Treaty contains two classes of fiscal provisions: (i) articles concerning fiscal policy during both the transition to monetary union (Stage Two) and monetary union itself (Stage Three); and (ii) articles which apply only to Stage Three. Stage Two began on 1 January 1994. Member states are to abolish all restrictions on capital movements and to adopt multiyear programmes designed to ensure the international convergence of their public finances. They are to begin strengthening the independence of their central banks. They are to avoid 'excessive deficits' and the accumulation of 'excessive debts' as defined above. Not later than 31 December 1996, the European Council must decide, by qualified majority vote, whether a majority of member states satisfies all the preconditions defined above in order to participate in the monetary union. If there is such a majority, the Council may set a starting date for Stage Three. If the date for inaugurating Stage Three has not been set by the end of 1997, it will begin automatically on 1 January 1999, so long as even a minority of member states satisfies the conditions.

The Council of Ministers is to exercise broad oversight over the process of movement through Stage Two towards attainment of Stage Three. The Council will be responsible for establishing whether 'excessive deficits' exist and ensuring that member states take appropriate action to eliminate them. Failure to do so may result in the Council requiring the member state to submit a programme of fiscal adjustment and a timetable for doing so. Continuing failure may be met with further penalties, including fines, and increasing difficulty of access to European Investment Bank funding.

These supervisory powers of the Council reflect the continuing priority it attaches to the objective of fiscal harmonisation. Eichengreen (1994) challenges the rationale for this supervision and asks why the member states cannot be relied upon to manage their fiscal affairs themselves? A concern which has featured prominently in the background papers to the Delors Report and the Treaty has been for the international macroeconomic spillovers of national fiscal policies which may be magnified as a consequence of economic and monetary integration. However, Eichengreen cites the empirical studies of international fiscal transmission of Oudiz and Sachs (1984) and Bryant *et al.* (1990) as evidence that such effects may be small and are unlikely to be significantly magnified by further economic and monetary integration.

Eichengreen (1994: 170–1) concludes that whether one believes that closer integration within the EU will create a bias towards excessive deficits, monetisation of public debt and inflation depends on the institutional setting and market structure one has in mind. He cites approvingly the model of Canzoneri and Diba (1991) as an approach to the problem. Essentially, this is an application of the Ramsey–Phelps optimal taxation problem to be solved by an optimising central bank. The model is predicated on increasing international capital mobility and the corresponding adjustments to domestic and foreign interest rates induced by capital mobility. This, in turn, will lead to higher taxes by domestic and foreign governments in order to pay the higher interest charges on outstanding debt.

MAINSTREAM THEORY OF TAX INCIDENCE

The framework, briefly summarised above, within which the analysis to date of the role of fiscal policy in a post-Maastricht Europe has been carried out, marks the critical nature of the difference between mainstream and PKK theory. Mainstream analysis seeks primarily to study the macroeconomic effects of relative price changes. This approach has dominated the mainstream since Harberger's (1962) two-sector general equilibrium model of corporate tax incidence in which the emphasis is on the response of factor flows to tax-induced changes in factor incomes.

The mainstream views on tax incidence are reflected are reflected in neoclassical theory of income distribution (Kotlikoff and Summers 1987). Whether taxes are levied on commodities, incomes or wealth (property), taxes ultimately affect the demand for, and supply of, factors and factor returns. A comparison of factor incomes before and after the imposition of a tax is used to determine the incidence of the tax. Within this family of models, the economic incidence of taxes may be less than, equal to or greater than the legal incidence, and this incidence is independent of who pays the tax, whether producer or consumer, or to which level of government the tax is paid (federal, state or local).

The neoclassical models of tax incidence range from standard partial equilibrium to general equilibrium to dynamic. These models are all supported by a core set of assumptions: that is, market clearing and the marginal product theory of income distribution. Moreover, when considering the effects of taxation in a general equilibrium framework, factors of production are assumed to be in fixed supply, and highly mobile and aggregate demand effects of tax changes are assumed to be nullified (Mieszkowski 1972). This dependence on the marginal productivity theory of income distribution means that neoclassical theory can only consider situations of continual full employment.

This limitation of the mainstream approach is recognised by Atkinson and Stiglitz (1980: 222):

> The general equilibrium analysis of tax incidence has to date been undertaken largely independently of the literature on macroeconomics. Thus, competitive equilibrium models, with all markets clearing, have been used to investigate the incidence of various taxes, whereas a quite separate literature, using aggregate demand/monetary models, has examined the implications of taxes for the level of employment and the rate of inflation. In other areas of economics, this gap has been narrowed ... but in public finance the gap has persisted much longer.

As we have suggested above, the discussion to date of the scope of fiscal policy in a post-Maastricht EU is being conducted within the mainstream paradigm and, as a consequence, suffers from the difficulty recognised by

Atkinson and Stiglitz. We think there is a need to introduce into the debate an alternative analysis based on what we consider to be a fuller integration of micro- and macroeconomic elements.

PKK MACROECONOMIC THEORY OF TAX INCIDENCE

PKK tax incidence theory has its origin in the realisation by Kalecki (1971/1937) that the publication of Keynes's *General Theory* required a reconsideration of the theory of taxation. Although his 1937 paper on the theory of taxation predates his later work on the degree of monopoly theory of income distribution, Kalecki recognised, in a way that Keynes never did, that Keynesian macroeconomic theory and marginal productivity income distribution theory are incompatible. And if we regard tax incidence theory as applied income distribution theory, then clearly a new theory of taxation was required, although Kalecki seems rather to have put the horse before the cart.

PKK macroeconomic tax incidence can be distinguished from the mainstream neoclassical general equilibrium approach on two grounds: (i) in the PKK paradigm, macroeconomic foundations are present in the incidence of various taxes; and (ii) neoclassical notions of market clearing and full employment are replaced with PKK institutional pricing and underemployment.

We begin with Kalecki's degree of monopoly theory of income distribution. This is expressed in the relationship:

$$\omega = 1/[1 + (k - 1)(j + 1)]$$

where ω is manual labour's share of value added, k is the ratio of aggregate proceeds to aggregate prime costs (that is the mark-up) and j is the ratio of expenditures on raw materials to expenditures on manual labour. Changes in the degree of monopoly factors affect k and thus lead to changes in ω. Reynolds (1984) has produced evidence in support of Kalecki's theory and this has been further confirmed in more recent work by Laramie *et al.* (1994).

Following Kalecki (1971/1937), Asimakopulos and Burbidge (1974) and Laramie (1991), we drop the assumptions of perfect competition, market clearing and fixed factor supplies; we allow for aggregate demand effects by assuming a non-homogeneous marginal propensity to consume; we replace the marginal product theory of income distribution with Kalecki's degree of monopoly theory of income distribution; and we recognise that the long run is made up of, and dependent upon, what has happened in many short periods. As a consequence, many of the standard neoclassical conclusions are reversed.

Kriesler (1989) argues that micro and macro foundations stand side by side in Kalecki's analysis of capitalist economies. The micro- and macroeconomic foundations feed into each other and both are present in the analysis of tax incidence. At the macro level, aggregate spending flows determine the level of profits. At the micro level, market power (as measured by the degree of monopoly) determines the distribution of income. Tax policies can affect the aggregate flow of spending and profits, but pricing decisions, as reflected in business mark-ups, determine the intra/interindustry and class distributions of income. Ultimately, the confluence of these factors determines the short-period incidence of taxes and this short-period incidence, insofar as it impacts on business investment, generates a long-period effect. Thus a dynamic Kaleckian theory of tax incidence identifies, in particular, the effects of taxation on depreciation and on the aggregate level of profits.

Kalecki's Contribution

Kaleckian tax incidence theory is concerned with the macroeconomic impact of taxation and demonstrates that the legal incidence and the economic incidence of taxes differ in both the short and long run. He analysed the effects of taxation on both the level and the distribution of income on the basis of a number of typically Kaleckian assumptions: a closed economic system operating with surplus labour and capacity; a balanced state budget with all state expenditure financed by taxation; any increase in taxation spent on officials' salaries or dole for the unemployed; investment determined prior to the period under consideration; a fixed capitalists' marginal propensity to consume, insensitive to changes in expectations of income; workers' savings equal to zero; and a perfectly elastic money supply.

Under these assumptions, Kalecki showed that an increase in the consumption tax rate, *ad valorem*, on wage goods does not affect the level of gross profits. The tax on wage goods represents a new type of prime cost. When this tax increases, prime costs and the value of sales increase, leaving gross profits and national income unchanged but reducing workers' real wage rate. An income tax on capitalists' incomes, which is not part of prime costs, increases gross profits by the amount of the income tax and leaves unaffected the part of gross profits received by capitalists. This increase in gross profits also leaves unaffected the expected profitability of investment and increases unemployment, while the effect on real wages is uncertain. Finally, the introduction of a tax on capital increases gross profits by the amount of the tax. In the short run, the portion of profits going to capitalists remain constant, but the expected profitability of investment increases, thus increasing future profits and employment.

From this analysis, Kalecki concluded that capital taxation is the best way to stimulate business and reduce unemployment as it has all the merits of financing state expenditure by borrowing but is distinguished from borrowing by the advantage of the state not becoming indebted. But he doubted whether any government would have the political will to introduce it on any significant scale. It is perhaps for this reason that Kalecki's theory of tax incidence has lain neglected for over 50 years.

Kalecki's original formulation and its subsequent extension by Asimakopulos and Burbidge (1974) are short-period equilibrium models in which it is implicitly assumed that prices are set in some unspecified way by price leaders and that the aggregate supply curve is perfectly elastic. Damania and Mair (1992) have rectified this shortcoming of the Kaleckian short-period model by means of supergame analysis of non-competitive behaviour. By introducing informational uncertainty and a trigger pricing strategy to punish deviant behaviour, Damania and Mair demonstrate how Kalecki's short-period model can be made dynamic in a way entirely consistent with Kalecki's expectations of the timing of price wars over the business cycle.

Dynamic Kaleckian Theory of Tax Incidence

Laramie and Mair (1996) have developed a dynamic Kaleckian model of tax incidence by integrating Kalecki's theory of tax incidence with his theory of the business cycle. The model builds on Laramie (1991) where he integrated the tax structure into Kalecki's (1971/1968) theories of the distribution and determination of income and showed that taxation of wages and salaries and profits, even with a balanced budget constraint, can impact on profits.

Taxation and government spending can be integrate into Kalecki's trade cycle theory in the following way. Kalecki (1971/1968: 171 *et seq.*) considered three determinants of new investment decisions: (i) entrepreneurial savings; (ii) the prerequisites for their investment; and (iii) an innovation factor. Whether entrepreneurial savings, E, are reinvested depends on the relationship between the actual level of investment, I, and the level of investment that generates the standard ('normal') rate of profits, $I(\pi)$. The extent to which the difference between investment that generates the standard rate of profits and actual investment impacts on investment decisions depends on r, the intensity of the reaction of entrepreneurs. To these are added innovations-induced investment decisions, $B(t)$, a semi-autonomous slowly changing function which depends on past economic, social and technological developments.

Fixed investment decisions, D, can be written as:

$$D = E + r(I(\pi) - I) + B(t) \tag{1.1}$$

Entrepreneurial savings can be written as a fraction of post-tax profits, P. Thus:

$$E = \lambda P \tag{1.2}$$

On the assumption of ample unused productive capacities, investment that generates the standard rate of profits will capture only a portion, n, of the new real profits generated, ΔP, augmented by productivity increases from new investment. These productivity increases will increase the real costs of using existing equipment and result in a shift of production and profits from old to new equipment. This transfer of profits is assumed to be proportional to real costs, the difference between national income, Y, and profits, P; that is $\omega(Y - P)$.

The profits generated by new equipment are $n\Delta P + \omega(Y - P)$ and the rate of profits on new equipment is $\pi = [n\Delta P + \omega(Y - P)]/\Delta K$, where ΔK is the change in capital stock. Investment that generates the standard rate of profits can be written as:

$$I(\pi) = [n\Delta P + \omega(Y - P)/\pi \tag{1.3}$$

Equation (1.3) can be rewritten by finding an expression for national income as a function of profits. Given mark-up pricing, profits are largely determined by capitalists' spending decisions independently of their pricing decisions. The latter, however, determine the wage share of national income. Given capitalists' spending and the resulting level of profits, the level of national income is determined by the wage bill which is generated by wages' share of national income. Recognising that total taxes are a function of both the pre-tax wage bill and profits, national income can be written as:

$$Y = P(1 - t_w)/(1 - t_\pi)(1 - t_w - \alpha) \tag{1.4}$$

where t_w = tax rate on wage; t_π = tax rate on profits; and α = the wage share.

Equation (1.4) shows that the tax system influences the relationship between profits and national income directly through the impact of taxation on wages and profits and indirectly through the wage share.

By substituting equipment (1.4) into equation (1.3), the level of investment generating the standard rate of profit can be rewritten as:

$$I(\pi) = [n\Delta P + \delta P]/\pi \tag{1.5}$$

where δ is the rate of depreciation in the sense that it represents the rate at which profits are lost to existing capital as the result of technical progress; it is expressed as:

$$\delta = \omega[\alpha + t_\pi(1 - t_w - \alpha)]/(1 - t_w - \alpha) \qquad (1.6)$$

Recognising that investment decisions in period t, (D_t), are translated into investment expenditures in period $t + \tau$, $(I_{t+\tau})$, so that $D_t = I_{t+\tau}$, equation (1.1) can be rewritten as:

$$I_{t+\tau} = \lambda P_t + r(\{[n\Delta P_t + \delta P_t]/\pi\} - I_t) + B_t \qquad (1.1')$$

As can be seen from equation (1.1′), the tax system impacts on investment through the level of profits and the rate of depreciation. The impact of taxation on depreciation is through the real tax bill associated with old equipment. Technical progress will raise the costs and reduce the profits of old equipment and accelerate its obsolescence. The extent to which changes in the tax rates on wages and profits affect the rate of depreciation depends on the extent to which either tax is shifted through an adjustment to business mark-ups. Laramie and Mair (1996) show that on certain shifting assumptions, changes in the taxation of wages and or profits will affect the rate of depreciation which, in turn, will have an impact on the level of investment and alter the structure of the business cycle.

The mechanism through which changes in taxes affect the level of profits is as follows. Kalecki (1971/1968) showed that aggregate profits, P, as measured by the difference between aggregate sales and prime costs, can be represented as the sum of gross profit investment, the government budget deficit $(G - T)$, the trade surplus and the difference between capitalist consumption and worker savings. We derive Kalecki's profit function by using a variant of Weintraub's consumption coefficient, a (Laramie 1991). Thus the level of profits is expressed as:

$$P = I + (G - T) + V(a - 1) \qquad (1.7)$$

Since the wage bill, V, is dependent on national income, Y, and assuming a balanced budget constraint $(G = T)$ and a zero trade balance, the profit function can be written as:

$$P = [1/(1 - a\alpha)][I(1 - \alpha) + \alpha G(a - 1)] \qquad (1.8)$$

The impact of taxation on the level of profits can be determined by differentiating equation (1.8) with respect to changes in the tax rates on wages and profits. Thus, with a balanced budget constraint, taxation impacts on the level of profits through changes in government purchases and the wage share. As with the depreciation effect, the impact of a tax change depends on the shifting assumptions, but there are tax changes which will have positive or negative effects on the level of profits.

Thus, taxation has an impact on profits through two channels: (i) the rate of depreciation and (ii) the level of profits. These taxation effects can be integrated into Kalecki's business cycle theory by differencing the profit function, equation (1.8), and then substituting the profit function and its difference form into the investment equation (1.1′). From this, it can be deduced that the impact of taxation on investment over the cycle depends on the following: (i) the cyclical variation in investment; (ii) the change in the cyclical variation in investment; (iii) a depreciation effect; (iv) a distributional effect, operating through changes in the wage share; and (v) a tax shifting effect, operating through changes in the mark-up.

To illustrate the effect of wage taxation on investment, we assume initially no tax shifting and that the consumption coefficient is greater than 1. In this case, a change in the wage tax rate has no impact on the rate of depreciation. As a consequence, a change in the wage tax rate alters investment and the structure of the business cycle through the distribution effect. It is inversely related to the wage share of income and, therefore, to the aggregate levels of profit and investment.

If investment is in an upswing or at its peak, where current investment determines current profits and current profits determine future investment, an increase/decrease in the wage tax rate reduces/increases the impact of current investment on profits and future investment. Thus, the increase/decrease in the wage tax rate dampens the upswing and reduces the peak of the business cycle. The opposite occurs during the downswing and at the trough of the business cycle. The opposite occurs during the downswing and at the trough of the business cycle. An increase/decrease in the wage tax rate dampens/heightens the amplitude of the business cycle.

With the same assumptions of no tax shifting and a consumption coefficient greater than 1, the effects of a change in the tax rate on profits are quite different. In this case, the impact of a change in the rate of profits tax on the structure of the business cycle is through the depreciation effect. The distribution effect is zero because the change in the profits tax rate has no direct impact on the wage share. If investment is in an upswing or at its peak, where current investment determines current profits and current profits determine future investment, an increase/decrease in the profits tax rate increases/decreases the impact of current investment and profits on future profits via an increase/decrease in the rate of depreciation. Thus, the increase/decrease in the profits tax rate increases/reduces investment during the upswing and at the peak of the cycle. The opposite occurs during the downswing and at the trough of the cycle. An increase/decrease in the profits tax rate heightens/dampens the amplitude of the cycle.

When tax shifting is introduced, the results change significantly. Again, with the consumption coefficient assumed to be greater than 1, shifting of an increase in the wage tax rate (where the mark-up is inversely related to the wage tax) increases the rate of depreciation and the rate of profits. Therefore, shifting of the wage tax reduces the dampening effect on investment of an increase in the wage tax rate described above. By contrast, the shifting of the profits tax rate has a negative impact on the level of profits and the rate of depreciation. Thus, an increase in the profits tax rate, if shifted, attenuates the rising amplitude of the business cycle. The consequence of introducing tax shifting is that the signs of the impact of taxation on investment all become indeterminate. The issue then becomes empirical.

With a balanced budget constraint, changes in the structure of taxation (as between wages and profits under certain shifting conditions) will have the effect of dampening or attenuating the business cycle. The important considerations to take into account are: (i) the stage of the cycle at which the economy happens to be; (ii) the long-run trend of investment; (iii) the direction of tax policy; and (iv) the process and degree of tax shifting (see Laramie and Mair (1966).

The most significant conclusion to emerge from the above analysis is that, with a balanced budget constraint, taxation has an impact on investment only in the presence of a non-zero trend. Under these circumstances, an unshifted changed in the tax on wages is inversely related to the trend level of investment and a change in the profits tax has an indeterminate effect on the trend level of investment, depending on the relative strengths of the depreciation and profits effects. Structural government budget deficit therefore acts as a stimulus, and not as a deterrent, to investment.

To summarise: we have presented a Kaleckian macroeconomic theory of tax incidence which has identified the channels through which changes in the structure of taxation will impact on the aggregate level of activity. This stands in contrast to the standard Keynesian balanced budget effect and/or various crowding-out effects. The model has highlighted the importance of fiscal incidence: that is, that the mix of government expenditures and tax receipts is important in determining macroeconomic effects. We proceed next to show how a PKK model of the macroeconomic incidence and effects of state taxes within a federal structure can be developed. We illustrate this model by reference to the US system of federal and state and local taxation as a starting point for the debate in Europe on the role of fiscal policy in Stages Two and Three of Maastricht.

PKK MACROECONOMIC THEORY OF INCIDENCE OF FEDERAL AND STATE TAXES

Following on from the PKK dynamic tax incidence model of the previous section, but allowing for taxes on wages, the share of profits and wages of industry value added are given as:

$$P/Y = [(k-1)(1+j) - O/W]/[(k-1)(1+j)+1] \quad (1.9)$$

$$W/Y = (1-tw)/[(k-1)(1+j)+1] \quad (1.10)$$

where P = aggregate industry profits; Y = value added; k = average industry mark-up; j = ratio of material costs to industry wage bill; O = industry overhead costs; W = industry wage bill; and tw = the tax rate on the wage bill. As reflected in equations (1.9) and (1.10), assuming profits taxes are not part of prime costs, the distribution of income is affected directly through changes in the tax rate on the wage bill and indirectly through the impact of taxation on industry mark-ups, k (see Mair and Laramie 1992); Laramie and Mair (1993).

The macroeconomic implications of Kalecki's theory of income distribution are as follows. The post-tax wage and salary share of gross private sector income is defined as:

$$V/Y = \beta/Y + \alpha \quad (1.11)$$

where V = wage and salary income; β = after-tax salaries (a part of overhead costs); α = wages' share of value-added. Assuming that k and j represent economy-wide aggregates, the right hand side of equation (1.11) is set equal to α. This term is used to derive the basic Kaleckian income multiplier $1/(1-\alpha)$, where the level of national income is given as:[2]

$$Y = (\beta + \Pi)/(1-a) \quad (1.12)$$

where $\Pi = P + T$.

National income is expressed as a function of expenditures by finding an expression for after-tax profits. If we define aggregate profits simply as corporate profits, like Levy and Levy (1983),[3] then:

$$P = I + X + (G - Tn) + D - Sp - Z \quad (1.13)$$

where P = post-tax gross corporate profits; I = gross private domestic investment less the inventory valuation adjustment; X = net foreign investment; Tn = net (of transfer payments) government receipts;

$G =$ government purchases; D = the sum of corporate net interest and dividends; Sp = personal savings; and Z = the sum of non-corporate consumption of fixed capital, wage accruals less disbursements, capital grants received and the statistical discrepancy. Then, the sum of corporate profits and tax receipts can be written as:

$$P = I + X + G + D - Sp - Z \tag{1.14}$$

Substituting equation (1.14) into (1.12) yields:

$$Y = [\beta + I + X + G + D - Sp - z]/(1 - \alpha) \tag{1.15}$$

If we assume that dividends and interest payments are payments are fixed in the short period,

$$D = Do \tag{1.16}$$

and that personal savings is a linear function of the national income,

$$Sp = Spo + s(Y) \tag{1.17}$$

then the expression for national income is given as:

$$Y = [\beta + I + X + G + Do - Spo - Z]/(1 - \alpha + s) \tag{1.15$'$}$$

From equation (1.15′) it can be seen that taxation plays no explicit role in affecting the level of national income but that the structure of taxation can affect the distribution factors, α and β (since β is after tax salaries, where pre-tax salaries are assumed to be fixed).

Thus, it can be seen from our PKK model that the equations critical for an examination of the macroeconomic incidence and effects of state and local taxation in a federal context are (1.14), (1.15) and (1.15′). We present below results we have obtained for the US as illustrative of the macroeconomic effects of state and local taxation.

THE MACROECONOMIC INCIDENCE OF STATE TAXATION

The macroeconomic incidence of taxation of profits is determined by two sets of effects (Laramie, 1994): (i) a public sector effect which depends upon the government's budget stance; and (ii) a private sector effect which, in turn, depends upon: (a) the reaction of personal savings to the tax/budget stance; (b) the reaction of investment to the tax in the long period; (c) the change in corporate mark-ups with respect to the tax; and (d) a foreign sector effect. As implied, a dollar increase in the taxes, holding other things constant, results in a dollar reduction in post-tax corporate profits, but this effect is mitigated depending upon the public and the private sector effects. If the government spends the tax receipts on final goods and services, the incidence of the profit tax on corporations is reduced depending upon the reaction of personal savings to the resultant change in aggregate income. Moreover, if corporations respond to a tax by altering mark-ups, then the economic incidence of the tax may further vary from the legal incidence. These various effects impact on future investment through their impact on profits, which may lead to cumulative incidence effects.

In determining the economic incidence of any tax, the relative strengths of these various effects must be considered. In the USA, the Federal government's budget stance is a policy decision, and typically little can be said about it, a priori. However, it is possible to indulge in some speculation about the relative strengths of the private sector effects. These are expected to be relatively weak. First, consider the behaviour of savings. If the marginal propensity to save is small, then a change in income, given a change in any tax, is likely to have a small impact on post-tax corporate profits. Second, the extent to which taxes impact on aggregate post-tax profits, via the degree to which taxes are shifted through changes in corporate mark-ups, is diluted by a number of factors.

For example, in considering the incidence of the US corporate profits tax, Pechman (1987) stresses that businesses only know their tax liability *ex post*, and, therefore, the immediate shifting of the profits tax through mark-up changes is unlikely; also, interfirm rivalry may inhibit the degree to which the tax is shifted forwards or backwards. These sentiments are also expressed by Sylos-Labini (1979) when he argues that non-direct costs may not be passed along due to interfirm differences. However, Coutts, Godley and Nordhaus (1978), in analysing the relationship between profit margins and corporate taxes with UK data, have suggested that little shifting occurs in the short period (a year or less), but that there is some full, or more than full, shifting in the medium and long runs respectively.

Even if full, or more than full, shifting is the outcome, then the extent to which such shifting impacts on the level of aggregate post-tax corporate profits depends upon: (i) the change in aggregate income with respect to the change in profit margins; and (ii) the extent to which personal savings change with respect to the change in aggregate income. Again, if the marginal propensity to save is relatively small, the change in corporate profits with respect to a change in corporate mark-ups is also expected to be relatively small. With the private sector effects relatively insignificant, the incidence of the corporation income tax depends largely upon the government budget stance. The economic incidence of the profits tax is determined politically or institutionally by the way in which these are reflected in the government's budget stance.

To consider the incidence of US state taxes on corporate profits, we re-examine equation (1.14) and consider the institutional/political factors that have determined the budget stances of state governments. Moreover, we reconsider some effects that develop in response to state government budget stances. The budget deficits of state governments are separated in equation (1.14):

$$\Pi = I + X + (G - T)_F + (G - T)_S + D - Sp - Z \tag{1.14'}$$

where the subscripts F and S represent respectively the federal and state governments.

The following factors, as mitigated by private sector reactions, will have an impact on the incidence of state taxes: (i) the structure of the tax receipts of State governments; (ii) the expenditure functions of state governments; (iii) the budget stances of states as determined by their permitted deficits and debt limitations; and (iv) intergovernmental relations between the federal and state governments. We examine each of these briefly in turn.

The Structure of State Government Receipts

To begin, we examine the impact of the structure of government receipts by assuming that tax receipts are simply held, not used, by the state governments. By doing so, we consider how the private sector responses to the structure of taxation alone impacts on corporate profits. Holding other things constant (on the right side of equation (1.14′), the change in State tax receipts is inversely related to corporate profits (dollar for dollar). The impact of taxation on corporate profits is mitigated by the extent to which personal savings change, given a change in state tax receipts. To consider the impact of state taxes on personal savings, we consider the incidence of these state taxes on household incomes.

State taxes can affect personal savings by altering the distribution of income to households which are affected in two ways: (i) through an income effect; and (ii) through a mark-up shifting effect. The income effect arises when the state tax reduces the income flows to households. For example, corporate businesses may reduce their dividends or owners of non-corporate businesses may have less personal disposable income following an increase in the state property tax. The mark-up shifting effect occurs when business alter their mark-ups in an attempt to shift the tax. A change in mark-up (see equation 10), alters the distribution of income and the flow of income to wage earners. Given wage earners' marginal propensities to save, the level of personal savings falls and the level of profits increases, *ceteris paribus*.

The Expenditure Functions of State Governments

As indicated above, one of the factors that influences the incidence of state taxes on corporate profits is the reaction of the private sector to the government budget stance. The private sector reaction depends on what state governments do with their receipts. If state governments receipts are saved and paid for via declines in consumption expenditures, corporate profits decline by the full amount of tax receipts, regardless of the source of tax receipts. If receipts are used to finance expenditures, then the impact of taxation depends on how these expenditures flow into the corporate sector. Government purchases of goods from the corporate sector, for example, flow directly back into the corporate sector, and, therefore, offset the negative impact of taxes on corporate profits. Government purchases from the non-corporate sector – ignoring the foreign sector, compensation to employees, government transfer payments and government interest payments – are payments to households, and the flow of these expenditures back to the corporate sector depends upon households' marginal propensities to save.

The functions of state governments are summarised in state government budgets, the bulk of which are devoted to government purchases. US data suggest that much of the incidence of state taxes on corporate profits depends on the relative impacts of taxes and expenditures on personal savings. The imposition of taxes reduces personal savings, whereas the spending of tax receipts increases personal savings. To determine the relative impacts of these, the state government budget stance and the relative marginal propensities to save (with respect to changes in various state tax receipts and expenditures) must be ascertained. We now consider the state budget stance and the impact of intergovernmental relations.

The State Budget Stance

As is well known, most states in the USA have some form of legal restriction, whether constitutional or statutory, that limits budget deficits. The existence of these restrictions have accounted historically for the surpluses in state budgets. State budgets have typically maintained a budget surplus over the 1980s from about 6 per cent to 12 per cent of gross receipts. In the 1990s, much of this surplus was eliminated. In 1992, the States' budget surplus was only about 0.8 per cent of gross receipts and can be attributed to the surplus in the state and local social insurance fund.

This government budget stance implies that the distribution of gross receipts to various uses (as reflected in expenditures) follows a pattern similar to the distribution of expenditures and that the impact of state taxes on corporate profits depends upon the redistributive effects of state budgets and the resultant impact on personal savings.

Intergovernmental Relations

Governmental relations between the federal and state governments encompass many activities, ranging from federal government mandates, to the deductibility of state taxes, to exclusion from federal taxes of state and municipal bonds, to grants-in-aid. During the 1980s, two of the major changes in fiscal intergovernmental relations that occurred were: (i) the elimination of the deduction for sales taxes; and (ii) consolidation and reduction in grants-in-aid to state governments. The elimination of the deduction for sales taxes appears to have had little impact. In contrast, the reduction in federal grants-in-aid has induced state governments to reduce their budget surpluses and to increase their reliance on income and property taxes in order to balance rising expenditures. Thus, in determining the incidence of state taxes, we are particularly concerned with the impact of federal grants-in-aid to state governments.

Federal grants-in-aid impact on the incidence of state taxes on corporate profits by altering the government budget stance. If the federal government has a marginal propensity to spend greater than the state governments, then the transfer of tax revenues from the federal to the state governments reduces the aggregate propensity to spend out of tax receipts and, thus, alters the impact of taxes on aggregate profits. Moreover, if state governments substitute federal grants-in-aid for other revenue sources, like personal and property tax receipts, the incidence of state taxes on corporate profits and other forms of income may be altered.

MEASURING THE SHORT-PERIOD EFFECT OF STATE AND LOCAL TAXES ON CORPORATE PROFITS

In order to estimate the impact of selected state and local tax receipts on personal savings, we estimate a personal savings function. Personal savings is expressed as a function of different definitions of personal disposable

Table 1.1 The impact of selected state and local tax receipts on personal savings in the USA, 1980: Q2 to 1993: Q1 (OLS estimates)

Constant	Y_D: *Def. 1*	Y_D: *Def. 2*	Y_D: *Def. 3*	*Corporate Profits Tax*	*Indirect Business Tax*	*Personal Savings (t – 1)*
79.402	0.0129					0.545
(3.126)	(0.256)					(4.630)
R^2 =	SER =	F = 11.2	DW =			
0.284	28.18		2.06			
113.83	–0.325	0.263				0.476
(3.196)	(–1.288)	(1.370)				(3.740)
R^2 =	SER =	F = 8.17	DW =			
0.296	27.94		2.06			
76.47	0.164	0.408		–2.130	–1.800	0.482
(1.71)	(1.350)	(1.540)		(–1.170)	(–1.460)	(3.820)
R^2 =	SER =	F = 5.58	DW =			
0.318	27.50		1.96			
73.06	0.163		0.330	–2.400	–1.790	0.499
(1.60)	(1.330)		(1.250)	(–1.310)	(–1.420)	(3.980)
R^2 =	SER =	F = 5.76	DW =			
0.310	27.6		1.97			

Note: *t*-statistics in parentheses.

income and of itself, all in current dollars, lagged by one quarter. The first definition (Y_D: Def. 1) of personal disposable income is the standard definition in the *US National Income and Product Accounts*. The second (Y_D: Def. 2) is the previous definition plus net state and local government transfer payments, which are defined as the difference between the sum of compensation to employees and transfer payments to persons and the sum of personal tax receipts and social security contributions. The third definition (Y_D: Def. 3) is the first minus US government transfer payments, defined as compensation to government employees and transfers to persons. The regression results are shown in Table 1.1.

As we see in Table 1.1, none of the coefficients, except those on the lagged dependent variable, is statistically different from zero. These estimates imply that the personal savings function, at least within one quarter, is not sensitive to changes in state and local net transfer payments and corporate and indirect business taxes. As a consequence, the incidence of state and local taxes, at least in the short period (one quarter), is determined by the difference between government expenditures and tax receipts.

To test for the robustness of this result, we estimate the average propensities to consume out of various incomes: (i) private sector compensation to employees; (ii) property incomes (the sum of corporate profits, proprietors' income, non-corporate net interest and rental income); (iii) federal government expenditures distributed directly to households (government compensation to employees, government transfers to persons and net interest paid by government); and (iv) state and local government expenditures distributed directly to households. To estimate these propensities, we use a variant of Weintraub's (1978, 1981) consumption coefficient.[4] In Weintraub's formulation, aggregate consumption expenditure is equal to the product of the consumption coefficient and the aggregate wage bill.

We alter Weintraub's formulation by including a random error term so that we write the consumption coefficient as:

$$C = a(V) + \varepsilon \tag{1.18}$$

where $C =$ aggregate consumption; $a =$ consumption coefficient; $V =$ aggregate wage bill (including salaries) and $\varepsilon =$ random error team. Since aggregate consumption can be defined as the sum of consumption out of private sector compensation to employees, consumption out of property income, consumption out of federal government distributions to households and consumption out of state and local government distributions to households, equation (1.18) can be rewritten as:

$$c_v(V) + c_p(P') + c_f(FD) + c_{sl}(SD) = a(V) + \varepsilon \tag{1.18$'$}$$

where $c_i =$ the average propensity to consume out of pre-tax incomes, where $i = v, p, f, sl$ and where $P' =$ property income, $FD =$ Federal government direct distributions to households and $SD =$ State and local government direct distributions to households. By rearranging (1.18′) and dividing sides by the wage bill, V, we derive:

$$a = c_v + c_p(P'/V) + c_f(FD/V) + c_{sl}(SD/V) + \varepsilon/V \tag{1/19}$$

By estimating equation (1.14), we are able to obtain estimates of the various average propensities to consume (see Table 1.12).

As can be seen from Table 1.2, over the sample period (1980: Q2–1993: Q1), all the estimates of the average propensities to consume were statistically different from zero, except the average propensity to consume out of property

Table 1.2 Estimates of average propensities to consume (maximum likelihood iterative technique)

c_v	c_p	c_f	c_{sl}
0.837 (6.850)	0.688 (0.599)	0.610 (2.658)	1.511 (2.838)
$R^2 = 0.971$	SER = 0.081	F = 568.909	DW = 1.80

c_v = private sector compensation to employees
c_p = property income
c_f = federal government direct distribution to households
c_{sl} = state and local direct government distribution to households
Note: *t*-statistics in parenthesis.

income. For US readers, the interest in these estimates lies in their numeral values. For European readers, the interest lies in the way in which Weintraub's consumption coefficient can be used to calculate estimates of the average propensities to consume for different categories of income and for different levels of government expenditures (federal, state and local).

We have looked above at ways in which US state taxation interacts with federal taxation. We now wish to consider some possible macroeconomic effects. As evidenced in equation (1.15′), State taxation has an impact on national income through these variables: (i) the post-tax salary bill, β; (ii) the wage share, α; and (iii) government purchases, G.

By differentiating equation (1.15′) with respect to β, G and α, we conclude that increases in tax rates that reduce the post-tax salary bill or the wage share have a negative impact on national income. In contrast, an increase in the profit tax, assuming the profits tax has no impact on the wage share, will increase national income, if the profits tax is used to fund an increase in government purchases.

This US result raises interesting questions for the future role of corporate profits taxation in post-Maastricht EU. In the USA, state governments make only minimal use of the corporate profits tax and it is their weakest revenue source. Due to capital mobility and the presence of local business and threats of exit, individual states are constrained in their ability to use the profits tax to fund projects even though such taxes are likely to stimulate growth and have no aggregate incidence impact on corporate profits. Instead, state governments clearly choose inferior policies which play income classes off against each other. For example, an increase in indirect business taxes, household property or sales taxes reduces household consumption on the one hand but is then redistributed back to households or to government purchases. The net effect is that some households, like middle or lower income households who do not receive transfer payments or have major stakes in corporations, are made worse off while corporate profits are unaffected. Corporate profits and household incomes, in aggregate, could be unaffected if the corporate profits tax were used to fund state government purchases. To the extent that the same pressures from the business sector will constrain the use of corporate taxation in a post-Maastricht EU, considerations similar to those that have arisen for the USA may arise.

The reluctance of state governments to use the corporate profits tax suggests an added rationale for federal grants-in-aid. The federal government has much greater latitude and does not face the same constraints, even in a global economy, as state governments in levying corporate profit taxes. The federal government could rectify the deficiency in public investment by increasing the corporate profits tax and by applying these funds to federal grants-in-aid. The result would be more balanced economic growth.

CONCLUSION

The purpose of this chapter has been to show that implementation of the Treaty of Maastricht raises important issues for fiscal policy. There are two levels at which we think the debate should proceed. The first is the theoretical, and we have shown here how a PKK model can be constructed to examine the macroeconomic incidence and effects of national fiscal policy in a federal Europe. It seems to us that this is an important theoretical issue. The widespread mainstream practice of grafting pre-Keynesian microeconomic assumptions – perfect competition, full market clearing, perfect factor mobility and so on – on to a Keynesian macroeconomic model seems to use to render mainstream theory incapable of analysing in any meaningful sense the macroeconomic effects of taxation. We argue for a PKK approach in which both micro- and macroeconomic elements are combined in the way we have demonstrated.

Our analysis suggest that stabilisation need no longer depend on the application of orthodox Keynesian policies of running budget deficits during recessions and surpluses during periods of recovery. Stabilisation objectives can be achieved within given volumes of public revenue and spending by altering the structure of taxation. Recognition of this possibility means that compliance by a member state to the 3 per cent budget deficit constraint of the Maastricht Treaty need not act as a constraint on its ability to use fiscal policy as an instrument of stabilisation. Appropriate and suitably timed switches between taxation of wages and profits, for example, could have the desired macroeconomic effects for member states.

A corollary of this PKK conclusion is that there would then be a tendency towards greater heterogeneity in the structure of taxation of member states. This, of course, would be at variance with the longstanding desire for fiscal harmonisation within the EU. However, this could provide an opportunity to address one of the major issues likely to delay successful completion of Stage Three: namely, the reluctance of certain member states, notably the UK, to surrender autonomy for economic and monetary policy to the EU. It would be possible for member states to exercise discretion over national macroeconomic priorities while still complying with the fiscal criteria of Stages Two and Three. The *quid pro quo* for the Council would be to forgo the quest for fiscal harmonisation.

If PKK theory is suggesting greater fiscal heterogeneity within a post-Maastricht EU as a means of reconciling member states' stabilisation objectives and the Council's convergence criteria, then it is important to recognise that the macroeconomic incidence and effects of EU taxation and spending may be quite different from the macroeconomic incidence and incidence and effects of the taxation and spending of member states. As we have shown in here, due to institutional and political factors in the USA, the macroeconomic effects and incidence of state and local taxes are different from the incidence of similar federal taxes. Due to statutory or constitutional requirements, state governments have deficit and debit limitations. The US federal government appears to have an *ad hoc* budget process with little apparent connection between the revenue and expenditure sides of the budget. These state fiscal constraints, coupled with federal grants-in-aid, cause the state governments' propensity to consume out of tax receipts to exceed one and, therefore, have a negligible, though positive, impact on corporate profits.

The fiscal policy implications for the EU of adopting the sort of PKK approach outlined in this chapter can only be identified after a detailed examination of the macroeconomic issues identified here. We have specified the sort of PKK model which can be estimated for the US (see Laramie and Mair 1995). A corresponding EU model would require to take into account: (i) a macroeconomic theory of the incidence of taxation; (ii) the structure of the tax receipts of the governments of member states; (iii) the expenditure functions of the governments of member states; (iv) the budget stances of the member states; and (v) the intergovernmental relations between the EU and its member states.

Notes

1. The Treaty contains provision for some relaxation of these conditions, but these are not important for our purposes here.
2. We are ignoring post-tax proprietor's income, rental income and non corporate net interest.
3. Levy and Levy (1983) show that manipulation of the savings and investment identity in the US National Income and Product Accounts yields the following expression for corporate profits:

   Post-tax corporate profits (with inventory valuation and capital adjustments) = gross investment + government budget deficit + dividends–personal savings – consumption of fixed capital – wage accruals (less disbursements) – capital grants received by USA (net) – statistical discrepancy.

   By recognising that the consumption of fixed capital can be broken down into corporate and non-corporate elements; and by adding the corporate component to both sides; and by subtracting the capital consumption and inventory valuation adjustments from both sides; and by adding corporate net interest to both sides, gross profit-tax corporate profits can be written as:

   Gross post-tax corporate profits (= undistributed corporate profits + dividends + corporate net interest + corporate consumption of fixed capital) = gross investment – corporate capital consumption adjustment + government budget deficit + dividends + corporate net interest – personal savings – non-corporate capital consumption allowance (with inventory valuation and capital consumption adjustments) – wage accruals (less disbursements) – capital grants received by USA (net) – statistical discrepancy.

   For more details, see appendix in Laramie (1994) for the complete derivation
4. Weintraub defines the consumption coefficient as the ratio of consumption expenditures to the wage bill in order to eliminate the standard Kalecki-Kaldor-Robinson assumption that capitalists do not consume and workers do not save. For further discussion of the theoretical and empirical relevance of the consumption coefficient, see Laramie, Mair and Toporowski (1996).

References

Asimakopulos, A. and Burbidge, J. B. (1974) 'The short-period incidence of taxation', *Economic Journal*, 84, pp. 267–88.

Atkinson, A. B. and Stiglitz, J. E. (1989) *Lectures on Public Economics* Maidenhead: McGraw-Hill).

Bayoumi, T. and Eichengreen, B. (1994) 'The political economy of fiscal restrictions: implications for Europe from the United States', *European Economic Review*, 38 (3–4), pp. 783–791.

Bryant, R., Henderson, D. W., Holtham, G., Hooper, P. and Symansky, S. A. (eds) (1990) *Empirical Macroeconomics for Interdependent Economies* (Washington, DC: Brookings Institution).

Buiter, W., Corsetti, G. and Roubini, N. (1993) 'Excessive deficits: sense and nonsense in the Treaty of Maastricht', *Economic Policy*, 16, pp. 57–100.

Canzoneri, M. and Diba, B. (1991) 'Fiscal deficits, financial integration and a central bank for Europe', *Journal of the Japanese and International Economies*, 5, pp. 481–503.

Coutts, K., Godley, W. and Nordhaus, W. (1978) *Industrial Pricing in the United Kingdom* (Cambridge: Cambridge University Press).

Damania, D. and Mair, D. (1992) 'The short period incidence of taxation revisited', *Cambridge Journal of Economics*, 16(2), pp. 195–206.

Eichengreen, B. (1990) 'One money for Europe? Lessons from the US currency and customs union', *Economic Policy*, 10, pp. 117–87.

Eichengreen, B. (1992a) 'Is Europe an optimum currency area?', in S. Borner and H. Grubel (eds), *European Integration: The View from Outside* (London: Macmillan), pp. 138–61.

Eichengreen, B. (1992b) *Should the Maastricht treaty be saved?, Princeton Studies in International Finance,* 74 (December).

Eichengreen, B. (1993) 'European monetary unification', *Journal of Economic Literature*, 31(3), pp. 1321–57.

Eichengreen, B. (1994) 'Fiscal policy and EMU', in B. Eichengreen and J. Frieden (eds), *The Political Economy of European Monetary Unification* (Boulder, Col.: Westview Press), pp. 167–90.

Harberger, A. C. (1962) 'The incidence of the corporation income tax', *Journal of Political Economy*, 70, pp. 215–40.

Kalecki, M. (1971/1937) 'A theory of commodity, income and capital taxation', *Economic Journal*, 47, pp. 444–50. Reprinted in *Selected Essays on the Dynamics of a Capitalist Economy, 1993–1970* (Cambridge: Cambridge University Press).

Kalecki, M. (1971/1968) *Theory of Economic Dynamics* (New York: Monthly Review Press).

Kenen, P. B. (1969) 'The optimum currency area: an eclectic view', in R. Mundell and A. Swoboda (eds), *Monetary Problems of the International Economy* (Chicago: University of Chicago Press), pp. 41–60.

Kriesler, P. (1989) 'Methodological implications of Kalecki's microfoundations', in M. Sebastiani (ed.), *Kalecki's Relevance Today* (London: Macmillan), pp. 121–41.

Kotlikoff, L. and Summers, L. (1987) 'Tax incidence', in A. J. Auerbach and M. Feldstein (eds), *Handbook on Public Economics, vol. 2* (Amsterdam: North-Holland), pp. 1043–92.

Laramie, A. J. (1991) 'Taxation and Kalecki's distribution factors', *Journal of Post Keynesian Economics*, 4, pp. 583–94.

Laramie, A. J. (1994) *The Incidence of the Corporate Profits Tax Revisited: A Post Keynesian Approach*, Jerome Levy Economics Institute, Working paper no. 109.

Laramie, A. J. and Mair, D. (1993) 'The incidence of business rates: a post Keynesian approach', *Review of Political Economy*, 5(1), pp. 55–72.

Laramie, A. J. and Mair, D. (1995) 'The short-period macroeconomic incidence and effects of state and local taxes', in G. Pola, G. France and R. Viaggi (eds), *Developments in Local Government Finance: Theory and Policy* (Chelthenham: Edward Elgar), pp. 135–58.

Laramie, A. J. and Mair, D. (1996) 'Taxation and Kalecki's theory of the business cycle', *Cambridge Journal of Economics*, 20(4), pp. 451–64.

Laramie, A. J., Mair, D., Miller, A. G. and Reynolds, P. J. (1994) 'Kalecki's degree of monopoly theory of income distribution: some new results', Department of Economics, Heriot-Watt University, mimeo.

Laramie, A. J., Mair, D. and Toporowski, J. (1996) 'Weintraub's consumption coefficient: some economic implications and evidence for the UK economy', *Journal of Post Keynesian Economics* (forthcoming).

Levy, S. J. and Levy, D. A. (1983) *Profits and the Future of American Society* (New York: Harper & Row).

Mair, D. and Laramie, A. J. (1992) 'The incidence of business rates on manufacturing industry', *Scottish Journal of Political Economy*, 39(1), pp. 76–94.

Mieszkowski, P. M. (1972) 'The property tax: an excise tax or a profits tax?', *Journal of Public Economics*, 1, pp. 73–96.

Qudiz, G. and Sachs, J. (1984) 'Macroeconomic policy co-ordination among the industrial economies'. *Brookings Papers on Economic Activity*, 1, pp. 1–64.

Pechman, J. A. (1987) *Federal Tax Policy*, 5th edn (Washington, DC: Brookings Institution).

Reynolds, P. J. (1984) 'An empirical analysis of the degree of monopoly theory of income distribution', *Bulletin of Economic Research*, 36(1), pp. 59–84.

Roberti, P. and Vissagio, M. (1994) 'Fiscal adjustments between fiscal harmonisation and the Maastricht convergence criteria', in M. Baldassarri and M. Roberti (eds), *Fiscal Problems in the Single-Market Europe* (London: Macmillan and New York: St Martin's Press), pp. 261–93.

Sala-in-Martin, X. and Sachs, J. (1992) 'Federal fiscal policy and optimum currency areas', in M. Canzoneri, V. Grilli and P. Masson (eds), *Establishing a Central Bank: Issues in Europe and Lessons from the US* (Cambridge: Cambridge University Press), pp. 195–220.

Sylos-Labini, P. (1979) 'Industrial pricing in the United Kingdom', *Cambridge Journal of Economics*, 3, pp. 153–63. Reprinted in M. C. Sawyer (ed.), *Post Keynesian Economics* (Aldershot: Edward Elgar).

Weintraub, S. (1979) 'Generalising Kalecki and Simplifying Macroeconomics', *Journal of Post Keynesian Economics*, 3, pp. 101–6.

Weintraub, S. (1981) 'An eclectic theory of income shares', *Journal of Post Keynesian Economics*, 4, pp. 10–24.

2 New Scale and Scope for Industrial Policies in the 1990s

Bruno Amable and Pascal Petit

INTRODUCTION

Industrial policies (IPs) are often considered as minor complements of macroeconomic policies. Low-key definitions, where IPs are limited to selective promotions of activities and support of R&D, are in accordance with what has been observed in the last four decades. This balance may be shifting as standard macroeconomic policies are losing momentum and effectiveness, while industrial policies are facing a new context.

We make a tentative assessment of the potential room for manoeuvre given to extended industrial policies. The growing openness of national economies to international competition, along with changes in technology and organisation, both reduce the room for standard national macroeconomic policies and present new opportunities for various kinds of monitoring (local, national or international). Even if one takes a comprehensive view of these opportunities, the macroeconomic result of these modern IPs still depends among other things on some order of magnitude, some continuity and coherence that requires a political will which may be lacking.

We shall start with a common definition of industrial policies such as that recalled by Sawyer (1992a: 51):

> any policy which seeks to influence industrial structure (e.g. merger policy, promotion of small business), to change the behaviour of enterprises or to improve industrial performance by micro-economic measures with macroeconomic measures such as interest rate changes excluded.

This definition mirrors a dichotomy rooted in the experience of most industrialised nations during the 'golden age of capitalism' period. It established that short-run demand management was a basic (Keynesian) tool of macroeconomic policy while an IP was a more 'local' means to ease in the longer run the structural change affecting the economy. For objective (the long-term aspect) or political reasons (the limits given to the role of the state) the macroeconomic effects of IP were not accounted for.

A central hypothesis of this chapter is to consider that changes in the economic and political environment invite us to reappraise the status that IPs can have in the making of contemporary macroeconomic policies. Such a perspective does not refer to the recent debate on demand or supply-side policies but could be referred back to the old post-war debate on various kinds of Keynesian policies. This is why we start with a presentation of this debate and survey briefly how, in various countries, the notion of the developmental role of the state was built up.

In spite of country differences, the new legitimacy of public intervention in the sphere of economic activity led to a general and continuous rise in the share of public expenditures (as a percentage of GDP) which only came to an end in the early 1980s. The third section looks back at this overall expansion of public spending during the 'golden age of capitalism' up to the crisis and slowdown of the 1970s and early 1980s. Looking at which categories of spending benefited most from this rise underlines the steady and general upward trend in social transfers and government consumption, while the share allocated to industrial policies seems to remain roughly constant. The next section then stresses how a new context since the mid-1970s – years of slow growth, where forms of competition have been drastically changed – sets opportunities to reshape IPs. This of course leads to questions on the scale and scope that these IPs can reach. The question of assessing the macroeconomic impact that coordinated IPs can achieve is tentatively addressed in the following section.

Even if 'realistic calibrations' on their own fall short of demonstrating that sound packages of industrial policies could fully reflate our economies, it seems useful in conclusion to point to some of the undergoing societal changes that could support the political will and enhance the magnitude of the policies as required for any sizeable change to occur.

THE DEVELOPMENTAL ROLE OF THE STATE

The room for public intervention in the economy was greatly enlarged in most developed economies in the aftermath of the Second World War. The crisis of the 1930s and the disasters and the destructions that followed made it clear that capitalism had to be reformed, to say the least. Keynesian ideas have been quintessential in placing increasing responsibility for economic performance on the governments' shoulders, with ambiguities which were an essential source of their widespread influence (to paraphrase Hall 1989). The forms and commitments to Keynesian policies vary from one country to another. Most policy packages and debates at the time were around the full employment issue, because unemployment had been a major cause of bellicose totalitarianism. Commitments to full employment at the beginning of the period and their evolution in the following decades therefore have been diverse.

Table 2.1 recalls the national characteristics of these commitments as they appear in times of relative full employment in the 1960s. It underlines that the main political concern (drawing a prevailing consensus within the population), as well as the form taken by the policies themselves, differ. Looking back on how these commitments had been implemented, Joan Robinson set a clear distinction between bastard and fundamentalist Keynesian policies. Only in the latter case were policies implemented at regional and micro levels, to ensure full employment in the spirit envisaged in the Beveridge plan of the 1940s. In the former case the commitment tends to boil down to sustaining economic activity by general fiscal and budgetary means of standard macroeconomic policies. Eatwell (1983) has rightly underlined that fundamental Keynesianism was much more long-term oriented than its more standard counterpart.

Some policy perspectives (as presented in Table 2.1) seem to be closer to IPs, as previously defined, than others. Countries that are more into a fundamentalist Keynesian tradition are expected to adopt more comprehensive IPs, while countries with a more standard Keynesian approach to macroeconomic policy are readily assumed to reduce IP to the correction of (micro) imperfections. Somehow this remark suggests that the distinction between restrictive and comprehensive IP (as drawn in Sawyer 1992a), distinguishing the market-failure origin of IP in the Anglo-Saxon tradition from the developmental IP tradition (more common in continental Europe), should correspond to sorting countries on the basis of what kind of full employment policies were pursued. It is therefore interesting to stress that such is not the case: countries that tended to pursue a radical full employment policy are not always considered as pursuing a comprehensive approach to industrial policy.

One can see from Table 2.1 that countries such as the Netherlands and the Nordic countries had radical full employment commitments but few comprehensive IPs, while some others, like France and Italy, with mild full employment commitments, could be considered as favouring developmentalist IP. Table 2.2 tries to feature the cross distribution of countries in the above categories; the importance of investment in public expenditures is taken as a rough indicator of a more or less comprehensive

Table 2.1 Full employment policies in the post-war period: highly country-specific

	Commitment to full employment by means of		
	Political concern	*Standard Keynesian policies*	*Specific interventions*
USA	For hegemony	Military expenditure Autonomy of Federal Reserve Board	Immigration
Japan	For growth	Administrative co-ordination of large firms	Life-time employment
Germany	For inflation	Strict monetary and budgetary policies *Länder* regional policies	Concerned action, immigration
France	For growth	Planning public investments	–
UK	For currency	Fiscal policy	–
Italy	–	Regional policy	Internal migration
Austria	Neutrality	Investment stimuli	Publicly owned business sector
Belgium	Free market	Tripartite management	None
Denmark	Employment	Fiscal stimuli	None
Netherlands	Employment	Tripartite management	Secondary concern
Norway	Employment	Subsidies to firms	Regional development plans
Sweden	Employment	Public investment	Direct intervention in labour market
Switzerland	Free market	Public investment	Immigration policy

Source: translated from Table I in Petit (1991). Appreciations are drawn from Therborn (1986), ch. III, and Esping-Andersen (1990), ch. 7.

industrial policy on one side, whereas the mention of full employment as an explicit political concern in Table 2.1 is taken as an indicator of radical Keynesian policy.[1] Even if this partition of countries is debatable, it should make the point that the two characteristics do not fully coincide. This observation leads to two remarks. First, it strengthens the highly country-specific nature of the full employment *accord* that took place in the post-war period. Second, it calls attention to the fact that the political concern for employment has been accompanied by a general and continuous rise in social transfers and government consumption, which contributed to improving, by means of public intervention, the condition of the wage earners. By contrast, public resources devoted to IPs more or less stagnated over the same 30 years (1950–80) in all countries. In effect, this structure of public intervention is a strong characteristic of the period, and the section which follows will return to this issue, stressing fundamental differences with the period that opened with the 1980s.

Table 2.2 Full employment policy and industrial policy: in the 1950s and 1960s

Full employment policy	*Standard Keynesian*	*Radical Keynesian*
Industrial policy		
Restrictive approach	USA, UK, Switzerland	Denmark, Sweden, Netherlands
Comprehensive approach	France, Italy, Japan, Germany	Austria, Norway

It is useful to question how policies operate within a given context and how these procedures change with a new context. More should be said about the periodisation we are hinting at. In effect, the context mentioned above is a long-term one as defined by the interplay of a set of institutions. Thus, the post-war period started with major changes in institutions, regulations and practices, which set the context for policies for three or four decades. This period may well have ended in the mid-1970s when the oil price shocks made clear the erosion of the old context in a world changed, among other things, by the internationalisation of economic activities, the emergence of a new technological system centred around information technology or the ensuing obsolescence of some institutions and regulations.

From the post-war experience, we usually tend to think that changes in context for a new 'growth regime' occur rapidly. The experience of the 1980s suggests that change may occur more gradually as shown by the trends of deregulation/regulation, the reorganisations of international relations, and the reshuffling of institutions which have been going on over more than a decade. In that perspective, where contexts are, by definition, highly country-specific, policies can be seen in different ways as trying more or less to make the best out of this context (or to overcome its shortcomings). These objectives vary with the theoretical perspective used. In a neoclassical perspective a change of context boils down to an exogenous shift of some aggregate production function. Policies should only cope with the imperfections brought along (such as market failures, information bias, externalities, and so on). In an evolutionary perspective *à la* Nelson and Winter, the whole shift operates through its impact on the learning process of the economy. The aim of policies to improve this learning process is thus to make the best of the context in a world of bounded rationality, imperfect information and strategic behaviour. Changes may accordingly deeply transform the initial context.

The *Régulation* Theory has a similar approach except that it emphasises the consistencies within one period between interacting sets of institutions and practices (founding productivity regimes and demand regimes) so that the above-mentioned learning process is given some meso-economic dimension (by means of structural forms). Policies are intrinsic parts of the institutional background of the growth regime prevailing over the given period; therefore, changes in what we called the context do not occur progressively but through (small and big) crises, which highlights the need for a periodisation.

These assessments are rather loose. Simple modelling can help to clarify the issue, as has been the case with the old Keynesian debate on the 'warranted' growth rate. In a context where rates of saving, investment, labour force growth and efficiency are fixed, the growth rate of the economy follows but the corresponding growth path is unstable (Harrod's knife edge) and has to be monitored. Built-in stabilisers most of the time include public interventions. Because of this threat of instability, economic policies appear necessary to keep economies on a steady growth path. Because the growth rate 'warranted' by the actual context does not eventually meet some 'natural' requirements, such as the full employment of the labour force, policies may also be aimed at promoting higher growth paths.

THE GOLDEN AGE AND THE EXPANSION OF WELFARE

Increasing Public Spending until the Early 1980s

The golden age period was characterised by an important rise in the share of the total public expenditures in GDP (see period 1960–74 in Table 2.3) in all of the industrialised countries. This rise took different forms but the bulk of it depended mainly on welfare and other payments allotted to wage earners. Thus the relative importance of indirect wages accounted for much of the differences between the levels of public spending reached in the mid-1970s

Table 2.3 Public expenditures as a percentage of GDP

	1960	*1974*	*1982*	*1990*	*Difference 1960–90*
Sweden	31.0	48.1	66.3	61.4	+ 30.4
Denmark	24.8	45.9	61.2	58.4	+ 33.6
Netherlands	33.7	47.9	61.6	55.6	+ 21.9
Norway	29.9	44.6	48.3	54.6	+ 24.7
Italy	30.1	37.9	47.4	53.0	+ 22.9
France	34.6	39.3	50.4	49.9	+ 15.3
Austria	35.7	41.9	50.9	49.6	+ 13.9
Canada	28.6	36.8	46.6	46.9	+ 18.3
Germany	32.4	44.6	49.6	46.0	+ 13.6
UK	32.2	44.8	47.0	42.1	+ 9.9
US	27.0	32.2	36.5	36.7	+ 9.7
Japan	17.5	24.5	33.6	32.3	+ 14.8

Source: OECD, National Accounts, various years.

(see Table 2.3). The countries where the share had increased most (Nordic and the Netherlands) were the countries classified as 'Radical Keynesian with a restrictive approach' (in Table 2.2). The countries where the share had increased less were previously classified as 'Standard Keynesian with a restrictive approach' to IP.

One should also notice that in most countries the rise in public spending, which occurred during a period of relatively rapid growth, continued until the early 1980s, well after the slowdown of economic growth which began in the 1970s. Some welfare payments kept their momentum, extending and intensifying coverage, while slow economic growth added new burdens on the budget (interest payments tied with rising indebtedness). Only in the last decade did public expenditure level off or start to decline as a share of GDP (see Table 2.3). In the early 1990s the geography of public spending could distinguish roughly three groups of countries: Northern Europe, Continental Europe and Anglo-Saxon countries.

The internal dynamics of public spending may also be changing. We can hint at these changes by looking at the composition of the spending. An examination of the figures in Table 2.4 reveals that industrialised countries have, in the early 1990s, different priorities in their public expenditure. The countries of the North of Europe favour government consumption and, to a lesser extent, social transfers. The latter have a much lower share in the

Table 2.4 Uses of total public expenditures in 1990 (% of GDP)

Government consumption		*Social transfers*		*Interests and subsidies*		*Investment*	
Sweden	27.1	Netherlands	26.3	Denmark	12.9	Japan	6.1
Denmark	25.2	France	21.4	Italy	12.8	Italy	4.9
Norway	21.0	Austria	19.9	Sweden	12.3	Austria	4.7
UK	19.9	Sweden	19.7	Canada	11.6	UK	4.0
Canada	19.8	Norway	19.0	Norway	10.9	Netherlands	3.9
Germany	18.4	Denmark	18.4	Netherlands	10.6	France	3.7
USA	18.1	Italy	18.0	Germany	8.9	Norway	3.7
Austria	18.0	Germany	15.3	Austria	7.0	Germany	3.4
France	18.0	Canada	12.5	France	6.8	Canada	2.9
Italy	17.3	UK	12.2	UK	6.0	Sweden	2.3
Netherlands	14.8	Japan	11.5	USA	5.9	Denmark	1.9
Japan	9.1	USA	10.8	Japan	5.6	USA	1.5

Source: OECD, National Accounts.

Anglo-Saxon countries or in Japan. This reflects differences in the wage-labour nexus of the different kinds of Fordisms under consideration (see Boyer 1988). In effect, the dynamic of the wage-labour nexus is central during this period. Within the set of institutions, set up at the beginning of the period, the dynamics of social progress and improvements for wage earners are taking place.

Over the 1960–80 period, social transfers have increased their share the most in public expenditure for the whole sample of countries, whereas investment has seen its share decrease slightly (see Table 2.5). Here again, the situation is contrasted according to countries. Public investment has seen its share decrease in some countries (Austria, Sweden, Denmark, Netherlands, Germany, USA) and increase in others. If one takes into account the average rate of change of each use in real terms, interest and subsidies have increased the most, followed by social transfers, consumption and, finally, investment. It is unfortunate that the figures given by the OECD do not distinguish between subsidies and interests, because the period under consideration is characterised both by an increase in the share of public debt in GDP for most countries, as well as by periods of important increases in real interest rates; two factors that contribute to increasing the debt service.

A more precise examination of the broad functions favoured by each European country can be done for the year 1986 (as given by Meraud 1994).

Table 2.5 Ratios of public expenditures to GDP: variations over three periods (in percentage points)

	Government consumption			*Social transfers*			*Interests and subsidies*			*Investment*		
Country	*1960/74*	*1974/82*	*1982/90*	*1960/74*	*1974/82*	*1982/90*	*1960/74*	*1974/82*	*1982/90*	*1960/74*	*1974/82*	*1982/90*
Denmark	+ 10.1	+ 4.8	– 3.0	+ 4.6	+ 6.1	+ 0.3	+ 5.1	+ 5.3	+ 1.8	+ 1.3	– 0.9	+ 1.9
Sweden	+ 7.4	+ 5.9	– 2.2	+ 6.3	+ 4.0	+ 1.4	+ 2.9	+ 7.8	– 1.2	+ 0.5	+ 0.5	– 2.9
Germany	+ 5.9	+ 1.3	– 2.2	+ 2.6	+ 3.1	– 2.4	+ 2.2	+ 2.3	+ 1.7	+ 1.5	– 1.5	– 0.9
Norway	+ 5.4	+ 1.1	+ 1.6	+ 5.7	+ 1.7	+ 4.0	+ 2.5	+ 2.3	+ 0.2	+ 1.1	+ 1.4	+ 0.5
Canada	+ 4.7	+ 3.0	– 1.3	+ 1.3	+ 2.5	+ 0.8	+ 1.9	+ 4.4	+ 1.5	+ 0.3	– 0.1	– 0.8
UK	+ 4.7	+ 1.7	– 1.8	+ 3.0	+ 4.2	– 1.8	+ 2.6	– 0.5	– 2.4	+ 3.4	– 3.2	+ 1.1
Netherlands	+ 3.6	+ 1.5	– 2.9	+ 7.2	+ 7.7	– 2.1	+ 3.9	+ 3.7	+ 0.5	– 0.5	+ 0.8	– 1.5
Austria	+ 2.8	+ 3.1	– 0.9	+ 2.6	+ 4.4	0	+ 0.6	+ 3.1	+ 0.6	+ 0.2	– 0.6	– 1.0
Italy	+ 1.8	+ 2.2	+ 1.3	+ 3.9	+ 2.6	+ 1.7	+ 2.5	+ 3.9	+ 2.0	– 0.4	+ 0.8	+ 0.6
USA	+ 1.5	+ 0.3	– 0.3	+ 4.5	+ 2.4	– 1.1	0	+ 2.0	+ 0.7	– 0.8	– 0.4	– 0.3
France	+ 1.2	+ 3.9	– 1.3	+ 2.0	+ 5.7	+ 0.2	+ 1.2	+ 1.8	+ 0.6	+ 0.3	– 0.3	0
Japan	+ 1.1	+ 0.8	– 0.8	+ 2.4	+ 4.8	+ 0.5	+ 1.7	+ 2.8	– 0.1	+ 1.8	+ 0.7	– 0.9

Source: Meraud (1994).

Seven functions are distinguished (health, housing, agriculture, defence, schooling, transport and security). Some models of public intervention can be inferred from the relative priority given to each function. For instance, the UK favours the traditional functions of the state (defence and security) and neglects a relatively more economic type of intervention (transport or agriculture). Italy has a ranking that is roughly the opposite of that of the UK, and the other European countries have intermediate positions.

Beyond this diversity the driving force remained centred in each country around the prevailing convention regarding the status of wage earners. The scope of other types of action, such as IP, remained somehow more limited.

The Approach of Industrial Policy in the 'Golden Age' Period

IPs at the time of the so-called 'golden age of capitalism' were mainly single-minded, searching to catch up either in diffusing the best practised techniques (those in use in the leading country, the USA) or in fostering national champions in promising hi-tech industries.

The main rationale for public intervention in industry during the post-war period had little to do with academic justification linked to market failures. In fact, the justification of industrial policy on academic grounds, which basically centred around the infant industry argument, was much less a problem than it is now, in a context of high internationalisation and rapidly changing technologies and organisations.

The problems facing European countries in the 'Golden Age' were linked to the necessity of a productivity catching-up *vis-à-vis* the USA. This was partially a problem of the size of national firms; hence the 'national champions' policies followed by some countries (notably in France and to some extent in the UK). In such a policy, the government promotes, via a control of (sometimes nationalised) industry or banks, the emergence of large industrial firms, more or less in line with the development of certain large industrial or technological projects (aerospace, nuclear energy, computers). This broad objective was also that of the Japanese government, but this government's monitoring of firms is less direct because of the lack of direct involvement of the state in the economy. The particular organisation of industry in Japan (*Keiretsu*) allows for the implementation of a less direct and centralised industrial policy. Large banks (each large firm has its main bank) can take up the role that was devoted to central agencies in Europe. This is also true for Germany where the banks are large and influential and where local governments have a large importance.

IP was mostly targeted; Japan and France are good examples, trying to favour the rise of industries with a high potential and to ease the structural change away from old industries. The recommendations in Japan's Ministry for International Trade and Industry's White Papers, for instance (Itoh and Kiyono 1988), led to policies in favour of activities with a high technological potential and high income elasticities. In many countries, the implementation of IP usually means a creation *ex nihilo* of large competitive firms. National champions are granted more or less directly a national monopoly, and benefit from a privileged access to credit, through nationalised or controlled banks, or equity. They are protected from foreign competition, invoking an infant industry argument in front of rising external competition. Such national champions policies had varying degrees of success across countries, across sectors and over time (electronics and computers were mostly failures). Some large projects could be technical successes and commercial failures (Concorde) or both technological and commercial failures (fast breeder reactors). Such a mixed record opened the way for criticism in the early 1980s when the relevance and soundness of public intervention was severely questioned. Nevertheless some successes (Japan in electronics, France in telecommunications, Europe as a whole in aerospace) have allowed Europe and Japan partially to catch up in industrial terms.

The 1980s thus appear as a transition period where IPs lost ground but gained new credentials when changes in the forms of competition which characterise the post mid-1970s context are taken into account.

IP: NEW ROOM FOR MANOEUVRE IN THE 1990s

The Context

The debate on IPs has been renewed during the 1980s and the 1990s, in a context where the internationalisation of firms' activity and the importance of technology were the dominant trends. One aspect that mattered during the 1980s, particularly in the USA (Shoch 1994) was whether IPs should be more of a support for sunset industries (such as steel, shipbuilding) or an aid to sunrise industries (such as electronics). Such discussion has an important impact on the political support for IPs, but it concerns the economic aspects too. It can be argued that because of some specific features of the new technologies involved in electronics, their now well-known 'generic' aspect, any action in this field cannot be strictly limited to a 'vertical' or targeted action. More horizontal actions are therefore required, which exert an influence on the economic environment of all the firms. In addition economics has recently focused on some long-term issues such as growth and competitiveness (see the endogenous growth literature, for instance).

Factors such as education and training of the labour force or an efficient network of public infrastructures have been brought to the fore as national competitiveness advantages.

The policy of national champions that some European countries had implemented has reached a limit. In order to grow, firms must necessarily operate outside the national territory and thus face foreign competition. The conditions for competitiveness abroad are very different from the peculiar competitive environment that allowed these firms to become the national champions. There is a contradiction between the protection they enjoy(ed) at home and the competitive pressure that is involved with external growth. The conflict between national champions from different countries must be resolved by economic competition, especially now that the context is one of deregulation. Another change concerns the instruments of IP. It has become increasingly difficult to implement targeted policies aimed at favouring a particular sector because of the size of firms concerned. Such a policy usually means favouring one or a few national firms, which leads to opposition from other (notably European) countries. On the other hand, an increased internationalisation of firms' activity means that they have more latitude for escaping the constraints set upon them by IPs. This limits the influence of an IP in its more restrictive aspects.

The question of the theoretical justification of IPs is raised with more insistence than in the previous decades. The ideological environment leads to questioning all kinds of public intervention and has implications in the different programmes of 'structural reform' advocated by international institutions such as the OECD or the European Commission. In order to be acceptable from an orthodox point of view, any support must not just favour the rise of a national competitor to gain market shares at the expense of another competitor, it must lead to an increase in overall welfare such as the consequence of a fall in production costs and prices. In such an environment, it is therefore not surprising that motivations of IPs in terms of market failures are called for more frequently. The fact that technology is increasingly perceived as a source of competitiveness and growth, with an emphasis put on 'non-price' factors of competitiveness,[2] favours such a point of view. Technology is not a free good. A cumulative learning process is required to appropriate it as it implies a certain amount of tacitness which limits its transferability. Such characteristics lead to the possibility and the desirability of a 'correcting' intervention. It is somewhat ironic that the usefulness of industrial policy is mentioned in an article written by Lucas (1988), which explores the possibility of diverging growth paths in a model with features relatively similar to the Kaldorian cumulative causation models. It illustrates how widespread, in the late 1980s, became the notions of New Competition and relevant cumulative processes as developed within what Sawyer (1992b) called the 'industrial strategy approach' to IPs (see also Best 1990).

Openness to trade and foreign investment implies specialisation in activity; if the prospects for productivity increases differ between activities, what a country makes (and exports) matters for its growth prospects. Indeed new growth theory, as acknowledged in its early seminal steps (see Romer 1986), retains, as Kaldor did, the idea that increasing returns can be fuelled in a dynamic process by some proper uses of the productivity gains generated in the process. While Kaldor had a comprehensive (and loosely defined) approach to these cumulative processes, where proper uses included in some ways all components of demand, new growth theory tends to develop around more specific factors (as with R&D investment and other sources of innovation) which are slightly more tractable but lack part of the widespread and complex nature of the growth factors in modern economies.

Moreover, technological change is an area where market failures are common, which matters a great deal considering the new context of economic policies. The existence of market failures gives a justification for some IP measures, even in a context of 'deregulation'. Externalities are also present where environmental protection measures are concerned. Changes in the forms of market competition in a world that is more open and more complex – a world increasingly concerned with its environment, its intangible assets – point towards comprehensive redefinitions of IPs.

The Measures

The channels of IP cannot be the same as those of the 'golden age'. Vertical measures tend to exacerbate the competition between nations, each defending its national champion. Therefore, in a world where fair trade practices are more and more imperative, only further horizontal measures are considered acceptable. The model of successful economic growth in the 1980s was Japan, and the example was that of the promotion of information exchanges between industry and policy makers. This indirect and indicative type of IP seemed more promising than the direct approach favoured in European countries so far. European initiatives in France and the UK and the definition of EC programmes supporting pre-competitive R&D were directly influenced by the Japanese approach, as exemplified by the fifth-generation computer programme.

One is struck by the diversity of structures of intervention among countries. These differences may be appreciated with the help of some EC surveys (as exploited by Dietrich 1991: see Table 2.6) on forms of IP interventions in European countries during the 1980s (a transition period).

Table 2.6 Industrial policy/aid by objective (average 1981–86) percentage of national GDP

	Innovation/ R&D	*Small/ medium enterprises*	*Trade promotion*	*Investment*	*Horizontal objectives*	*Sector aid*	*Total*
Denmark	0.11	0.12	0.08	0.01	–	–	0.32
Germany	0.18	0.06	0.01	0.01	0.02	0.02	0.30
France	0.04	0.01	0.33	0.15		0.05	0.58
Italy	0.15	0.15	0.27	0.25	0.98	0.08	1.88
Netherlands	0.07	0.19	0.02	0.04	0.01	0.01	0.34
UK	0.10	0.02	0.14	0.03		0.01	0.30

Source: Dietrich (1991).

It is clear that European countries differ in the objectives assigned to IPs. Germany favours innovation and R&D policies, with an emphasis on diffusion of technology in the direction of small firms. France prefers to put the emphasis on export promotion and general measures favouring firms' investment. The UK has an intermediate position, favouring both export promotion and R&D. Italy is distinguished by the horizontal character of its IP interventions.

The sums involved differ considerably. Over 1981–86, Germany spent six times as much as France on innovation and R&D measures, and France ten times as much as Germany on export promotion. The total share of IP interventions in GDP vary from 0.30 per cent for the UK and Germany to 1.9 per cent for Italy, with France at 0.6 per cent.

Even if these expenditures may have important leverage effects, the sums remain relatively small. But in the perspective taken here, the definitions retained above for IPs are rather restrictive. Another type of horizontal intervention concerning the networks of public infrastructures is also relevant. Some recent contributions[3] have thus stressed the importance of infrastructures in the determination of the productivity of private firms and on the rate of growth. All channels contributing to supporting the relative competitiveness of one particular territory could also be considered.

The limits for such interventions are not yet clearly set. Three areas can be distinguished. One has to do with the organisation of markets, a broad sphere including the setting of infrastructure networks (such as telecommunications) but also going down to support for small and medium firms. The second area concerns innovation policy, and has received much attention in the course of the present diffusion of the new technological system centred around the technologies of information and communication. The third area is environmental issues, even if the massive scale and scope for intervention still lies ahead of us.

ASSESSING THE POTENTIAL MACROECONOMIC DIMENSION OF IPS

At some level, macroeconomic policies and IPs have similar objectives: stablilise the economy and promote its development. Macroeconomic policies act on demand, whether on investment or consumption. The pressure of international competition on goods and services as well as financial markets limits the room for manoeuvre of standard fiscal and budgetary macroeconomic policies. Too high levels of public debt reinforce this limitation. Conversely, in economies where markets and production processes are more differentiated, more complex, there is a growing need for IPs not only to accommodate market failures but also to upgrade developmental parameters and facilitate institutional and organisational change. Even if such re-balancing is widely admitted, the magnitude and potential effects of IPs are difficult to assess. We saw that the public expenditures that specifically concern IPs are, in Europe, spread between 0.2 per cent and 2 per cent of GDP. A more comprehensive figure, including all public expenditures in 1990, devoted to investment ranges from 6.1 per cent of GDP in Japan to 1.5 per cent of GDP in the USA. Relevant subsidies and training expenditures could also be added.

The expenditures related to IPs, even broadly defined, cannot be compared with the 16 per cent of GDP spent on average on social transfers, or with the 18 per cent of GDP devoted to government consumption. To have a macroeconomic impact they must have a major leverage effect. To become effective this multiplying-effects potential may well require co-ordinated measures of a scale and scope not yet well perceived. Much of what we can do at the early stage of a new period is to take a schematic view of the issue in order to stress some important trade-off and calibrate the effects.

To clarify our view on the respective role of policies through time we can feature the 'multiplier effects' mentioned above in a simple model. We did suggest in the previous section that IPs have extended their role in the last decades from easing the catching-up of less advanced economies to co-ordinating and promoting learning processes in fully modernised open economies. We also posited the role of economic policies in a growth model where the conditions of steady growth required a precise matching between aggregate behaviours of firms and consumers (investment and saving ratios) which could not be met without public interventions. This Harrod scheme is not only very crude in its assumptions on technical change but it does not try to account for the kind of co-ordination that public intervention is going to promote. When macroeconomic policies had some meaningful room for manoeuvre, this omission did not seem problematic. At times when one needs to conceptualise more specific types of intervention, the above scheme is too crude. We shall basically use a Kaldorian framework of cumulative causation, adapted to account for the specificity of productivity and demand growth regimes during the two large periods under view, as well as for the specificity of the windows opened to public interventions in these two periods.

The whole exercise remains very sketchy and the use we will make of these models does not pretend much more than to draw some perspectives for further research.

Let us assume for the first phase that standard macroeconomic policies can more easily be effective in promoting economic growth when applied by economies lagging behind and aiming to catch up with the leading country (or set of countries) in a world relatively open to trade but with little capital mobility. Closing progressively their productivity gap, thanks initially to a policy favouring – directly or indirectly – investment, these countries increase their price competitiveness and expand their share of world markets, which together stimulate their internal economies, reinforcing their efficiency in a cumulative way, which in turn brings credit to the policy for this growth dynamic.

Conversely, within a set of economies that are all relatively close to upper levels of development, policies that in general favour investment will not be so easily effective and policy makers will have to resort to inventive IPs, favouring R&D, market organisation and productive networks. All these actions should be aimed at improving the non-price competitiveness of countries. It follows that in the first case/period policies will mainly help to improve the efficiency of productive capacity while in the second case/period the effects of IPs will show in a greater ability of economies to take advantage of national and foreign demands (improving competitiveness mainly by means of product differentiation, and also improving marketing and distribution), all of which can be formalised as follows.

Let G_c be the contribution to the overall productivity growth of a given economy brought by what we called standard proactive policies. This contribution shows the capacity of an economy to stimulate some catching-up in modernising the overall process of production; it is therefore a positive function of the productivity gap and of the means devoted to this policy.

Conversely, let G_g be the contribution of a consistent set of IPs to the overall competitiveness of the economy under view. This contribution shows the capacity of an economy to target expanding markets (which include product innovation) and to efficiently adjust marketing and distribution. This contribution is a positive function of the means devoted to these policies but also of the leading 'edge' of the productive efficiency at each economy above the average (some kind of opposite of the productivity gap). This last assumption implicitly refers to the characteristics of the new technological system centred around the technologies of information and communication. On the one hand, mastering these technologies is crucial to organising markets efficiently; on the other, technological gaps between countries are less easy to fill and it requires more rather than fewer specialisations and public interventions than before.[4] If the mastering of these technologies occurs, as it seems, in the first place in the more efficient countries, then productivity gaps tend to widen during a first phase of the diffusion of the new technological system.[5]

The previous hypotheses lead to expressions of the law of productivity gains and demand expansion as follows:

$$Z = AQ^a e^{bt} G_c \qquad \text{productivity regime} \qquad (2.1)$$

$$Q = D + X = P_{I^d} P_{e^f} Q_{e^k} G_g \qquad \text{demand regime} \qquad (2.2)$$

with Z the productivity of labour, Q the level of national production, X the level of exports, D the level of internal demand net of imports, P_I price index of national productions, P_e price index of foreign production, and Q_e the level of world demand.

These formulae are expressions of productivity growth in case of increasing returns, and of demand growth in a fully open economy where internal as well as external demand is mainly determined by the competitiveness of the economy (for example, terms of trade and elasticity to world income). These rather standard expressions of demand and productivity growth regimes are augmented respectively by the impact of IPs and standard macroeconomic policies.

To complete the model formed by equations (2.1) and (2.2) one only needs to express some law of price formation to seize the price effect of productivity gains, assuming to begin with that the wage rate, W, is exogenously given, as is the price index of world competitors, P_e. P_I, the price index of national productions, can then simply be given as resulting from a mark-up over labour costs of production

$$P_I = W(1 - t)/Z \qquad (2.3)$$

We still have to express how G_c and G_g encapsulate the leverage effects of public interventions in the two spheres of standard macroeconomic policy and IPs. We shall express G_c and G_g as functions of differences in development levels and of different types of public expenditures. For the sake of simplification we shall express directly the contributions of G_c and G_g in terms of growth rates, g_c and g_g:

$$g_c = -c_1(Z/Z_m) + c_2V_c \tag{2.4}$$

$$g_g = g_1(Z/Z_n) + g_2V_g \tag{2.5}$$

with c_1, g_1, c_2 and g_2 positive parameters showing the relative efficiency of public intervention in each case or the impact of productivity differentials, Z_m the *level* of productivity in the country 'at the frontier' (and, as usually assumed in the catching-up literature, Z_m will be exogenous) and Z_n a benchmark of slow productivity growth (which is more unusual and could refer to the expected slow productivity of the worse of the developed countries in the subset of developed economies under view). V_c represents the effort made in standard proactive macroeconomic policies and V_g the cumulated efforts in IPs.[6]

At this stage of the growth model of a fully open economy, as given by equations (2.1)–(2.5), P_e, Q_e, W, V_c and V_g are exogenous variables while Z, Q, P_I, G_c and G_g are endogenous variables. Written in growth rates, this growth model turns into a system of differential equations that are linear relative to the growth rates of the five unknown variables.[7] It can thus be solved analytically and it leads to a differential equation for the productivity level in an economy i:

$$\begin{aligned} z_i(1 + ad) = {} & ad(w_i + \tau) + afp_e + b \\ & + ag_1Z_i/Z_n - c_1Z_i/Z_m + c_2Vc_i + ag_2Vg_i \end{aligned} \tag{2.6}$$

where Z_m, Z_n and Z_i are, respectively, the level of productivity in the frontier country, the 'lowest' productivity path among the small set of developed trading partners under view and the level of productivity observed in country i, while w_i and τ are, respectively, the wage rate and the mark-up rate of country i and z_i is the growth rate of productivity.

This equation could be estimated in order to calibrate the various coefficients if one assumes that equation (2.6) applies to a set of developed trading partners. All coefficients are expected to be positive. Furthermore we made strong assumptions on the periodisation of the effects. We thus assumed that catching-up effects were only relevant in the first period during which time standard economic policies were effective; meanwhile in the second period technological advantage played positively, widening the gap for a while during which only IPs were really effective. The time horizon of the model is thus given by two dates: t_1, end of phase 1, and t_2, end of phase 2. So far these dates are exogenously given. These assumptions can be translated into the following assumptions concerning the coefficients c_i and g_i (which respectively mark the efficiency of standard macroeconomic policy and of IPs):

$$c_i = 0 \text{ if time } t > t_1$$

$$g_i = 0 \text{ if time } t < t_i \text{ or } t > t_2$$

The relevant expression for the differential equation of the productivity gains in country i should thus be written in two parts:

$$z_i(1 + ad) = ad(w_i + \tau) + afp_e + b - c_1 Z_i/Z_m + c_2 V_i \text{ if time } t < t_1$$

$$z_i(1 + ad) = ad(w_i + \tau) + afp_e + b + ag_1 Z_i/Z_n + ag_2 V g_i$$
$$\text{if time } t_1 < t < t_2 \tag{2.7}$$

The productivity gap is a stimulating factor in the first period. The productivity differential is a limitating factor in the second period. Since we take into account this change in the effect of productivity differentials on economic growth, the leverage effect of economic policies, V_c or V_g, varies over time. The differential equation (2.7) can be solved, leading to the following simplified expression for the growth rate z_i:

$$z_i = A/(BCe^{At} + 1) \tag{2.8}$$

where A represents all terms in (2.7) that are not factors of Z_i/Z_m and B represents, if positive (respectively negative), the coefficient of Z_i/Z_m (respectively Z_i/Z_n), while C stands for a constant of integration.

B is positive if time is such that: $t_1 < t < t_2$ and negative before t_1. A and C are positive coefficients. It implies that, in the first period, the growth rate decreases,[8] in principle, down to $z_i = 0$.

Conversely, B is negative if time is such that: $t_1 < t < t_2$, and z_i increases[9] until time $t = t_2$. The model takes as given this time limit t_2 when the competitive advantage of high productivity level peters out as the diffusion of the new technological system has reached a certain level. IPs can help to make the best of this competitive advantage for all countries able to master the new technologies rapidly. Still, the impact of both types of policies has rather similar expressions in this model (with the relevant elasticities included in coefficient A of Equation (2.8). In other words, the model does not embed the difference in nature between the two policies.

The question then bears on the magnitude of these effects: their comparability and evolution along time. Studies helping to estimate these effects are quite few. Evidence backing our assumptions and formalisation has (unfortunately) to be looked for in two directions: changes over time in investment and marketing behaviours, and efficiency of public interventions.

On one side we have studies stressing that times have changed for key issues of our concern. The determinants of investment have changed in the 1980s to appear more diverse, varying, uncertain and therefore responding less well to general incentives of governments (Catinat *et al.* 1987; Fazzari, Hubbard and Petersen, 1988; Fayolle 1991; Ford and Poret 1991). At the same time the process of catching-up within developed economies has petered out in the 1980s (see Gittleman and Wolff 1995; Pianta 1995) and the non-price dimension of competitiveness has increased. On the other side we have a growing set of studies insisting that government consumption (Ram 1986), public expenditures (Ashauer 1989) and infrastructure investment (Munnell 1990, 1992) have a meaningful positive impact on economic growth.

We agree with Dowrick (1993), following Abramovitz (1986), that such studies on the effect of policies (standard economic policies or IPs) on growth should be limited to a set of countries within a similar range of development[10] and we refer to the more developed OECD countries. Orders of magnitude can be derived from some estimations of elasticities, for instance of output to public infrastructures, which are close to 0.3/0.4 for Aschauer (1989). Several studies have refined the approach, using different methods (data, estimation). Some studies find a very low elasticity (0.05) but their results are debatable; others find figures roughly of the order of 0.3. One may refine this by distinguishing different types of public capital. The most useful type corresponds to a 'core' of infrastructures (roads, transport, and so on), with elasticity roughly equal to 0.2/0.3 (Munnell 1990).[11]

It suggests that impacts can be sizeable. This literature points to the great variance in results. It stresses the role of differences in the architecture of the financial systems (markets' short-termism versus banks' long-termism), the method of management (old style hierarchies versus more horizontal management) and the systems of education (Boyer and Caroli 1995). If failures and successes are entrenched in peculiar combinations of these institutions, the room for industrial policies remains severely conditioned.

With these two kinds of evidence we are left with a good sample of reasons to say that the dynamics of investment and incentives have changed and that new forms of interventions may be effective: that is, of sizeable impact.

Nevertheless, whether IPs could be turned into fully-fledged employment policies also depends on the possibility of expanding their field of actions towards work organisation and participation of the labour force.

TOWARDS NEW DEALS

Most of our arguments are meant to back a few propositions: IPs, seen as a means to develop proper learning processes, have a new potential at a macroeconomic level. This is all the more important since the old means to fuel economic growth have lost most of their stimulating power. The impact of IPs mainly tends to transform markets. This helps countries not only to be more competitive, but more innovative, which can expand demand. It is not necessarily a zero sum game in a developed world where competitiveness has accrued its non-price dimension (product innovations/differentiation, bundling of goods and services, lasting customer/producer relations, and so on).

Still, a strong political support for such interventions requires some enlargement of their impact, where their effect on employment, ways of life and incomes will be more obvious. The ways in which IPs could monitor the product markets and the forms of competition are diverse and rapidly concern the working of the labour market itself as well as the nature of the industrial relations. We can give two examples showing how far-reaching in effect are these fields of intervention.

The first example has to do with the organisation of the fabric of small an d medium firms. It is an objective of most governments to help set up networks, infrastructures which will ease their organisation, their access to the new technologies, to external markets and so forth. The model is often, somehow, to reproduce all the good interactions noticed in old 'historical' industrial districts, except that new forms have to be invented. The policy means are diverse. It may have a major impact on employment, regional development and industrial relations according to the methods used and the interactions developed. Pragmatic trial and error processes seem to lead most development. Still, a variety of good recipes are slowly maturing in the first place in hi-tech industries, in modern services and, with a greater degree of difficulty, in mature manufacturing industries where price competitiveness remains strictly binding. New deals in this field concern access to finance and to qualified human resources (in-house or pooled and/or outsourced), mainly supported by local authorities.

Setting up and organising a qualified workforce is the second example of a major objective. Two principles have become crucial: a qualified labour force has to respond to specific local needs, and training has to be regular to keep up with a world continuously renewing its practices and techniques. This can only be achieved by means of policy deeply changing the functioning of labour market. Organising the time for training impinges on the reorganisation of working hours; it is even a crucial issue in the debate over the reduction in working hours.[12] Taking into account the specificity of local needs leads to favouring interactions among local firms and this has cumulative effects, with the policy supporting a dynamic fabric of small to medium-sized enterprises (SMEs). Some forms of organisation of this qualified workforce can represent outsourcing capacities for large as well as small firms. Keeping in mind that improving collective learning processes is one direct objective of IPs, it is enough to show their potential range of action.

Still, the same latitudes, which show such virtuous growth cycles, could as well turn into vicious cycles, where firms will tend to specialise more and more in some kind of work organisation and industrial relations, increasing a dualism between good jobs and bad jobs in a same region, if not between regions. How to avoid that is a clear challenge of central national policies, which have to redistribute public means so that difficult local situations do not worsen, while already successful regions further improve.

Notes

1. Two corrections have been introduced: the UK has been straightforwardly classified among the countries with a restrictive approach to IP despite a relatively high ratio of investment to GDP; Austria has been considered as practising a radical Keynesian approach to full employment because of the importance of the public sector in keeping unemployment low despite the absence of any official political commitment.
2. See Amable and Verspagen (1995) for an empirical investigation of technology as a source of 'non-price' competitiveness.
3. See Aschauer (1989) and Munnell (1990) among others.
4. See Archibugi and Michie (1995).
5. Another way to put it is that when the diffusion of a new technological system presents some meaningful challenge of organisations to one country, then productivity gaps for a while do not represent the advantage of a straightforward potential to be reaped but, somehow, the disadvantage of backwardness, as in the argument made by Abramovitz (1986) to explain that the catching-up thesis over a long period of time did not apply across the board of all countries but only to those who could build up their own access to the technology.
6. Note that because of differences in nature of interventions V_p cumulates the efforts done each year while V_e registers the effort done in the period under view.
7. An interesting expression of the model can be obtained by reducing by substitution the system to three equations:

$$Z_i = aq_i + b - c_1\, Z_i/Z_m + c_2V_e$$
$$q_i = dp_i + fp_e + g_1\, Z_i/Z_n + g_2V_p$$
$$p_i = w_i + \tau - z_i$$

8. The asymptotic properties of our very sketchy model are of course of no interest for our argument.
9. t_2 must be such that z_i remains within 'realistic' boundaries.
10. If one does not distinguish between poor economies, middle economies and rich economies, results may well be erratic much because beyond the statistics of standardised national accounts the nature of economic activities, transactions and learning practices are too separated.
11. A special mention should be made of the study by deLong and Summers (1991) which compares the relative efficiency of equipment investment (found highly productive with a 30 per cent rate of return) and investment in public transport and infrastructure (much less productive). In a schematic way one could derive from our assumptions that this ranking could be reversed, or be much less marked in the period of the 1980s and 1990s. In all cases the high gross return of global investment in equipment does imply (when private returns to investment are obviously much lower) strong externalities and positive effects of public investments.
12. See the interesting (and much debated) measure of sabbatical leave set up by the Danes in the 1990s. More generally see Esping-Andersen (1990) to assess the extent of 'decommodification' of labour that some reorganisations of labour practices can represent.

References

Abramovitz, M. (1986) 'Catching-up, forging ahead and falling behind', *Journal of Economic History*, 46, pp. 385–406.

Amable, B. and Verspagen, B. (1995) 'The role of technology in market shares dynamics', *Applied Economics*, 27, pp. 197–204.

Archibugi, D. and Michie, J. (1995) 'The globalisation of technology: a new taxonomy', *Cambridge Journal of Economics*, 19(1) pp. 121–140.

Aschauer, D. A. (1989) 'Is public expenditure productive?', *Journal of Monetary Economics*, 23, pp. 177–200.

Best, M. (1990) *The New Competition* (London: Polity Press).

Boyer, R. (ed.) (1988) *The Search for Labour Market Flexibility* (Oxford: Clarendon Press).

Boyer, R. and Caroli, E. (1995) 'Production regimes, education and training systems: from complementarity to mismatch', in C. Buechtemann (ed.) *Human Capital and Economic Performance* (New York: Sage Foundation Press).

Catinat, M., Cawley, R., Ilzkovitz, F., Italianer, A. and Mors, M. (1987) 'Les déterminants de l'investissement', *Economie Européenne*, 31 (March).

DeLong, J. B. and Summers, L. H. (1991) 'Equipment investment and economic growth', *Quarterly Journal of Economics*, 106(2), pp. 407–43.

Dietrich, M. (1991) 'European economic integration and industrial policy', *Review of Political Economy*, 3, pp. 418–38.

Dowrick, S. (1993) 'Investment and resource allocation as sources of long-run growth', paper presented at the conference on 'Catching Up, Forging Ahead and Falling Behind', Oslo, May.

Eatwell, J. N. (1983) 'The long period theory of employment', *Cambridge Journal of Economics*, 7 (3–4) pp. 269–285

Esping-Andersen, G. (1990) *The Three Worlds of Welfare Capitalism* (London: Polity Press).

Fazzari, S. M., Hubbard, R. G. and Petersen, B. C. (1988) 'Financing constraints and corporate investment', *Brookings Papers on Economic Activity*, vol. I.

Fayolle, J. (1991) 'Taux d'intérêt, financement et performances des enterprises', *Economie et Statistique*, 239 (January).

Ford, R. and Poret, P. (1991) 'L'investissement des entreprises: performance récentes et conséquences pour l'action des pouvoirs publics', *Revue Economique de l'OCDE*, 16 (Spring).

Gittleman, M. and Wolff, E. (1995) 'R&D activity and cross country growth comparisons', *Cambridge Journal of Economics*, 19(1) 188–208.

Glyn A., Hughes, A., Lipietz, A. and Singh, A. (1990) 'The rise and the fall of the golden age', in S. Marglin and J. Schor (eds), *The Golden Age of Capitalism*. (Oxford: Clarendon Press).

Hall, P. J. (ed.) (1989) *The Political Power of Economic Ideas*, (Princeton University Press).

Itoh, M. and Kiyono, K. (1988) 'Foreign trade and direct investment', in R. Komiya, M. Okuno and K. Suzumura (eds), *Industrial Policy of Japan* (Tokyo: Academic Press).

Lucas, R. (1988), 'On the mechanics of economic development', *Journal of Monetary Economics*, 22, pp. 3–42.

Lucas, R. (1993) 'Making a miracle', *Econometrica*, 61(2) (March) pp. 251–72.

Meraud, J. (1994) 'La Dépense Publique en France: Evolution sur trente ans et comparaison internationale', *Avis et Rapports du Conseil Economique et Social*, Paris, Journal Officiel, 26.

Munnel A. (ed.) (1990) *Is There a Shortfall in Public Capital Investment?* (Boston: Federal Reserve Bank of Boston).

Munnell, A. (1992) 'Policy watch: infrastructure investment and economic growth', *Journal of Economic Perspectives* 6(4), pp. 189–98.

Pianta, M. (1995) 'Technology and growth in OECD countries, 1970–1990', *Cambridge Journal of Economics*, 19(1), pp. 175–187.

Petit, P. (1991) Les politiques de plein emploi appartiennent – elles au passé?, *Cahiers de Recherches Sociologiques* (Montreal), 17.

Ram, R. (1986) 'Government size and economic growth: a new framework and some evidence from cross section and time series data', *American Economic Review*, 76, pp. 191–203.

Romer, P. (1986) 'Increasing returns and long run growth', *Journal of Political Economy*, 94, pp. 1002–37.

Sawyer, M. C. (1992a) 'Reflections on the nature and role of industrial policy', *Metroecomica International Review of Economics*, 43, pp. 51–73.

Sawyer, M. C. (1992b) *On the Theory of Industrial Policy and Strategy* (Manchester University Press).

Shoch, J. (1994) 'The politics of the US industrial policy debate 1981–1984 (with a note on Bill Clinton's "industrial policy"', in D. Kotz, T. McDonough and

M. Reich (eds), *Social Structures of Accumulation. The Political Economy of Growth and Crisis* (Cambridge University Press).

Therborn, G. (1986) *Why Some People Are More Unemployed Than Others* (London: Verso).

3 Industrial Policies and the Macroeconomic Effects of Taxation: Some Comments

Johan Deprez

Keynesian economic policies are currently in disrepute because of a tendency to define such policies in terms that are too narrow and uncreative and because the theoretical underpinnings have been inadequately understood by many so-called 'Keynesian' proponents. While one could argue that there was never any real problem of the relevance of Keynesian economic policies for those who thoroughly understood Keynes and the major related thinkers, there is undoubtedly a need to convince many others of the relevance of Keynesian policies today. Part of the challenge is to articulate and extend the theoretical foundations and explanations of Keynesian policy options. Another part of the challenge is to extend the policy options to deal with the ever-changing realities of the modern world. The studies by Amable and Petit (Chapter 2) and by Mair and Laramie (Chapter 1) both make interesting contributions in this direction.

Amable and Petit examine the alternative and changing ways in which industrial policies of a Keynesian character have been applied in different countries. They point out that economic policy traditions can be separated according to whether there is a standard Keynesian emphasis on general macroeconomic health or whether there is a radical emphasis on full employment. Similarly, IPs in certain countries have aimed only at addressing 'market failures', while the focus in other places has been less restrictive and more comprehensive by working on the developmental elements of IPs. They also point out that what was possible during the golden age period of 1960–1974 has increasingly come under pressure from international competition, budget constraints and a changing political environment. Out of that analysis suggestions have emerged for the future direction of industrial policies to be more comprehensive and long term in orientation, favouring R&D, market reorganisation, and institutional flexibility.

Mair and Laramie re-examine the tax incidence of different tax regimes within federal states from a Kaleckian perspective. Comparisons are made between the USA and the proposals for the EU. From this perspective, the fundamental conclusion is reached that current discussions of tax policy are seriously flawed because they are built upon an inadequate theoretical framework. The key shortcomings of the neoclassical approach lie in its failure to have macroeconomic foundations, combined with its implicit or explicit belief in the full employment tendencies of capitalist economies. Moving beyond these restrictions also leads one to alternative views of firm behaviour, pricing and market dynamics. Once one gets the theory right – by moving to a dynamic Kaleckian perspective – then the interesting policy discussions can begin. There are significant possibilities for rejuvenating tax policy in ways that are presently being ignored, including the ability to create counter-cyclical and other macroeconomic effects even within a balanced-budget situation. They also see the ability to levy a profits tax without a negative impact upon household income.

A key point of Keynes's (1964/1936) analysis is that production, employment and investment decisions are driven by expectations. Short-term expectations determine production and employment decisions, long-term expectations determine investment decisions, and user cost provides for a path of interrelationship between the two. Actual price and sales results give a feedback mechanism through which such expectations may be modified. The resulting policy conclusions are that it is important to set up structures and influences that will create business expectations which are as positive as possible and, if this is not feasible or desirable, for social institutions to carry out the required activities that the private sector fails to implement. From this perspective certain comments can be made on both chapters.

From the Kaleckian perspective of Mair and Laramie, the ability of capitalist firms to mark-up above costs gives them the ability to pass on taxes to their customers. Consequently, taxes on firms can be an effective mechanism for raising revenue for governments without creating any disincentive for firms in terms of production, employment and investment. Mair and Laramie have specified plausible conditions under which this would be true. While briefly recognising the question, they have, however, not addressed the impact of tax changes on the short-term expectations that drive current production and employment decisions, on the long-term expectations that determine investment decisions and purchases, or on the expectations that influence the consumption behaviour of workers. Within the context of an uncertain world there is a wide possible range of scenarios. Depending upon the particular economic structure, it could be argued, certain reactions may be more likely. As Kalecki (1972/1943) pointed out, we should be quite sceptical about capitalist firms' willingness to carry out and support policy that will benefit their sales and profits. They may perceive overriding considerations.

Even if taxes on firms should logically not have production, employment and investment impacts in the aggregate and can theoretically be used to raise tax revenue to whatever level is desired by the authorities in order to support socio-economic programmes, there still is an important regional question. Local authorities throughout the world use tax breaks and subsidies as a way to attract firms and plants to their jurisdictions. Under such conditions, tax policy is not focused on raising revenue, redistribution of income and wealth, or any other socio-economic goals other than attracting these enterprises. Even if there were to be no aggregate output/employment effect from increasing taxes, differential taxes between areas can be expected to lead to regional redistributions of production, employment and investment. Consequently, local authorities will be very wary of tax increases that will cause such effects. In an increasingly open global economy, the same can be said for national authorities. Such 'location competition' will tend to generate uniform local tax structures within a federal state at some lowest common denominator level. If this tendency is correct, then the Mair-Laramie thesis that taxes can be used in a creative and differential fashion within a federal state to promote social and economic welfare is, unfortunately, not true. One needs general agreement from the different taxing authorities in order to have a successful tax policy of that type.

This regional consideration can be exasperated by the differential nature of the context in which industries operate. Tax policy will be more effective when used on industries that are locked into a particular area, as opposed to footloose industries. That, of course, leads to the danger of excessive or insufficient taxes on particular industries from a social point of view. A multi-industry approach to the Kaleckian tax analysis of Mair and Laramie would be an interesting and useful extension. Similarly, the formal modelling of multiregional tax consideration would also be an appropriate extension.

Chapter 2 is consistent with three ideas in this context. First, business expectations are formed and modified in different ways and generate different results depending upon the particular form of a capitalist economy with which one is dealing. Second, the particular approach to economic policy that a country employs also influences the formation of expectations and business reaction to outcomes. Third, IPs are a mechanism by which the context of business behaviour is modified and potentially constrained to be consistent with social goals. While there is no explicit discussion of expectations formation, the discussion of institutions and structures, as well as the focus on long-term development and sustainability of economic health, is consistent with Keynes's perspective. Creative policies aimed at modifying rules, institutions, and structures – as compared with traditional discretionary fiscal policy – repeatedly show up in Keynes. These are the mechanisms by which the uncertainty of the real world is made manageable. Such IPs are consistent with Keynes's (1964/1936: 378) desire for investment activities to meet social needs. This view of policy is also consistent with Keynes's view of how to set up international structures, rules and institutions.

Keynes (1973: 408–11) emphasised that he was dealing with a monetary production economy which is 'an economy in which money plays a part of its own and affects motives and decisions and ... the course of events cannot be predicted either in the long period or in the short, without a knowledge of the behaviour of money between the first state and the last' (Keynes 1973: 408–9). When discussing any component of Keynesian policies one must look at the interrelationships with monetary and financial considerations. This is only briefly mentioned in Chapter 2. In order to carry out certain IPs, there must be an access to finance. Promoting certain industries, firms, or regions may not receive the participation of commercial banks. Setting up state banks to meet this need then becomes a necessary complement to these IPs. The socialisation of investment (Keynes 1964/1936: 378) needs to be associated with a socialisation of finance.

In Chapter 1, the monetary considerations are also left in the background. In particular, there is the important issue of funding and finance. Does the state need to raise funds before it can spend? If so, then taxing power and effectiveness are the keys to the ability to spend. If, on the other hand, the access to finance is key, then tax revenues play only a legitimising role and are not a prerequisite to spending. On this issue there are a number of contradictory views among Post Keynesians and Kaleckians. Re-examining the issues raised in this study in the light of those debates would be highly illuminating.

Both chapters point to the internationalisation of economies and the economic integration that is occurring in major parts of the world. They also recognise that it is an open question whether or not this process will lead to divergent growth between different regions within these trading areas or to a convergence of living standards. As long as this is an open question, Keynesian policy must stand ready to provide for the economic development of lagging areas. In the modern context it is clearer than ever that it is not sufficient to worry about the macroeconomic magnitudes for an economy as a whole. One must look at what is happening in the particular subregions. Furthermore, international economic integration highlights the commonality of interest of peripheral areas in different countries in opposition to the centre regions.

Within today's context of rapid development of communications and related technology, there is also the opportunity to move economic activity away from the centre to the periphery. While there are tendencies to move production from high-cost to low-cost areas, it can also be an effective mechanism to promote development in poorer areas. The ease of modern communication is increasing these possibilities. This is true both within countries and trade groups, as well as outside. Proper IP would promote such a pattern of development, although it would run into the political interest of centre politicians and bureaucrats, as well as centre capitalists and corpocrats.

Both Chapters 1 and 2 point out that Keynesian policies have been, are, and can be much more creative and have greater depth than the current lines of orthodox thinking. They show the sterility of the orthodox view that a *laissez-faire* policy is the best by either assuming that such conditions already exist and corporations can be left to do what they feel is best, or that policy should focus on creating the appropriate conditions for *laissez-faire* to flourish, or to create the conditions so the world can function 'as if' it is in a pure *laissez-faire* state. The point of the work of Keynes, Kalecki, Robinson and many other post-Keynesians is that it is exactly these *laissez-faire* conditions that are a significant contributor to the economic problems in both the abstract and the real world. There are creative alternatives that provide for a much more realistic hope to create truly effective policies. Amable and Petit have pointed to the capabilities of comprehensive Keynesian IPs. Mair and Laramie indicate certain ways in which one should be suspicious of the orthodox disincentive view of taxes and that one can make effective use of tax policy for greater economic and social health. They all point out that the irrelevance of Keynesian policies only comes from the orthodox straitjacket in which they have been put and the lack of creativity with which policy makers have applied Keynesian ideas. Moving to truly Keynesian foundations allows the full range of policy requirements and possibilities to flourish. There is hope for activist policies and no need to 'let the market do it'.

References

Kalecki, M. (1972/1943) 'Political aspects of full employment', in M. Kalecki (ed.), *The Last Phase in the Transformation of Capitalism* (New York: Monthly Review Press), pp. 75–83.

Keynes, J. M. (1964/1936) *The General Theory of Employment, Interest, and Money* (New York: Harcourt Brace Jovanovich).

Keynes, J. M. (1973) *The Collected Writings of John Maynard Keynes*, vol. XIII, *The General Theory and After: Part I Preparation* (London and Cambridge: Macmillan and Cambridge University Press).

4 'Socialization of Investment' and 'Euthanasia of the Rentier': The Relevance of Keynesian Policy Ideas for the Contemporary US Economy

Robert Pollin*

INTRODUCTION

Evaluating the current relevance of Keynesian economic policies first depends, of course, on what one means by such policies. In the USA today, for example, economists often considered to be mainstream Keynesians are among the prominent exponents of the view that the most fundamental macroeconomic problem facing the country is its inadequate saving rate, due to both public and private profligacy. However, this 'Keynesian' perspective is actually consonant with the central tenets of pre-Keynesian thought, which, reaching its apogee during the 1930s as the British 'Treasury View', held that the pursuit of full employment policies was necessarily constrained by an economy's level of saving. Perhaps the fundamental innovation of Keynes's *General Theory* and the subsequent Keynesian revolution was to overthrow the Treasury View, and to put in its place the argument that, as Joan Robinson said, 'firms are free, within wide limits, to accumulate as they please, and the rate of saving of the economy as a whole accommodates itself to the rate of investment that they decree' (Robinson 1962: 82–3).

Another misconstruing of Keynesian economics followed more directly from Keynes's assault on the Treasury View and other versions of a 'causal saving' perspective. This was the notion – enshrined in a generation of mainstream macroeconomic textbooks relying on Hicks's IS-LM framework – that because Keynes argued that saving rates *per se* did not constitute a barrier to capital accumulation, Keynesianism therefore held that there were no financial constraints on activity. From this perspective, Keynesian economic policy should be focused on stabilising consumption, which, through the multiplier, would in turn stabilise investment and thereby aggregate fluctuations.

This view, in fact, is equally incongruous with the writings of Keynes himself in the *General Theory* and elsewhere. It has been widely recognised that Keynes does not concentrate on monetary and financial market issues in the *General Theory* as much as he does elsewhere in his writings. Nevertheless, even in the *General Theory* Keynes offers a painstaking critique of speculative financial market practices, particularly inasmuch as they exert a malign influence on the prospects for channelling resources towards, as he put it, 'a steady stream of enterprise' (Keynes 1964/1936: 159); that is, towards the expansion of the stock of productive plants and equipment. The conclusion Keynes drew from this critique was that strong market intervention policies were necessary to channel financial resources away from speculative markets and towards productive activity. Keynes, in fact, was firm, if not very specific, on this question. Among the few explicit policy statements that he offers in the concluding chapter of the *General Theory* are his calls for 'the euthanasia of the rentier' (Keynes 1964/1936: 376) and for a 'somewhat comprehensive socialization of investment' (Keynes 1964/1936: 378).

The question I therefore wish to pursue in this chapter is whether *these* Keynesian policy themes – the 'somewhat comprehensive socialization of investment' and the 'euthanasia of the rentier' – are relevant today, specifically as regards the US economy. My short answer is that they are quite relevant indeed, provided that these ideas are flexible. For example, the proposals advanced here would not bring the rentier class to an 'easy and painless death' (the literal meaning of euthanasia) since, on the one hand, few rentiers would consider such proposals as easy to accept, while, on the other, their extinction is not among the agenda items. The issue, again, is policies relevant for today, and I interpret that to mean that we are operating within the realm of what is feasible within the existing political and economic environment.

Over the past 20 years, the US economy has experienced a historically unique form of economic stagnation, combining declining investment growth, more severe business cycles, increased financial instability, higher interest and unemployment rates, falling average wages, and a widening income distribution.[1] The central argument of this chapter is that the structure of financial markets and institutions in the USA has played a major role in generating these trends, although by no means has it alone caused them. Focusing on policy matters in particular, I contend that the existing US financial structure constitutes a major barrier to the successful implementation of policies that could work to counteract these trends, including policies to promote full employment, financial stabilisation and an egalitarian growth path.

In the next section, the major body of this chapter, I first show that while the growth of domestic net investment has been stagnant since the 1970s, this has not been because the corporations faced a shortage of funds available for investment. Indeed, over the last full business cycle, corporate internal funds were fully sufficient to pay for *all* of the corporation's fixed investment. Corporations also borrowed to an unprecedented degree over this period but, in the aggregate, these funds were channelled primarily towards mergers, take-overs, and related speculative activities.

Drawing from that experience, I then present what I consider to be the three financial constraints on full employment and other egalitarian policy measures emanating from the financial system. The first is that financial forces create a bias towards short-term horizons and towards speculative take-overs rather than new investments. The second is that these same forces encourage a long-term tendency towards increased financial fragility, meaning that expansions are inhibited by speculative financial activity and downturns are more severe than they would be otherwise because of the vulnerability of the financial system. The third is that the structure of the financial system has weakened the ability of the primary tools of interventionist policy: that is, deficit spending and loose monetary policy. This has resulted in part because the increased power of financial market interests within the realm of macro policy formation has created a deflationary bias in the setting of macro policy.[2]

I make these arguments by way of contrasting the US financial system with those of other capitalist economies, drawing on the by now voluminous literature that compares the Anglo-American 'capital-market'-based financial system with the 'bank-based' systems of, among other countries, Japan, Germany and France. To a significant degree, the bank-based systems have successfully controlled the tendencies towards speculation and financial instability, as well as the deflationary policy bias that is prevalent in the USA.

While many useful lessons can therefore be gleaned from the bank-based systems, in the concluding section I nevertheless argue that these economies do not offer a viable model for the USA, either on the grounds of feasibility or, more importantly, desirability. The most unfavourable aspect of the bank-based systems is that their success has rested in large measure on the fact that policy making was dominated by a narrow elite and that the policies were targeted at serving a correspondingly narrow set of priorities. I therefore conclude by offering a sketch of policy proposals which attempt to combine the useful aspects of the bank-based systems with policies that would also promote democratic accountability and egalitarianism.[3]

FINANCE, INVESTMENT AND SPECULATION

In evaluating the US economy since the 1960s, it is important to note that, amid an array of theoretical and empirical controversies over the nature and extent of long-term stagnation, two matters are not in dispute: the rate of investment growth for US corporations declined over the last two full business cycles; and spending on mergers, take-overs and similar asset transfers, financed primarily with borrowed funds, rose correspondingly over the same period. Differences emerge, of course, in trying to explain these phenomena and their possible connections.

To a significant extent, mainstream analysts, including in particular the 'Keynesians' among them, rely upon a causal saving argument in explaining this experience. Thus, the prominent mainstream Keynesian Lawrence Summers wrote:

> The channel through which low national saving leads to reduced investment is through increases in the *cost of capital*. When low national saving leads to a reduced supply of capital, the cost of capital rises ... High costs of capital lead investors to set high hurdle rates of return that cheat the future. Consider this comparison: A U.S. investor, given his or her costs of capital, would be willing to invest only 37 cents in return for receiving one dollar six years from now, compared with 66 cents for his or her Japanese counterpart. It is hardly surprising that Japanese managers often appear to take a longer view than their U.S. counterparts do. (Summers 1990: 159)

Summers is correct to focus on short-term horizons by corporations as a cause of their poor investment performance and their thrust towards speculative finance. The problem with this perspective is that it depends completely on three presuppositions: that official National Income Accounting measures of national saving will determine cost of capital; and that cost of capital will determine both the rate of fixed investment and the inducements of speculative asset transfers. None of these positions can be adequately supported on the basis of either the theoretical or empirical literature.

In other recent work, I have considered in some detail the various factors that will cause market-clearing interest rates to change independently of officially measured saving rates, based on changes in the institutional structures through which both sources and uses of funds are channelled as well as through policy interventions.[4] The notion that the cost of capital can itself explain both investment behaviour and a bias towards speculative finance is equally problematic. For one thing, within the contemporary econometric literature, standard neoclassical cost of capital models do not perform well in explaining investment behaviour relative to models focusing on demand influences (that is, variants on an accelerator model) or models focusing on changes in internal funds or profitability (that is, variants of cash flow models).[5]

Building in part on the profitability and demand theories of investment, I would rather propose that there are two basic sources for the short-term bias in the contemporary US financial market. The first is contemporary profitability trends which have rewarded asset transfers over asset creation. The second is an organisational structure that similarly rewards short-term measures to raise equity returns over long-term commitments to productive enterprise. We will consider these in turn, as well as explore the relationship between these phenomena and the related trend towards increased financial instability. We begin by examining the contemporary finance and investment patterns of non-financial corporations.

Declining Profitability and Rising Interest Rates

Table 4.1 reports data on corporate financial patterns over the past five full business cycles. Beginning with the data on corporate profitability, we see that from a 1960s' peak of 12.2 per cent, corporate profitability fell in the early 1970s to 8.1 per cent. The next row presents data on a proxy for Tobin's *Q* ratio. Tobin's *Q* measures the market value of firms – including equity and debt valued in financial markets – relative to the value of firms' assets at replacement cost. Because of measurement difficulties, this proxy includes the value of bonds, and reports the market value of equities relative to firms' net work at replacement cost. This proxy ratio is still a good reflection of the financial market's perception of future corporate profitability. Between the 1960s and early 1970s, we see that this proxy *Q* ratio fell, along with the profit rate, from 0.96 to 0.84.

The growth rate of gross capital expenditures also fell between the first and second cycles, but not by as much as the decline in profitability. Because of this disjuncture between profitability – the primary source of corporate internal funds – and capital expenditures, corporate borrowing relative to their capital expenditures rose sharply over this period from 30.2 to 38.7 per cent.

The first upward shift in corporate debt financing is an instance of what we may call *compensatory* credit demand: in the face of declining internal sources, corporations financed capital expenditures increasingly through debt. To a small degree, this tendency may have been promoted by the

Table 4.1 Profitability, investment and finance for non-financial corporations

NBER cycles	*1960–69*	*1970–73*	*1974–79*	*1980–81*	*1982–90*
Pretax profit rate (%)	12.2	8.1	5.9	6.0	8.6
Proxy Q ratio	0.96	0.84	0.41	0.44	0.63
Growth of gross capital expenditures (%)	6.2	4.3	4.1	0.4	2.2
Borrowed funds/capital expenditures (%)	30.2	38.7	28.8	30.1	37.2
Internal funds/capital expenditures (%)	93.8	82.8	87.7	82.8	100.7
Net new equities/net increase in liabilities (%)	4.9	14.0	3.8	–1.2	–50.0
Real interest rate (average of commercial paper and bond rates)	2.6	2.3	–0.1	1.8	5.8
Net interest/pre-tax profits (with IVA + CCA) (%)	10.9	27.2	29.7	50.7	51.0

Sources: US National Income Accounts, Flow of Funds Accounts, and Balance Sheets; Citibank Economic Database. Profit rate calculation follow Pollin (1986).

decline of real interest rates, falling on average from 2.6 to 2.3 per cent. But such a sharp increase in debt financing cannot be attributed primarily to the small interest rate decline.

In the second half of the 1970s, profit rates fell even further and the proxy *Q* ratio plunged: the stock market here is valuing the current cost net worth of firms at only 41 cents on the dollar. The growth of capital expenditure again falls, now to 4.1 per cent. In this period, however, corporations as a whole did not increase borrowing to sustain capital expenditures, even though real interest rates were negative. They primarily cut back capital expenditures, but also relied to a somewhat greater extent on internal funds.

Beginning in 1982, a fundamental shift occurred in corporations' finance and investment strategies. Their commitment to financing capital expenditures remained weak. For the full period, capital expenditures grew by only 2.2 per cent, and *all* of that growth was due to a 35 per cent increase in spending between 1983 and 1984. Otherwise, capital expenditures declined by an average of 1.5 per cent annually.

At the same time, new opportunities opened in this period for what we will term speculative finance: that is, borrowing to purchase existing assets with the expectation of capital gain. With the net worth of corporations for sale at an average of 44 cents on the dollar over 1981–82 (as shown through the proxy *Q*), firms borrowed to an unprecedented degree to buy up existing assets rather than create new capital stock. The borrowed funds/capital expenditures ratio thus jumped to 37.2 per cent, despite the paltry growth of capital expenditures itself. At the same time, the ratio of internal funds to capital expenditures rose to an average of over 100 per cent. This means that, in the aggregate, *none* of the growth of debt over 1982–90 was necessary to finance new capital expenditures; *all* of it was devoted to mergers and buy-outs as well as current operations. This is the most important sense in which the corporate borrowing patterns of the 1980s were unique. We observe this rise of speculative finance through considering the ratio of net new equity issues/net increase in liabilities. This ratio turns negative in the 1980s, dramatically so, at negative 50 per cent, over the last full cycle. This means that one-half of the increase in corporate liabilities was devoted only to buying back outstanding equities.

This surge in speculative borrowing corresponded with the run-up in real interest rates to an average of 5.8 per cent, a level unprecedented over the past 100 years of US history. The rise of speculative credit demand over 1982–90 was clearly not significantly inhibited by this unprecedented increase in real interest rates.

As to the effects of this investment and finance pattern, profitability did increase somewhat over this period. However, gains in profitability were not nearly adequate to outweigh the growing burden of corporate debt. As Table 4.1 shows, net interest payments absorbed 51 per cent of non-financial corporations' pre-tax earnings over the 1980s, a figure more than double the average of 19.8 per cent for the previous two decades.

These descriptive data then suggest a fairly straightforward story. US corporations became reluctant to invest in new plant and equipment in the 1980s because of the decline in profitability, beginning in the early 1970s, and the high level of interest rates, sustained through the 1980s. However, firms were not reluctant to borrow, despite the relatively weak profitability performance and high interest rates. But in the aggregate, they borrowed predominantly to finance corporate take-overs.[6]

Financial Structure, Corporate Time Horizons and Instability

Exit and Voice in Financial Markets

The US financial system is organised primarily through arms' length relationships in capital markets. It is, as John Zysman (1983) has put it, a 'capital-market' dominated system, similar to Great Britain in which 'financial institutions tend to manage portfolios of stocks, spreading their risks across companies rather than investing in the future of specific companies that they nurture through hard times' (Zysman 1983: 63).

Such an institutional arrangement contrasts sharply with the 'credit-market' or 'bank-based' systems that had prevailed in Japan, France and Germany prior to the 1980s' wave of financial innovation and deregulation.[7] In these systems, financial firms interacted closely with non-financial firms and the state in forging commitments to long-term investment projects. The pressures for short-term profitability or capital appreciation were therefore substantially lower.

The exit/voice analytic framework developed by Hirschmann (1970) is an illuminating tool for understanding these alternative systems. The US/British system is dominated by 'exit' as a means of exercising influence. Thus, dissatisfied share or bondholders will typically express their displeasure through selling their claims to the company. By contrast, the credit-based systems of corporate finance were premised on the exercise of influence by 'voice'. Major financial institutions and state agencies have been actively involved in charting a non-financial firm's long-term plans and then committing themselves to the process of implementing those plans.

The point here is not that credit market systems necessarily encourage voice while the capital market system must rely on exit; rather that in the current US system, there is no institutional framework parallel to that which prevailed in Japan, France and Germany for encouraging the exercise of voice. This absence – embedded within a capital market based system – has biased the US financial structure towards short-term thinking.

Short-Termism and Financial Instability

The market and institutional interactions associated with bank-based systems induce, among other things, a greater tolerance on the part of the lenders/investors for higher leverage ratios (Grabel 1996: Table 10). At the same time, the capital-market based systems are more susceptible to financial instability than the bank-based systems. Why is this so?

The underlying source of financial instability, at the simplest level of accounting, must be that debt commitments are systematically outstripping the income flows necessary to service them. In turn, the basic explanation for the systematic deviation between debt commitments and income flows (that is, borrowed funds) is used disproportionately to finance speculative and compensatory spending (that is, borrowing to purchase existing assets with the expectation of capital gain and to compensate for declining income streams or other internally generated funds). Put another way, instability results when debt is used insufficiently to finance productive spending (spending that enhances the income-generating capacity of firms and individuals). When credit is extended for speculative and compensatory spending to a disproportionate degree relative to productive spending, the result will be income streams inadequate to finance the growth of debt.

Considered within a cyclical framework, the most influential treatment of this problem has been the work of Minsky.[8] He argued that, as an economy shifts into a growth phase, and, in particular, as full employment is approached, 'euphoric expectations' take hold. The growth rate of debt exceeds that of profits since, for a given distribution of income between wages and profits, profit opportunities are constrained by the growth of productivity, whereas the extension of credit is not so constrained. The financial structure thus becomes increasingly fragile: that is, vulnerable to an interactive debt deflation which induces a generalised depression.

In the absence of government intervention or other administrative arrangements, an economy dominated by free capital markets thus proceeds normally from a cyclical trough to an unsustainable boom characterised by speculative financial behaviour. The cycle culminates in a debt deflation and depression. But the depression itself creates the conditions for a return to financial robustness and recovery. Thus, and here Minsky's position is perfectly consistent with that of Schumpeter and Marx, depressions are functional: they are the destructive but necessary mechanism – the 'slaughtering of capital values' as Marx put it – that returns financial structures to balance.

Note here that the basic source of difficulties is not the rise of debt *per se*, or even the rise of debt relative to income or assets. High leverage ratios are therefore sustainable as long as, over time, a return flow of revenue is generated to service them. As a general model, the bank-based systems are better designed to avoid mismatches between debt commitments and income flows. This is because the thrust towards speculative finance is reduced inasmuch as finance is dedicated to a greater degree to long-term productive projects. Moreover, the commitment to long-term projects means that the projects will have a longer grace period before they have to generate returns to their lenders.

Evidence on Short-Termism and Instability

A wide range of research has accumulated in recent years to support the view that the bank-based systems have promoted longer time horizons and greater financial stability. To begin with, survey evidence of corporate Chief

Executive Officers (CEOs) in the USA, Japan and Europe developed by Poterba and Summers (1992) found that US CEOs believe that their time horizons are shorter than those for their counterparts in Europe and Japan.

According to the US CEOs, their relatively short horizons derive to a significant extent from the financial market environment in which they operate. These managers contend that US equity markets undervalue long-term investments. Were the firms valued more in accordance with the perceptions of managers, the managers believe that their long-term investments would increase, on average, by perhaps as much as 20 per cent.

The survey also found that for the US CEOs, the minimum expected rate of return that would induce them to commit to a new investment project – that is, the 'hurdle rate' – is substantially higher than standard cost-of-capital analysis would suggest. On average, US CEOs reported that their hurdle rate was 12.2 per cent. This compares with an average real return over the past 50 years of less than 2 per cent on corporate bonds and around 7 per cent for equities.

Moreover, as Porter (1992) reported, this difference in time frames and hurdle rates is associated with a striking difference in managerial goals: US managers rank return on investment and higher stock prices as their top two corporate objectives, whereas Japanese managers rank improving existing and introducing new products, and increasing market share, as their two highest priorities. Higher stock prices is ranked last by Japanese managers among the eight objectives included in the study.

These survey findings are also consistent with evidence from corporations' actual operations. Porter (1992) found that the share of investment going to R&D, intangibles (especially investment in 'corporate training and human resources') and plant and equipment is lower in the USA than in Germany and Japan. In addition, the proportion of total R&D expenditures going to long-term projects is lower than in the USA. In the USA, 22.6 per cent of the total R&D budgets were allocated to such projects, while in Japan and Europe, the figures were 46.8 and 60.5 per cent, respectively.

Studies have also found that, at least over the 1970s and 1980s, the real after-tax cost-of-capital is higher in the USA than Japan and Germany, and that differences in these countries' financial systems are seen as a major contributing factor. McCauley and Zimmer (1989), for example, wrote that greater integration of industry and finance has permitted higher leverage without raising bankruptcy risks equivalently, and also greatly reduced liquidity risks of non-financial firms. Moreover, according to McCauley and Zimmer, the Japanese and German governments are more actively involved in mitigating the direct costs associated with non-financial firms' periods of financial distress.

Economic Policy under Alternative Systems

The McCauley and Zimmer evidence on interventionist policies raises the more general question of policy differences between the bank- and capital-market-based systems. Examining such differences involves considering both the constraints on policy imposed by the financial system in place, and the policy options pursued, given such constraints.

Broadly speaking, bank-based systems are structured more suitably than capital-market-based systems for achieving favourable results from two primary policy tools: expansionary policy and industrial strategy. The basic source of the advantages inherent in bank-based systems is the greater integration between non-financial and financial firms, which engenders a commonality of purpose that is absent in capital-market based systems.

Expansionary Macro Policy

There are basically two macroeconomic policies to achieve growth and employment goals: manipulating government spending relative to tax receipts and thereby the level of an economy's aggregate demand; and using central bank policies to adjust both the quantity and price of credit.[9] Here we focus on the limitations and, in particular, the diminishing capacities over time, of fiscal and monetary policy as instruments of full employment policies.

What are the reasons for the diminished capacities of expansionary policy? To begin with, it will be helpful to return to Minsky's analysis of systemic financial fragility. As Minsky has pointed out – drawing on Kalecki's well-known accounting identity wherein profit equals investment plus the government deficit – the effect of deficit spending is to establish a floor for profits. More favourable profit expectations in turn encourage investors' animal spirits, which should then break the downturn. At the same time, expansionary monetary policy will counteract the liquidity shortages of distressed financial firms.

What Minsky stresses here, however, is that these interventionist policies will not promote a full employment equilibrium. Rather, the interventionist policies will tend to validate the existing fragile financial structure: problems emerging out of the fragile structure are allowed to continue and even deepen. As a result, the effectiveness of full employment policies will deteriorate over time: government policy is called on increasingly to bail out the fragile system and thereby avoid a depression, but this very policy encourages more fragility and thus increases the burdens placed on future policy interventions.[10]

This analytic framework helps us to explain the extraordinary rise of innovative finance over the second half of the post-war period, including, for example, the rise we observed of asset and liability management within the US financial market.[11] The incentives for innovative finance are a constant, since innovation is essentially a means of lowering the transaction costs of moving funds between surplus and deficit units. Historically, however, the collapse of financial markets and subsequent increase in risk-aversion by market participants constrained such activities. This constraint has been diminished over the contemporary period. Innovative financial practices, in turn, have weakened the ability of central banks to maintain either price or quantity targets in pursuing expansionary policies.

In bank-based systems, since banks hold equity positions and are active in the management of firms, the banks, along with the non-financial firms, will be more favourably disposed towards expansionary macro policies. In the Anglo-American system, where financial firms are not directly linked to industry, the financial firms are more likely to favour restrictive policies. The values of outstanding financial assets are more important to the Anglo-American financial firms than the growth prospects of non-financial firms and, as such, they are more concerned about the threat of inflation than comparable institutions in bank-based systems.[12]

These attributes have been reflected in the central bank policies of different types of country. In the USA and UK, the central bank has had a relatively high degree of independence. Over time that independence has evolved into a close alliance with financial interests. These central banks have therefore tended to favour restrictive policies. In the bank-based systems, where there is a strong link between bank and industry, biases towards restrictiveness have tended to be weaker, though Germany, with its combination of a bank-based system and a highly independent central bank, is a clear exception to this general tendency.[13]

Related to this, in the USA/UK model, the independence of the financial system has led to a strong international orientation for its financial sector. In both cases, the domestic currency is used extensively for international transactions, and a formidable industry has developed around international finance. Maintenance of confidence in the currency is therefore given greater priority than in bank-based systems.[14]

It also appears that the negative collateral effects of expansionary policy tend to be stronger in the Anglo-American than the bank-based systems, although more research is needed to establish this point. This is, first, because capital market systems have a lower tolerance for leverage and increases in spending or lower interest rates are more likely to lead firms (and households) to reduce their indebtedness rather than increase expenditures.

The relatively greater degree of speculative activity also makes it more difficult in capital market financial systems to affect long-term interest rates. Expansionary policies in these countries are more likely to be met by rising long-term interest rates due to inflationary fears, and this will reduce the effectiveness of monetary policy. The most general problem is that expansionary policies in capital-market-based systems are more likely to engender an allocation of credit towards speculative finance, such as mergers, buy-outs and real estate investments.[15]

Credit Allocation and Industrial Policy

The advantage of bank-based systems here is that they are more amenable to public credit allocation policies as the centre-piece of industrial strategy. Public credit allocation policies, in turn, can be an effective instrument of an industrial strategy that promotes growth and employment.

At the same time, in considering the historical experience, the actual causal relationships between a country's financial structure, its degree of public credit allocation and its efforts and attainments in the area of IP are not clear-cut. That is, while it may appear that countries with bank-based systems are more successful at implementing credit policies and industrial strategy, this appearance may primarily result from the fact that the same countries are more actively engaged in both credit allocation and industrial strategy. Relatedly, the historical record is not clear on the extent to which countries with capital-market systems can deploy credit policies to compensate for the capital market's distortions: that is, engaging credit policies to replicate the desirable features of a bank-based system within the existing capital market institutional framework.

Thus, the USA has had considerable experience since the 1930s with public credit allocation policies, despite its status as the prototypical capital-market-based financial system. Indeed, considering all forms of credit allocation (direct loans, guaranteed loans and government-sponsored enterprise loans) the federal government is the largest creditor in the US financial market, lending or underwriting on an annual basis between about 15–30 per cent of all loans. Major recipients of funds have been the housing sector, agriculture and education. These programmes, moreover, have achieved considerable success relative to their stated goals. For example, they have contributed substantially to the unprecedented access to home ownership enjoyed by a high proportion of the non-wealthy in the USA.[16]

The extent and successes of these programmes demonstrate that credit policies can be implemented effectively within a capital-market-based financial system. At the same time, while these policies have been crucial to the development of targeted sectors, they have not been used to the USA to guide an overall industrial strategy. It is therefore difficult to gauge the extent to which a broader-based set of credit/industrial policies might be frustrated by the structure of US financial markets. However, the success of these programmes on their own terms suggests that the ability to implement credit allocation policies successfully may not be dependent on whether a country's financial system operates as a bank- or capital-market-based system.

THE RUDIMENTS OF FEASIBLE AND DESIRABLE POLICY

The financial system in the USA does present formidable obstacles – the tendency towards short time horizons, speculation and financial instability – to the successful pursuit of full employment and other policies to promote stability and an egalitarian growth plan. As I have argued, these constraints are diminished in countries using bank-based financial systems. However, there are several reasons why it would be neither feasible nor desirable for the USA to seek to appropriate as much as possible from the bank-based model.

At the most basic level, it is not realistic to assume that the existing highly developed US financial market could be converted as a piece to a bank-based framework. This is particularly true in light of the trend towards the globalisation of financial markets, which widens the opportunities for asset and liability management and innovation, and thereby increases the difficulties of imposing a full break with the existing institutional structure.

More importantly, despite the many successful features of bank-based systems, these systems also have serious deficiencies, in particular from the perspective of seeking to achieve full employment and other egalitarian ends. The close interlocking relationships between major firms, banks and government bureaucracies create wide opportunities for clientism in credit allocation and the associated phenomena of industrial collusion and oligopoly. Such an environment obviously limits access to external funds for small and new industrial enterprises and, as a result, may diminish opportunity and the prospects for innovation. In addition, as Stiglitz (1993) argued, the credit subsidy programmes associated with bank-based systems face problems because the costs are diffuse and difficult to calculate.

However, even more objectionable from the perspective of constructing an egalitarian programme is the fact that bank-based systems have been most successful in East Asian countries such as Japan and South Korea, where government planners were completely independent from democratic decision-making processes. In the USA, such policies would be desirable only if they could also extend accountability within the financial system.

The aim of US policy should therefore be not to emulate the bank-based systems, but rather to reproduce within the US context the elements of these systems that are central for implementing full employment policies. Within this context, policies would be needed to accomplish three things: lengthen time horizons and reduce the tendency towards speculative finance; reduce the conflict of interest between industrial and financial capital; and counteract the factors that weaken the effects of expansionary fiscal and monetary policy.

The policy interventions that would be most important for accomplishing these aims would include the following.

1. A set of financial regulatory policies which 'levelled the playing field upward' among all financial intermediaries. A substantial inducement towards financial innovation has been simply to exploit differences in how intermediaries are regulated. A consistent regulatory environment would obviously eliminate such opportunities, and would therefore strengthen the impact of any given set of regulations.[17]
2. Credit allocation policies to increase incentives towards productive investment and weaken those for speculative asset transfers. Several instruments could be used here, many of which are already part of existing law.

One instrument would be the existing Community Reinvestment Act (CRA). This law obliges banks to lend for projects among underserved areas of the communities in which they are located. This law has not been seriously enforced by the Federal Reserve, the agency responsible for enforcement. But if the CRA were extended to include all intermediaries, not just banks, and were then seriously enforced on a uniform basis, it would have a significant impact on the composition of both lending and investment throughout the country.[18]

A similar approach could be taken with the investment of pension funds. Although pension funds are heavily subsidised by government policy, they are not required to consider the social rate of return on their investments. This is so, despite the fact that such a calculation is fully consistent with what Barber and Ghilarducci described as 'fund participants' 'whole identities: as workers who need employment to accumulate retirement income, as citizens whose quality of life depends on the economic health of their communities, [and] as parents who want their children to have as much or more opportunity than their parents had' (Barber and Ghilarducci 1993: 291). It is true that vexing problems stand in the way of implementing such an approach to pension fund investing. For example, how would a single pension fund capture, for its own community, the social rate of return accruing to that funds' investments? But these problems are becoming less formidable as experience is gained with such investment strategies.

A third instrument of this kind could be Federal Reserve policy itself (see Pollin 1993). The Federal Reserve could use discount window lending and asset requirements for financial institutions to promote investments with high social rates of return, and discourage short time horizons and speculation. Something like this has already been implemented on a large scale in the USA with, for example, the longstanding asset requirements that were applied to the Savings and Loan (S&L) industry. Up until they were deregulated in 1980, the S&Ls were required to concentrate their lending almost entirely on individual family home mortgages. These policies were extremely successful in promoting home ownership among the non-rich to an unprecedented degree. Comparable policies could be successful in promoting investments with high social rates of return, including high employment multipliers, and to discourage speculative finance.

All of these policies would increase the power of government regulators over the financial system. It would therefore be necessary to increase the accountability of the regulators to the public, which would then also increase the accountability of the financial system more broadly. Several proposals for extending accountability have been formulated, including within the US Congress. One that I have suggested (in Pollin 1993) calls for direct election of the Boards of Directors of the regional Federal Reserve Banks. Such increased accountability would also address – though never entirely solve – the legitimate concerns that public allocation policies would degenerate into rent-seeking and other hidden costs to the economy.

A securities transaction excise tax would also discourage speculative finance. Depending on how high the tax was set, one could trade off between discouraging speculative finance against generating revenues for the government. Thus, for example, given existing US financial markets, a transaction tax on equity trades of 0.5 per cent, which was then scaled down appropriately by maturity for all bonds and derivative instruments, would raise roughly $30 billion a year, even after assuming that securities trading would fall by half after the tax was implemented.[19]

All of these policies to channel private investment towards productive activities would have to be complimented by increased public investment. Note, however, that the public investment policies could now be financed, at least to a significant degree, by the securities transaction tax.

Taken as a whole, this policy approach would also make conventional expansionary fiscal and monetary policies more effective in promoting full employment. The following effects would be central.

1. The increase in public investment would create a guaranteed domestic outlet for increased government spending policies. This reduces the import leakage of expansionary policies.
2. Investments induced by the accelerator effects of expansionary policies would be channelled increasingly towards investments with high social rates of return, and away from asset transfers that absorb financial resources but do not increase output and income. This would reduce the 'speculative leakage' of expansionary policy.
3. Creating more accountability within the financial system would weaken the power of financial capitalists in the system. This, in turn would reduce the bias against expansionary policies.

In short, even given the existing conditions in the US financial system, important steps can be taken towards the Keynesian policy goals of 'a somewhat comprehensive socialization of investment' and 'the euthanasia of the rentier'. However, such policy aims are not desirable in their own right. The argument here is that their success would weaken the now formidable barriers imposed by the financial system on the achievement of full employment and other egalitarian goals. The compelling nature of these goals is what, ultimately, makes the case for the continuing relevance of Keynesian policy ideas.

Notes

* I am grateful to comments by participants at the 19 May 1995 conference at University of East London, 'The Relevance of Keynesian Economic Policies Today'; and the 24 May conference at Robinson College, University of Cambridge, 'Restoring Full Employment: Rebuilding Industrial Capacity'. I especially wish to thank Jonathan Michie, Professor Brian Reddaway, Philip Arestis and Malcolm Sawyer for their careful reading of an earlier draft. A longer paper which incorporates much of the present discussion is Pollin (1996d).

1. In somewhat different form, a similar pattern of stagnation has been experienced throughout the OECD economies.
2. The evidence for this within the Clinton administration is provided in abundant detail in Woodward (1994).
3. This paper is a survey that draws on some of my recent research, including Pollin (1993; 1996a; 1996c) as well as Pollin and Dymski (1994), Dymski, Epstein and Pollin (1993), and Baker, Pollin and Schaberg (1995).
4. See Pollin and Justice (1994) and Pollin (1996b) for lengthy analytic treatments of this question, and Pollin (1996d) for a more policy-oriented discussion.
5. Two recent innovative studies, which find support for accelerator and cash flow/ profitability perspectives, are Fazzari (1993) and Gordon (1996).

6. Pollin (1996a) provides a fuller discussion of these patterns, as well as an extended discussion of the relationship between profitability declines and corporate take-overs.
7. The effects of globalisation and deregulation on the viability of the credit-market-based systems remains an open question. See Goldstein (1994) for some interesting observations on the Japanese case.
8. Minsky's position is most fully presented in his *Stabilizing an Unstable Economy* (Minsky 1986). See Pollin and Dymski (1994) for a fuller treatment of the Minskian argument presented here.
9. These policies were accompanied in the post-war period by two types of financial regulatory regimes. The first, of course, was the Bretton Woods international monetary framework, designed to provide administrative procedures for maintaining balance of payments and exchange rate equilibrium between countries. The second was the array of financial regulatory systems developed within domestic economies. These latter are discussed briefly in this chapter's concluding section, and are considered at length from a range of perspectives in Dymski, Pollin and Schaberg (1993).
10. Pollin and Dymski (1994) considered these arguments empirically within the US experience between 1875 and 1989, dividing the full period into 'small government' and 'big government' eras. The general finding is that, by several measures, instability had been ameliorated substantially in the post-Second World War 'big government' era up until the 1970s. But the 1980s emerge as a unique period, in which government remains large, but the indicators of instability approximate those of the small government era.
11. This world-wide development is analysed in, for example, De Cecco (1987).
12. This argument was developed theoretically and empirically in Epstein and Schor (1990).
13. Epstein (1994: 259) ranks the central banks of OECD countries according to their degree of independence. By his ranking in the early 1990s, Germany has the most independent bank, followed by the USA and the UK. This situation has been evolving since the time of Epstein's ranking, given that the establishment of independent central banks has become a major policy aim within the international banking community, including policy makers at the IMF and those directing the movement towards EMU. As one important measure of this change, legislation was enacted in France in 1992 mandating that its central bank become independent, and steps towards implementing this policy change have been advancing steadily. This development will have important implications for the future viability of bank-based systems. Here, however, we are primarily concerned with the lessons to be learned from recent past experiences with bank-based systems.
14. This point was developed by Fine and Harris (1985: 61–2) with respect to the UK and in Epstein and Schor (1990) with respect to the USA.
15. The bank-based systems have high degrees of speculation as well. But as Goldstein (1994) explained with respect to the Japanese model, at the core of this credit market system is a bifurcation, in which speculative market activity does not exert significant influence over the use of funds for productive purposes. Epstein (1993) discussed what he called the 'inflation', 'external' and 'domestic financial market' constraints on the pursuit of expansionary monetary policy in the US context.

16. Bosworth, Carron and Rhyne (1987) is a basic reference on the development of federal credit programmes in the USA.
17. Discussion on this question began with the innovative work of D'Arista and Schlesinger (1993).
18. See Campen (1993) on this question.
19. The details of designing such a tax are presented by Baker, Pollin and Schaberg (1995).

References

Baker, D., Pollin, R. and Schaberg, M. (1995) 'The case for a securities transaction exercise tax: taxing the big casino', manuscript, Department of Economics, University of California Riverside.

Barber, R. and Ghilarducci, T. (1993) 'Pension funds, capital markets, and the economic future', in G. Dymski, G. Epstein and R. Pollin (eds), *Transforming the US Financial System: Equity and Efficiency for the 21st Century* (Armonk, NY: M. E. Sharpe), pp. 287–320.

Bosworth, B. P., Carron, A. S. and Rhyne, E. H. (1987) *The Economics of Federal Credit Programs* (Washington, DC: Brookings Institution).

Campen, J. T. (1993) 'Banks, communities and public policy', in G. Dymski, G. Epstein and R. Pollin (eds), *Transforming the U.S. Financial System: Equity and Efficiency for the 21st Century* (Armonk, NY: M. E. Sharpe), pp. 221–52.

D'Arista, J. and Schlesinger (1993) 'The parallel banking system', in G. Dymski, G. Epstein and R. Pollin (eds), *Transforming the U.S. Financial System: Equity and Efficiency for the 21st Century* (Armonk, NY: M. E. Sharpe), pp. 157–200.

De Cecco, M. (ed.) (1987) *Changing Money: Financial Innovation in Developed Countries* (New York: Basil Blackwell).

Dymski, G., Epstein, G. and Pollin, R. (eds) (1993) *Transforming the U.S. Financial System: Equity and Efficiency for the 21st Century* (Armonk, NY: M. E. Sharpe).

Epstein, G. (1993) 'Monetary policy in the 1990s: overcoming the barriers to equity and growth', in G. Dymski, G. Epstein and R. Pollin (eds), *Transforming the U.S. Financial System: Equity and Efficiency for the 21st Century* (Armonk, NY: M. E. Sharpe), pp. 65–100.

Epstein, G. (1994) 'A political economy model of comparative central banking', in G. Dymski and R. Pollin (eds), *New Perspectives in Monetary Macroeconomics: Explorations in the Tradition of Hyman P. Minsky* (Ann Arbor, MI: The University of Michigan Press), pp. 231–76.

Epstein, G. and Schor, J. (1990) 'Macropolicy in the rise and fall of the golden age', in S. Marglin and J. Schor (eds), *The Golden Age of Capitalism: Reinterpreting the Postwar Experience* (New York: Oxford University Press), pp. 126–52.

Fazzari, S. (1993) 'Monetary policy, financial structure and investment', in G. Dymski, G. Epstein and R. Pollin (eds), *Transforming the U.S. Financial System: Equity and Efficiency for the 21st Century* (Armonk, NY: M. E. Sharpe), pp. 35–64.

Fine, B. and Harris, L. (1985) *The Peculiarities of the British Economy* (London: Lawrence & Wishart).

Goldstein, D. (1994) 'The impact of financial structures on corporate behavior', manuscript, Department of Economics, Allegheny College.

Gordon, D. (1996) 'Must we save our way out of stagnation?', in R. Pollin (ed.), *The Macroeconomics of Finance, Saving and Investment* (Ann Arbor, MI: University of Michigan Press), forthcoming.

Grabel, I. (1996) 'Saving and the financing of productive investment: the importance of national financial complexes', in R. Pollin (ed.), *The Macroeconomics of Finance, Saving and Investment* (Ann Arbor, MI: University of Michigan Press), forthcoming.

Hirschman, A. O. (1970) *Exit, Voice and Loyalty: Responses to Decline in Firms, Organizations, and States* (Cambridge, MA: Harvard University Press).

Keynes, J. M. (1964/1936) *The General Theory of Employment, Interest and Money* (New York, Harcourt, Brace & World, first Harbinger Edition).

McCauley, R. N. and Zimmer, S. A. (1989) 'Explaining international differences in the cost of capital', *New York Federal Reserve Bank Quarterly Review*, Summer, pp. 7–28.

Minsky, H. P. (1986) *Stabilizing an Unstable Economy* (New Haven, CT: Yale University Press).

Pollin, R. (1986) 'Alternative perspectives on the rise of corporate debt dependency: the U.S. postwar experience', *Review of Radical Political Economics*, 18 (Spring and Summer) pp. 205–35.

Pollin, R. (1993) 'Public credit allocation through the Federal Reserve: why it is needed; how it should be done', in G. Dymski, G. Epstein and R. Pollin (eds), *Transforming the U.S. Financial System: Equity and Efficiency for the 21st Century* (Armonk, NY: M. E. Sharpe), pp. 321–54.

Pollin, R. (1996a) 'Borrowing more but investing less: economic stagnation and the rise of corporate takeovers in the U.S.', manuscript, Economics Department, University of California Riverside.

Pollins, R. (1996b) 'Financial Intermediation and the Variability of the Saving Constraint', in R. Pollin (ed.), *The Macroeconomics of Finance, Saving and Investment* (Ann Arbor, MI: The University of Michigan Press), forthcoming.

Pollin, R. (1996c) 'Financial structures and egalitarian economic policy', *International Papers in Political Economy*, forthcoming.

Pollin, R. (1996d) 'Saving and finance: real and illusory constraints on full employment policy', in J. Greive Smith and J. Michie (eds) *Restoring Full Employment: Rebuilding Industrial Capacity* (Oxford: Oxford University Press), forthcoming.

Pollin, R. and Dymski, G. (1994) 'The costs and benefits of financial instability, big government capitalism and the Minsky paradox', in G. Dymski and R. Pollin (eds), *New Perspectives in Monetary Macroeconomics: Explorations in the Tradition of Hyman P. Minsky* (Ann Arbor, MI: The University of Michigan Press), pp. 369–402.

Pollin, R. and Justice, C. (1994) 'Saving, finance, and interest rates: an empirical consideration of some basic Keynesian propositions', in G. Dymski and R. Pollin (eds), *New Perspectives in Monetary Macroeconomics: Explorations in the Tradition of Hyman P. Minsky* (Ann Arbor, MI: The University of Michigan Press), pp. 279–310.

Porter, M. (1992) *Capital Choices: Changing the Way America Invests in Industry* (Washington, DC: Council on Competitiveness).

Poterba, J. and Summers, L. (1992) 'Time horizons of American firms: new evidence from a survey of CEOs', manuscript, Department of Economics, Massachusetts Institute of Technology.

Robinson, J. (1962) *Essays in the Theory of Economic Growth* (London: Macmillan).

Stiglitz, J. (1993) 'The role of the state in financial markets', manuscript, Department of Economics, Stanford University.

Summers, H. (1990) 'Stimulating U.S. personal saving', in C. E. Walker, M. A. Bloomfield and M. Thorning (eds), *The U.S. Saving Challenge: Policy Options for Productivity and Growth* (Boulder, CO: Westview Press), pp. 153–76.

Woodward, R. (1994) *The Agenda* (New York: Simon & Schuster).

Zysman, J. (1983) *Government, Markets and Growth: Financial Systems and the Politics of Industrial Change* (Ithaca, NY: Cornell University Press).

5 Globalisation, Polarisation and US Policy Activism

Gary A. Dymski*

INTRODUCTION

Money, goods, and ideas cross national borders with ever more ease; ever more economic activity is conducted outside national regulatory jurisdictions. Mainstream macroeconomists agree that increased income inequality is the consequence of this globalisation: technical change and freer cross-border flows of capital and goods have increased the demand for technically-adept labour, and decreased that for less-skilled labour. Social policies interfering with the free play of market forces can temporarily stave off greater income inequality, but only at the expense of increased longer-run unemployment and stagnation.

Figure 5.1 uses an aggregate-demand/aggregate-supply (AD/AS) approach to present this argument. The mainstream view amounts to an argument that globalisation shifts the AS curve out and flattens it (since there are more labour units per dollar of GDP, *ceteris paribus*). Policy moves that shift the AD curve might be temporarily effective in raising GDP; but it is important to avoid AD-shifting policies that interfere with market forces such as the trend towards more income inequality.

This chapter disagrees with this prognosis. It argues that the deepening inequality associated with globalisation has had perverse macroeconomic effects overlooked in this mainstream argument. Specifically, increasing inequality has led firms to shift to production and financial-product strategies which have increased spatial polarisation and reduced the size of the fiscal and monetary policy 'multipliers'. These trends, in turn, have widened gender and racial rifts in the control of resources, and reduced access to capital for lower-income households and for smaller firms.

In Figure 5.1, these trends shift the AD curve in. They also shift the AS curve in, and make it steeper. So any short-term macroeconomic benefit from greater inequality leads to cumulative, longer-term structural costs.[1]

So because of deepening racial and gender polarisation, traditional fiscal and monetary stimuli lose some of their potency in restoring generalised prosperity. Other critics of mainstream economics have pointed out that

Figure 5.1 AD-AS shifts due to increased inequality

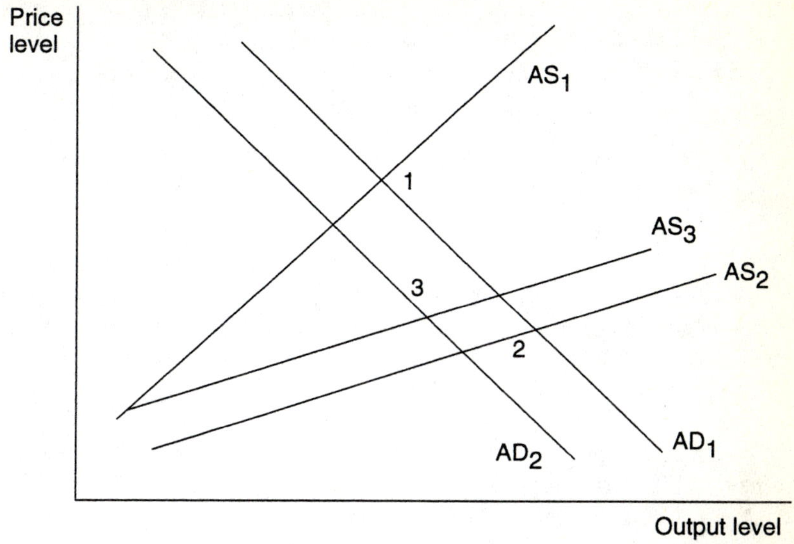

Note: In the mainstream interpretation, increased inequality shifts equilibrium from point 1 to point 2. Here, we argue that further effects shift it again to point 3.

restoring the viability of Keynesian policy means reducing the instability associated with a globalised economy. This chapter adds the point that making policy activism viable again also requires that racial and gender inequality be reduced. This is no small charge, since racial and gender inequality have festered throughout US history.

Race and gender have been characterised recently as 'identity' issues that distract political attention from shared economic concerns (Brinkley 1995; Piore 1995). But US class processes have always been channelled through matrices of gender and racial exclusion. Minorities and women have long lacked equal access to resources, even during the nostalgically-remembered 'Golden Age'. Race and gender exclusion give rise, in turn, to path-dependent growth which steadily widens spatial and class disparities. Inequality will only deepen, unless policy activism is rethought, because industrial and government-policy shifts have largely eliminated channels of economic mobility within US society – such as job security, and access to financial or human capital – for those on the outside looking in.

The next section reviews mainstream arguments about globalisation, inequality and policy irrelevance, while the following section examines US racial and gender inequality in the context of globalisation. After that, we set out the increasing-returns framework that underlies our argument, and then move on to examine the implications of globalisation and polarisation for Keynesian fiscal policy, and subsequently for monetary policy. The final section concludes, and discusses implications for policy activism.

GLOBALISATION, INCOME INEQUALITY AND UNEMPLOYMENT: MAINSTREAM VIEWS

The last 20 years have seen not just accelerated globalisation, but the adoption of representative-agent and general equilibrium models within mainstream macroeconomics and, not coincidentally, growing scepticism about policy activism among macroeconomists. Because of the Lucas critique and capital mobility, stimulative shifts of the AD curve will be countered by offsetting AS shifts; and because of the Barro critique and the 'twin deficits' argument, attempts to shift the AD curve may create feedback effects, shifting this curve back to its original location.[2]

Against this background, some economists have lionised increasing income inequality as a way to improve macroeconomic outcomes; see Bean (1994), Federal Reserve Bank of Kansas City (1994), and Federal Reserve Bank of New York (1995). The argument is that European nations have had persistently higher unemployment rates than the USA since the 1980s because income inequality has increased in the USA more than in Europe.

The US 'employment miracle' scenario begins with the assumption that consumer preferences and rapid technical change are inducing shifts in work organisation, and encouraging the globalisation of real and financial activity.[3] These changes, in turn, have increased demand for high-skilled labour and reduced demand for low-skilled labour. In Europe, these shifts have resulted in higher rates of unemployment, for longer periods, especially for less-skilled workers.[4] Less-skilled workers have been laid off, not hired for lower wages, because of the more inflexible and egalitarian European wage structures. US unemployment rates, by contrast, have not tended upwards. The flexible US wage structure has accommodated the reduced demand for less-skilled workers by permitting their real wages to fall. In effect, the USA has a wider income distribution with a lower floor.

US and European wage structures differ, in turn, because their labour-market institutions differ. In the USA, unions are weak, and bargaining units lack market power; hence low and flexible wages. The corporatist and heavily unionised economies of Europe have had more inflexible wage bargaining, and thus more unemployment. Further, government oversight of the labour market is more intrusive in Europe. European minimum wages are much higher (relative to the average wage) than the US minimum wage, and constitute binding constraints in the labour market.[5] Further, European systems have generally provided generous and extended income maintenance to the long-term unemployed, encouraging them to become detached from the labour market.

Mainstream arguments about inequality extend to the globalisation not only of capital and goods, but also of labour. The USA now has an immigration boom unprecedented in scale since the 1920s (Borjas 1994: 1668). Earlier US immigration waves consisted primarily of Europeans and Canadians, but Latin Americans and Asians dominate this wave. Furthermore, this wave is bifurcated: for example, it contains high numbers of both high-school drop-outs and college graduates, though on average the new immigrants' education level is below that of the native population.

Borjas (1994) shows that new immigrants contributed to, but did not single-handedly cause, the 1980s increase in US income inequality. He suggests that US income inequality may actually help the USA to reduce its labour-supply mismatch. Countries with egalitarian income distributions and progressive income taxes will lose talented residents to countries with light tax burdens for the wealthy; countries with generous welfare benefits and high minimum wages will attract low-skilled migrants. So policy measures that induce greater income inequality increase the flow of desirable, upper-end immigrants, and reduce that of lower-end migrants.

RACE/GENDER POLARISATION IN THE USA, BEFORE AND AFTER GLOBALISATION

The idea that widened income inequality conveys a competitive labour-market advantage to the US economy rests on a historically naive understanding of the US labour force. It ignores both class conflict and the racial and gender divides, or zones of exclusion, that have historically characterised the US class structure.

Other political economists have presented very compelling discussions of the evolution of class conflict *per se* in the USA. These 'Golden Age' models (reviewed in Amin 1994) describe a capitalist-worker accord (or, alternatively, 'Fordist' era) which originated amidst the Depression and persisted until about 1974. However, these stylised accounts also ignore gender and race exclusion, despite the fact that the 'Golden Age' never arrived for women and minorities as it did for white men.[6]

Figures 5.2 and 5.3 starkly illustrate these divides. Figure 5.2 shows that black unemployment rates have steadily diverged from those for whites since

Figure 5.2 Unemployment by race and gender, 1969–94

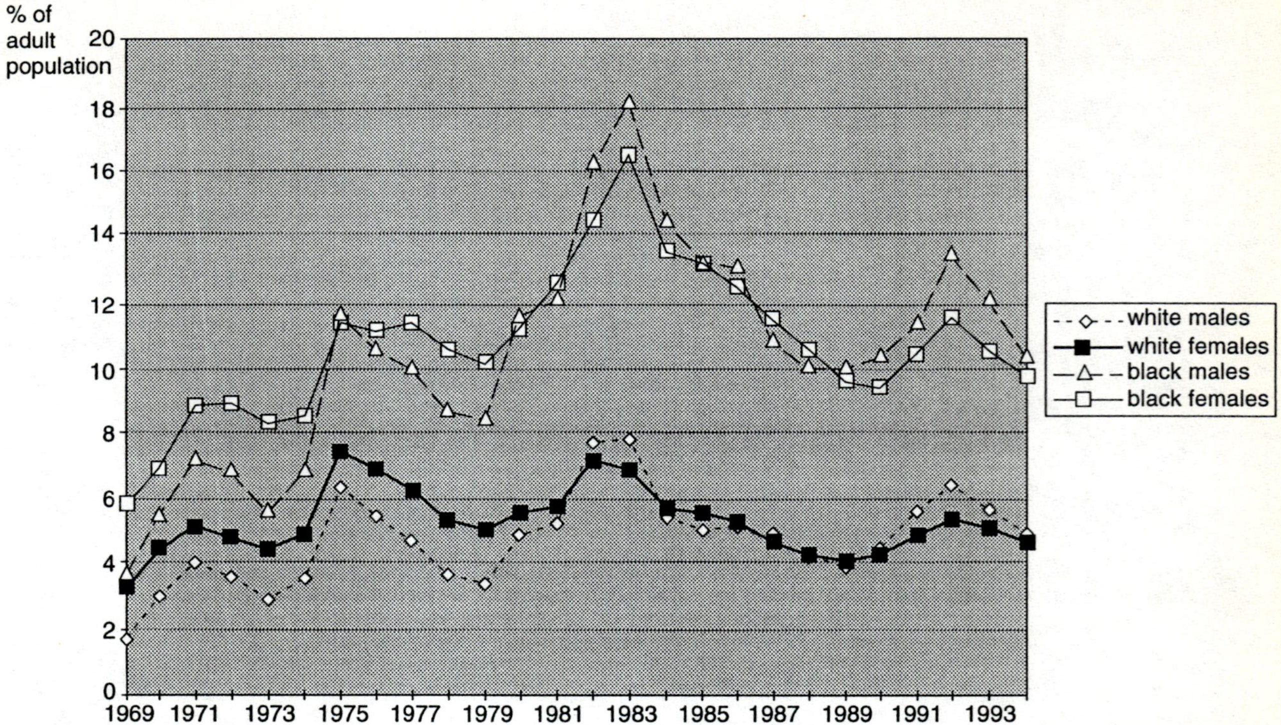

Figure 5.3 Labour-force participation by race and gender, 1969–94

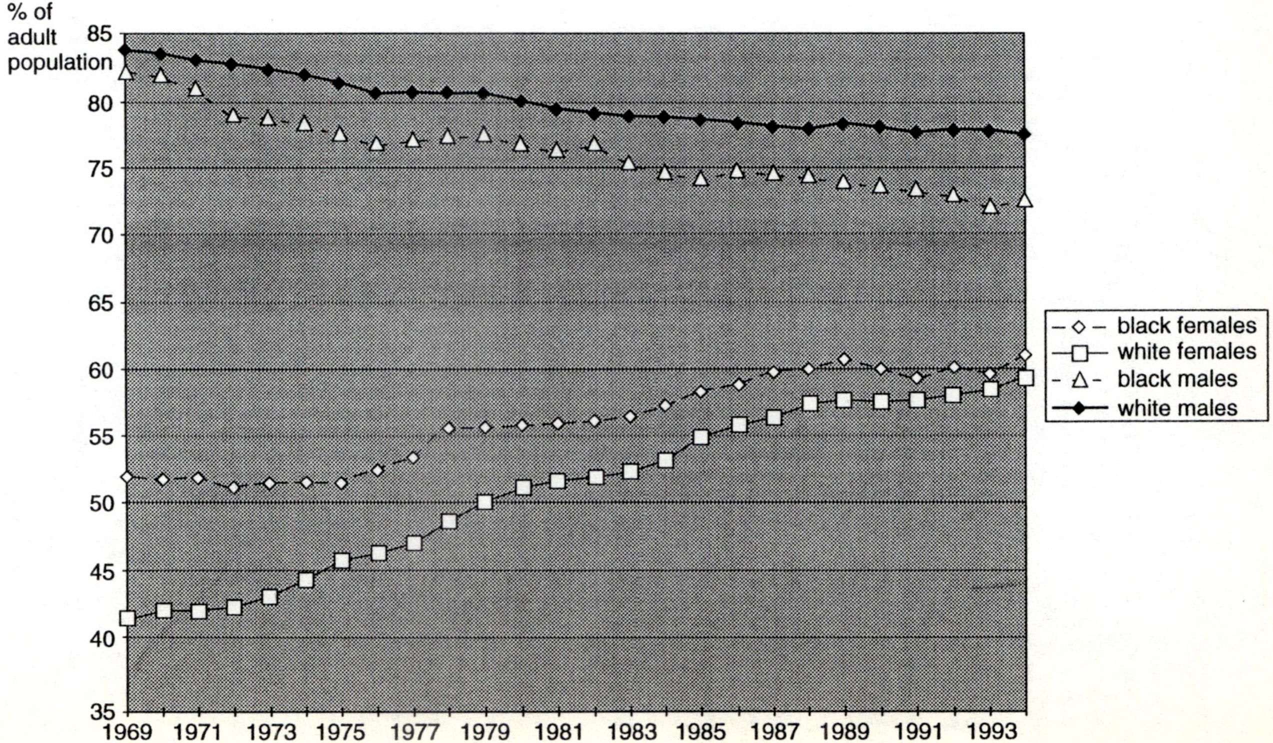

1969. Figure 5.3 presents some secular race/gender trends in labour-force participation: those of all males are declining, though those for black males are declining faster; and those for all females are rising, though rates for white women are rising faster.

In the early years of the twentieth century, women were categorically excluded from numerous jobs and occupations. While women of colour chronically participated in the labour force, white women usually did not, until wartime mobilisation and subsequent labour shortages increased the demand for female labour (see Figure 5.3). The gender division of labour shifted to accommodate women's entry: several previously 'male' occupations (for example, clerical and sales work) were redefined as female jobs. Generally, women were integrated into the work force through expanding numbers of low-paying, dead-end jobs. Symptomatic of women's unequal participation in the formal labour force was their near-universal difficulty in gaining independent access to credit (Chesler and Goodman 1976: ch. 11).

There are several telling parallels between the economic experience of US minorities and that of women. Like women, minorities were excluded categorically from the mainstream economy through most of the century.[7] In the South, blacks' second-class economic status was reinforced by *Jim Crow* social laws and by a political power structure that effectively precluded the black vote. In the West, Asians and Mexicans confronted numerous economic barriers, including *de facto* racial exclusion.

Many minority workers and families moved to cities in response to the labour shortage accompanying the two world wars. When these wars ended, returning white workers displaced minority workers in most stable, well-paying jobs. Segregated minority ghettos emerged, spurred by racial unrest and exclusionary covenants. Ghetto residents had difficulty in finding decent work; banks often did not locate, and would not make loans, there; and social and physical infrastructures were inadequate.

Segregation had contradictory implications for class structure and inequality. Minority communities were a labour reserve for white industrial employers, and had lower income flows and wealth levels than white communities. At the same time, minority communities had complex internal class structures and their own income/wealth hierarchies, as Boston (1988) documents. Teachers and doctors faced housing segregation as did labourers, so minority communities had some degree of social integration. They also had a significant base of businesses owned by community residents; hence much of the cash flow generated by ghetto residents was retained within these communities.

Legislative reforms attacking race and gender discrimination, passed in the 1960s and 1970s, opened channels of labour-market and residential opportunity for women and minorities just as globalisation was gathering force. For example, women have filled a disproportionate number of managerial positions in both the 1970s and 1980s (Appelbaum 1981; Shaw *et al.* 1993), and some categories of households – especially upper-income families, and married couples – have experienced rising median income, spurred largely by women's entry into the labour force.[8]

Nonetheless, the dominant distributional trend has been the declining median income of households across the entire bottom of the income distribution. The number of low-income households has risen sharply.[9] Restructuring firms have laid off workers; increased the use of contractual labour; and eliminated many lower-level managerial positions, which provide ladders for career advancement (Shaw *et al.* 1993).

This trend deepened economic polarisation, especially along gender and racial lines. For example, while an increasing share of men – 16.3 per cent in 1993, versus 8.1 per cent in 1974 – work full-time for less than the minimum wage, even now many more female than male workers occupy this category (26.7 per cent in 1993). More poor women either work full-time or combine welfare with occasional or part-time work.[10]

Female-headed households, which have grown from 10 per cent of all households in 1951 to 18.1 per cent in 1993, have a special plight. In 1993, female-headed households' median income was just 40.1 per cent of married couples'. The bottom 80 per cent of these households experienced declining real income in the 1979–89 period, and their poverty rates have increased due to declines in transfer payments (Hanratty and Blank 1991).

The same broad pattern – greater opportunity for some, combined with worse outcomes for most – has characterised minorities' recent experience. While wage-rate differentials between *all* black and white males have narrowed (Jaynes 1990), among *young* workers the black-white wage differential has increased: from 10.3 per cent in 1973 to 16.4 per cent in 1989 (Bound and Freeman 1991).[11] Further, black and Hispanic median family income has fallen relative to that of whites at least since 1967; and the median black wealth level has fallen to 5 per cent of the overall median as of 1989 (Wolff 1995: 17).

The disparate minority wage-gap and family income trends are explained, in part, by the higher incidence of female-headed households among minorities, and in part by the declining labour-force participation of black males (compared with whites). Black male joblessness has been a long-standing problem. By 1960, prime-age black males' labour-force participation rate already lagged behind that of whites (93 per cent as against 97 per cent), and their unemployment rate was double that of white males.[12] Over time, an increasing proportion of black males have reported no employment-based income; in 1990, Jaynes found this proportion to be one in six.

As Jaynes observes, black male workers fall into two segments: one keeping pace with white males, another increasingly isolated from the labour market. Clark and Summers have argued that this labour-force bifurcation, especially along racial lines, is central to the entire US unemployment problem. They find that non-whites must wait twice as long as whites to find work when they are unemployed; and observe that: 'unemployment is high because a relatively small number of workers are out of work a large part of the time, although the remainder of the labor market clears. Even over fairly long periods, the burden of unemployment is highly concentrated' (1990: 39).

These changes in income flows are associated with structural geographic shifts. The effects of de-industrialisation have been felt disproportionately in the central cities, as Tables 5.1 and 5.2 show; further, job losses in cities have been concentrated in minority areas.[13] Meanwhile, job gains – including the new growth 'technopoles' at the technological cutting edge – have emerged primarily in suburban and ex-urban areas (see Gordon and Richardson 1991; Scott 1993). In consequence, a disproportionate number of the unemployed, and of working-age adults out of the labour force, are found in central cities (and rural areas). Accompanying this shift in jobs is a parallel population shift. As Table 5.1 shows, the US working-age population and labour force have shifted steadily to the suburbs, and away from central cities and rural areas.

Decreased residential segregation has allowed more minorities to move to suburbs. Table 5.2 shows, for example, that the proportion of minorities in central cities has not risen in recent years, even with the overall population shift to the suburbs. But racial isolation remains high among blacks and Hispanics. Suburbanisation has not significantly reduced social segregation among blacks (Farley 1991). And Massey and Denton (1993) and Denton (1994) find most blacks to be 'hypersegregated' in the period 1970–90, with the blacks becoming less centralised but more isolated and concentrated over time.

Another facet of the globalisation process is a new immigration wave, composed (unlike earlier ones) primarily of ethnic minorities. Most new arrivals fall into two categories: those with low skills and few financial assets, who sell their labour in the most poorly paid jobs; and those with skills, education and financial assets. Immigrants in the latter category often establish either family-owned businesses, or professional practices that cater to ethnically-homogeneous clienteles in 'ethnoburbs' (Li 1995). This new immigration has complicated the racial divide, because the zones of racial exclusion now include minority subgroups, even within ethnic 'categories'.

Table 5.1 Population and labour force by degree of urbanisation

	Metropolitan areas		Rural
	Central cities	*Suburbs*	*areas*
Percentage of population (16–65 years old) in:			
1973	30.8	37.8	31.4
1988	31.0	47.0	22.1
1993	29.8	47.9	22.2
Percentage of civilian labour force in:			
1973	30.5	38.8	30.7
1988	30.4	48.7	20.9
1993	29.3	50.0	20.6
Percentage of unemployed:			
1973	36.3	36.0	27.7
1988	37.2	39.2	23.6
1993	32.4	41.6	25.9
Percentage of not-in-labour-force:			
1973	31.4	36.3	32.3
1988	32.0	43.7	24.3
1993	31.3	44.7	24.1
Unemployed and not-in-labour-force as % of labour force:			
1973	72.1	64.6	72.1
1988	61.1	50.9	66.4
1993	63.2	52.2	72.1

Sources: *Employment and Earnings* (various issues), US Bureau of Labour Statistics.

PATH-DEPENDENCE, INCREASING RETURNS AND SOCIAL POLARISATION

The previous section has suggested several points. First, there have always been race and gender divides in the US labour force. So in the US 'employment miracle' literature, the contrast between flexible US labour markets and 'structural' European unemployment is overdrawn: much of the US flexibility is itself 'structural' (the result of the unequal and contingent inclusion of minorities and women). Second, the last 20 years have seen a deepening of these divides and a bifurcation in incomes. The increasing inequality celebrated in the mainstream argument has operated, to a large extent, along well-established race/gender rifts in the US working class.

Table 5.2 Central-city concentrations of minorities, women, and teenagers

	Black	*Hispanic*	*Female**	*Male**	*Teenage*
Percentage of central-city population (16–65 years old):					
1973	21.7		49.1	40.8	10.1
1988	20.8	12.4	49.6	42.9	7.5
1993	21.6	14.0	49.7	43.8	6.5
Percentage of central-city labour force:					
1973	21.5		37.5	53.9	8.6
1988	20.0	12.5	43.3	50.8	5.9
1993	20.0	13.8	44.0	51.3	4.7
Percentage of central-city unemployed:					
1973	34.7		35.3	37.6	27.2
1988	37.5	16.2	37.8	45.2	17.0
1993	34.2	18.7	36.4	49.7	13.9
Percentage of central-city not-in-labour-force:					
1973	21.8		66.4	21.1	12.5
1988	22.1	12.4	61.2	28.5	10.3
1993	24.5	14.5	60.0	30.2	9.8

*includes females and males 20–65 years old in numerator.
Sources: *Employment an Earnings* (various issues), US Bureau of Labour Statistics.

Third, what makes racial and gender divides especially important is that, thanks to segregation, they have a uniquely spatial character. For example, female-headed households and black male deproletarianisation are concentrated in inner cities.

These trends have consequences overlooked in mainstream discussions of the viability of Keynesian policy. This section confronts the central conceptual question for our argument: since gender and race inequality has always characterised US class relations, why does its deepening now make activist policy less effective than before?

Mainstream macroeconomics approaches this or any question of temporal change by looking for breakpoints in time series.[14] In this case, deepening inequality and ineffective Keynesian demand management are traced to the same exogenous shocks: globalisation and technical change. This approach assumes that certain outcomes are necessary, given initial conditions: that is, behavioural functions are assumed to be linear (or log-linear), and hence to have precise equilibria (or determinate steady states).

There is little empirical support for this linear, exogenous-shock view in this case. Figures 5.2 and 5.3 present key statistical aspects of this puzzle. These graphs show that both black/white and male/female labour-market experience has steadily diverged, without a single detectable 'break point'. It is possible to salvage the regime-shift approach by positing – as the real-business cycle theorists do – that linear behavioural relations are continually bombarded with exogenous shocks (typically due to unobserved technology shocks), to which they instantly react. But without disputing that technological change has occurred and is important, we will forgo this temptation in favour of the explanatory alternative: the possibility that change is not driven by one-time exogenous pushes, but by continual endogenous adjustments.

That is, we will suppose the US economy is replete with economic mechanisms which turn differences in degree, eventually, into differences in kind. As Card and Freeman put it, 'small differences matter [because] individuals and institutions respond in economically significant ways to incentives ... [and because] small differences interact in various ways' (1993b: 9).

The idea that elements such as globalisation and polarisation might be linked endogenously requires that we identify processes of what Myrdal (1957) termed cumulative causation: market dynamics that can lead in more than one direction. Arthur (1994) observes, in his book on increasing returns, that market outcomes can be viewed as the result of necessity, of chance, or of both: necessity, to the extent that market fundamentals like resource endowments determine what happens; and chance, to the extent that different initial conditions can lead to very different outcomes.

Mainstream theory presupposes that market outcomes are necessary; but an alternative is to suppose they depend to some extent on 'chance': that they are path-dependent. One area may become a Silicon Valley, and another not, because the former has small advantages at some early stage; momentum builds almost accidentally at first. Models taking this approach – which include most Keynesian models, conflict models and information-based models – generate multiple equilibria and are sensitive to initial conditions.

Here we will make the case for why polarisation can have perverse, unintended effects by suggesting the importance of two different models of path-dependence: Verdoorn's Law, and its mirror image; and spatial and credit-market externalities.

Kaldor (1967: 12) attributed the uneven pace of economic development between nations to the varying responses of supply to changes in demand. So 'productivity increases in response to increases in total output because of economies of scale or increasing returns'. This is Verdoorn's Law:

productivity growth is a function of output growth. Self-sustained growth requires increasing returns and elastic commodity demand. For our purpose here, the mirror image of Verdoorn's Law is also relevant: another possible economic constraint is the varying response of AD to changes in AS. Specifically, AD responses vary, as we argue below, because they are filtered through firms whose behaviour tends to amplify initial differences.

Spatial and credit-market externalities are a second, more 'micro', source of path-dependence. Uneven growth can worsen initial imbalances *within* metropolitan areas.[15] Uneven intra-metropolitan development follows from several interlinked features of urban economies. Specifically, when investment in urban areas depends on whether small firms can obtain credit for geographically-specific (unmoveable) assets, urban growth may be uneven and path-dependent (see Dymski 1995a; Dymski and Veitch 1995b). These uneven patterns will be more pronounced if urban investment generates spillovers due to demand stimulus or refurbishment effects.

In this event, every bank faces a co-ordination problem: maximising returns from lending means lending where its competitors do; but these competitors are faced with the same dilemma. The solution to this problem is likely to be guided by the perceived prospects of different areas, and perceived prospects turn, in part, on their racial composition. The past is most often prologue in the credit market.

Spillovers also arise in urban areas because of factor market interlinkage. Any prospective borrower's creditworthiness depends, *ceteris paribus*, on her expected success in the labour market: repayment is more certain the better one's earnings. Success in the labour market also depends on success in the credit market: borrowing is a key to financing an education and enhancing human capital, and to financing a business and succeeding as an entrepreneur. In effect, economic opportunity itself – access to capital or labour markets – is path-dependent.

Gendered economic dynamics exaggerate these uneven development trends further. The factors favouring suburbs over central cities led not just to uneven development, but to the social and economic isolation of women in suburbs. Women's entry into the work force, in both female-headed households and dual-earner households, has meant often a return to central-city living, since costs and work/residence tensions are lower there (England 1991). The problem is that the growth industries in central cities (advanced corporate and retail services) disproportionately offer part-time and casual employment opportunities (Sheets, Nord and Phelps 1987). This sort of underemployment accommodates the time-space constraints of women facing household *and* workplace responsibilities (Pratt and Hanson 1991), but it does not permit these workers to 'catch up' with workers in more privileged jobs.

In effect, urban economies are spillover factories. Taken together, even small structural differences between areas – in residents' incomes, the character of schools, the types of businesses, racial composition, and so on – lead to differential rates of community growth and individual economic opportunity.

THE PRODUCTION/CONSUMPTION NEXUS AND THE FISCAL-POLICY MULTIPLIER

The incremental structural changes associated with globalisation (see above) have eroded the effectiveness of Keynesian policies over time, through path-dependent processes described in the previous section. Here we discuss the fiscal multiplier; the next section considers the money multiplier.

The argument here answers two questions. First, given the longstanding gender and racial exclusion in US society, why was fiscal policy potentially more effective in the earlier post-war years? Second, why does greater polarisation make fiscal policy less potentially effective now?[16]

We cite five reasons why the potential effectiveness of fiscal policy was not compromised by race and gender inequality in the earlier post-war period. First, the minority labour-force was better integrated into primary-sector jobs in the earlier post-war years. Minorities, especially males, often held stable jobs capable of supporting families; yet these workers were 'last hired, first fired'. So their labour-force participation rates and earnings were more pro-cyclical than those of whites.[17] Second, uniform racial segregation created dense economic interdependencies and cash flows within minority communities. In effect, these communities realised benefits from local spillover effects.

Taken together, these two factors suggest that recessions would hit minority communities hard, while expansionary fiscal policy actions would yield rapid income gains among minority workers. Minority communities' internal economic heterogeneity and interconnections would, in turn, ensure a large fiscal multiplier.

A third factor was the US political atmosphere. The relatively stable and relatively high growth rates of the earlier post-war years spread prosperity broadly among US households. An idea like 'ending poverty in our time' (John F. Kennedy) was part of national political discourse; Richard Nixon even proposed a European-style income floor. The 'War on Poverty' was tolerated because living standards were rising for most households.

The fourth factor is related: most counter-cyclical government spending and transfer programmes were not specifically aimed at minorities and women. Public expenditure programmes for highway construction, defence and military procurement directly benefited white males more than any other labour-force category.[18] Eligibility rules for Social Security favoured the elderly with a longstanding labour-force attachment.

Appelbaum and Schettkat (1994, 1995) suggest a fifth factor. These authors modify Verdoorn's Law to explain the OECD employment crisis. The authors argue that industries' elasticities of demand depend on income levels. In the earlier post-war period, when incomes were low, Verdoorn's Law operated as a 'virtuous circle': increased AD led workers to purchase goods from high-productivity industries, thus spurring output and employment growth simultaneously. But as incomes have risen over time, the income-elasticity of demand for high-productivity commodities has declined, while that for low-productivity industries has risen. So demand stimulus increasingly leads to expanded output and employment in low-productivity industries which pay lower wages and produce less output per worker.

This argument suggests that the expenditures of the larger numbers of lower-income households should expand high-productivity employment. However, globalisation has led firms to eliminate many high-wage jobs in sectors producing tradables, in favour of low-wage jobs in these same sectors. So spending by lower-income households creates multiplier effects for other lower-income households, either at home or abroad.

This does not mean that fiscal stimulus is now ineffective in re-igniting growth in the polarised US economy. Freeman (1991) recently found that in urban areas whose unemployment rates were cut to 4 per cent or less by demand expansion, youth unemployment rates fell by half and employment/population ratios nearly doubled.[19]

Nonetheless, the sensitivity of minority communities to fiscal stimulus has been eroded. For one thing, minorities are less likely to be employed in primary-sector manufacturing jobs. So the 'last hired, first fired' effect has been diluted: fiscal stimulus no longer generates a demand for minority workers to staff third shifts in plants that have been shut or disassembled. Further, following Boston (1988), minority communities have less integrated class structures. Consumption is less likely to occur within the minority community; so any spending injection will have smaller multiplier effects for impacted minority communities. Both of these arguments, together with inner-city residents' lower labour-force participation, imply that a larger stimulus will be needed to reduce unemployment to any given target level. In effect, local spillover effects from growth have been diminished through the accumulated effects of structural change.[20] On top of this, the Appelbaum–Schettkat argument implies that a stimulus of any magnitude will have a higher cost in price inflation because consumers are purchasing lower-productivity commodities.

The rise of dual-earner households in the privileged sectors of the labour force also weakens the support for counter-cyclical stimulus. Wheelock (1990) observes that when single-earner households predominated, recessions had devastating, widespread effects; but with the rise of dual-earner households, savings rather than consumption suffer during recessions. Because higher and more stable incomes insulate them from cyclical downturns, members of dual-earner households are less likely to support fiscal stimulus, and more likely to want reduced public expenditures.

The final consideration in the decline of fiscal effectiveness is the transformation of the political climate. Real-income stagnation and 'white male angst' due to globalisation and de-industrialisation have fed a political backlash. Political support for war on poverty has been replaced by a political war *on* welfare (Katz 1989).

MONETARY-POLICY IMPLICATIONS OF FINANCIAL TRANSFORMATION

US monetary policy has always operated through the banking system. Until globalisation pressures mounted in the 1960s, this system was based on two principles: market segmentation and universal coverage.[21] Depression-era reforms had separated banking markets geographically and strictly limited banks' competition for savings and for loans. Thanks to deposit insurance and federal guarantees, most US households held financial assets in two forms: transaction balances in commercial banks, and savings balances in S&L associations (thrifts). The former provided, in the main, short-term financing for business; the latter provided long-term financing for the housing market.

This New Deal banking system provided a stakeholding vehicle for the broad mass of Americans. Further, banks and thrifts generated positive economic spillovers for the communities they served by providing integrated local mechanisms for gathering and channelling small savings.

This stakeholding vehicle did not extend evenly to all. As noted, women had extremely limited access to credit. Further, banks and thrifts often did not locate or lend in minority neighbourhoods. Wealth-building within minority communities was further compromised by government policy: federal mortgage guarantees explicitly discriminated against minority areas until the 1960s; and since residential segregation was widespread, home-ownership subsidies were of little use to blacks and Hispanics.

From the mid-1960s on, macroeconomic pressures and the growing sophistication of banks and their larger customers gradually broke down the key features of the New Deal banking system, such as the banks' monopoly over household savings, and their primary role in credit provision.

Bigger banks reacted by adopting aggressive new management philosophies: they sought out new loan customers – especially in less-developed countries (LDCs) – to replace lost 'blue chip' borrowers; and they replaced deposits with bought funds. Beginning in the 1970s, leading-edge banks such as Citibank and Wells Fargo changed their marketing strategies in response to these shifting fundamentals: they designed 'retail banking' services for upper-end customers, closed branches in 'marginal' locations, and reduced non-fee services for lower-end customers.

The 1980s brought bank and thrift stress, as interest rates and hence the cost of bought funds rose to unprecedented levels. Thrifts were especially compromised because of their specialisation in long-term, fixed-rate mortgages. The LDC lending crisis broke out when Mexico defaulted in August 1982. And after banks had shed their LDC exposure in 1987, they plunged into a lending binge for an ill-fated bubble in the commercial real-estate market (which collapsed in the 1990 recession).

Four banking acts were passed in the 1980s to prop up the US banking system. Broadly, these acts extended public funds and guarantees, supervised the closure and merger of failed institutions, and aggressively liberalised banking practices. For example, market segmentation has been gradually eliminated, and bank rates have been deregulated (see Dymski, Epstein and Pollin 1993).

Some aspects of this transformation of US banking pertain to economic polarisation and path-dependence. First, fewer banks and thrifts remain in operation. Gradually, the thrift and banking industries are consolidating; larger banks with multiple product lines and broad geographic coverage are becoming the norm.

In consequence, the retail banking business has also been transformed. The major banks have shifted 'upmarket' towards wealthier, upper-income customers. Indeed, New Deal banking markets, which featured (near-) universal access and standardised savings/transactions instruments for all, have broken into three distinct segments. At the top end are the wealthy, whose financial needs are catered to personally by diverse sets of brokers, bankers and advisers. Most households fall into a middle segment, which has ready access to standardised savings/borrowing options (credit cards, mutual funds, money market accounts, and so on). A broader range of product choices is available to this segment than in the previous banking system, and more firms (and types of firm) compete to offer these standardised services.

As a result, these households enjoy some continued benefits from cross-product subsidies.[22] On the bottom are the unbanked, who are unable to maintain bank accounts due to low savings rates and rising bank service fees.[23] The unbanked conduct their financial business through a network of informal firms – cheque-cashing outlets, money-order firms, grocery shops – at substantially higher fees than banks typically charge.

Not only have banks been segmenting their customer bases, they have been downsizing. Branches have been closed, especially in lower-income areas and hence in minority communities. In effect, banks have responded to shifts in the US income distribution by cutting their effective customer base to include only its upper portions. Caskey and Peterson (1994) show that the proportion of all households with a bank account dropped from 90.5 per cent in 1977 to 86.5 per cent in 1989. This entire decline was accounted for by the bottom sixth in income terms, 70.3 per cent of whom had bank accounts in 1977, versus 59.2 per cent in 1989.

In addition to customer shedding, banks have shed credit risks and, in some credit markets, shifted from an intermediary to a broker role. Banks have shed risk in part by making variable-rate loans, and by expanding their use of loan securitisation. In some markets – credit-card and mortgage debt – most loans are now bundled and sold by the lenders who originate them. This has redefined the relationship between banks and the communities within their market areas. Banks and thrifts no longer are the focal point for integrated, localised savings/investment processes. Instead, they are the localised purveyors of standardised financial contracts and services. Some smaller banks retain the older model, but these banks find it difficult to attract deposit funds from wealthier borrowers, who have so many savings options.

In sum, banking system adjustments to globalisation have deepened polarisation in the USA. Only some households qualify for preferred bank accounts; these same households are most likely to be eligible for mortgages and other securitised debt. Among businesses, the larger and better-established firms have direct access to credit markets; others must rely on intermediated credit, since securitisation of small business loans has not occurred (see Beshouri and Nigro 1994).

This polarisation has occurred not just on the basis of income, but also along racial lines. Numerous studies of residential mortgage lending have found evidence of racial discrimination and redlining; Dymski (1995b) reviews this literature. Studies also suggest that minority businesses rely on family financing and lending circles because they cannot procure bank loans.

As a consequence of these patterns of banking change, lower-income and minority communities are experiencing spillover losses due to redlining and discrimination, branch closures, bank consolidation and securitisation.

Externalities in local credit markets lead to the erosion of economic development possibilities in communities populated by critical masses of the unbanked, even as financial infrastructures blossom in communities populated by the wealthy.

These changes in the banking system – whose root is the globalisation process that began in the 1960s – reduce the money multiplier, and compromise the effectiveness of monetary policy interventions. Reducing the discount or interbank rate, and freeing lending capacity in the banking system, will be less effective in spurring economic activity now than under the abandoned universal-access system. Fewer households and businesses hold balances with, and borrow from, banks than under the old system. Further, the large banks that increasingly dominate the banking system are turning away from intermediation, and instead playing the role of a broker between financially capable customers and secondary markets. These customers, and the larger businesses, have immediate access to the direct credit markets, regardless of the state of monetary policy. Vast numbers of smaller firms and lower-income households still depend on bank credit markets to increase their spending. But the smaller banks that extend loans to these economic units are disappearing in the bank consolidation wave.

Expansionary monetary policy will still increase credit flows; but these will go, increasingly, to upper-income households and communities, whose members are seldom credit-starved in the worst of times. Conceivably, monetary stimuli could feed speculative price bubbles more than in the past, and do less good in providing credit for small businesses and lower-income households. The loss of financial capacity in minority and lower-income communities implies smaller money multipliers there due to local spillover effects involving housing values, business viability and job creation. Increased numbers of informal financial firms offering fragmented costly services cannot duplicate the synergies of the now-dismantled integrated banking system.

CONCLUSION AND POLICY IMPLICATIONS

Adding more income inequality into a society already polarised along race and gender lines has created not simply a 'solution' to an economic problem, but also more extreme, self-reinforcing social polarisation, which has become an incendiary situation for the polity.[24] While this has compromised the effectiveness of monetary and fiscal policy, it has made policy activism a more urgent necessity.

In the midst of the Second World War, Michal Kalecki wrote an essay considering why democratic governments would not pursue the expansionary policies needed to permanently attain full employment. He observed that with full employment, ''the sack'' would cease to play its role as a disciplinary measure' (Kalecki 1943). The deepening polarisation in US society suggests another political constraint on policy activism. That is, as polarisation deepens, the political will to redress inequities and resource deficits in undeserved areas deteriorates. The problems of the poor are not just out of sight (because of racial and gender exclusion in the USA, the poor don't look like 'us' and warrant no political attention); the economic divide becomes a political divide, which in turn constrains the use of policy activism to address economic problems. These dual divides are hardly salutary for the 'land of opportunity'.

We have argued that fiscal policy has become less viable for several reasons: slippage in the economic integration of minorities into 'primary sector' jobs; reduced spillover capture within minority communities; a vindictive political environment, aimed especially at categorical (as opposed to universal) programmes; the reversal of Verdoorn's Law. Monetary policy has become less effective as well, for related reasons: banks have moved upmarket, and the banking structure is no longer a broad-based stakeholding vehicle; the formal banking sector has downsized and withdrawn from lower-income and minority areas, triggering spillover losses there; banks and thrifts increasingly play a broker role and not an intermediary role, which restricts the number of households and businesses that pass creditworthiness criteria.

These changes reduce the size of the fiscal and money multipliers. And as noted in the first section, they shift back the AD and AS curves. It should also be stressed, however, that because of changes in the workplace and in financial intermediation, there are fewer mechanisms of economic opportunity now than in the past. Access to 'good' jobs and access to 'capacity-building' capital is increasingly scarce.[25] What should be done about employment and opportunity, in light of these changes?

One response, consistent with the mainstream analyses, is *nothing*. The income-inequality trend is inevitable, and its peculiar race/gender coding is just an unfortunate historical coincidence. The higher unemployment rate, and lower labour-force participation, of minorities can be improved only if the lessons of market flexibility sink in, in the ghetto: work cheaply or die. Feldstein (1976) first made this argument over 20 years ago. He argued that rising welfare-state benefits have increased workers' reservation wages, so structural problems (that is, the culture of poverty) and not inadequate demand account for the impermeability of youth unemployment, especially among minorities. Borjas's analysis of immigration offers two new defences of increased US income inequality. First, the flood of low-skilled workers into the US *proves* there is a supply of low-wage jobs available; so domestic residents without jobs must be choosing not to supply their labour. Second, increased returns to wealth should attract more capable immigrants.

This approach is fatally flawed, however. Feldstein's hypothesis about the benefits of reduced welfare-state benefits on reservation wages has had a natural experiment in the form of Reaganomics: and there is no evidence that it is true. Further, it blames the victim, but ignores the long history of structural inequality that has brought us to this juncture. It pits one sector of the excluded against another, providing neither with mechanisms of opportunity. Given the path-dependence of community growth and stagnation, and the racial/gender coding of economic transactions in the USA, the second Kaleckian political constraint will simply bite more and more deeply.

Borjas's points similarly do not hold up. His own study (1993) of comparative US-Canadian immigration shows that *Canada* has been 'outcompeting' the USA in terms of the 'quality' of its immigrants. But this should not be: Canada has pursued a resolutely corporatist/welfare-state policy approach during the recent past, while the USA engaged in its supply-side tax-reform experiments. Further, Borjas does not consider that the rush of immigrants to take low-wage jobs in the USA may reflect 'push' factors – the dissolution of social structures elsewhere in the world – more than 'pull'. How many cab-drivers in New York and Boston were once engineers in Eastern Europe?[26]

A second, polarly opposite approach is to run a 'high-pressure' economy. The study by Freeman (1991) suggests that a high-pressure economy *will* dramatically reduce the unequal labour-force participation and unemployment rates between minorities and whites, including young workers. High employment pressure could be generated in lower-income communities in one of two ways. First, the zones of exclusion and weak fiscal/money multipliers in lower-income communities could be left untouched, and the requisite AD stimulus applied to the US economy as a whole. This would fly in the face of the mainstream consensus about the evils of deficit spending. Second, government spending could be reapportioned so as to generate high-pressure conditions in lower-income areas: for example, by downsizing the military and using the savings for inner-city training, education and jobs programmes.

Both these high-pressure economy approaches are problematic because they would require political commitments violating the second Kaleckian constraint. As Folbre has observed, 'Racial and ethnic conflict provides the strongest explanation for United States "exceptionalism," its significant divergence in social policies from even ... Great Britain' (1994: 196).

An alternative to demand stimulus is a purely supply-side approach, emphasising training and transition programmes for the unemployed. Programmes of this sort, widely advocated by the Labor Secretary, Reich, will undoubtedly assist some workers. However, the spatial zones of race and gender exclusion matter for training strategies. The world economy may be headed for cyberspace; but a large proportion of the unemployed, as Clark and Summers observed (1990), are trapped in spatially differentiated communities, without access to the information superhighway. Training programmes will help for the 'truly disadvantaged', but only if they are linked to support mechanisms which allow young workers to overcome their inexperience, the burden of their dependent children, their lack of health care, and to get and hold jobs.

Policy choices in capitalist economies are squeezed between the two Kaleckian political constraints discussed above. Another, more feasible, path may exist, however, if indeed increasing returns are systematically present and quantitatively important in the US economy.

As discussed above, increasing returns imply that outcomes are path-dependent, not pre-given: so outcomes are institutionally contingent, and hence policy-sensitive. Hence 'small differences matter'. Card and Freeman (1993a) used this insight to identify why Canada's family income inequality and poverty rates fell during the 1980s, but rose in the USA. What motivated the comparison was the many similiarities of these two countries. They indeed found small differences: both countries adopted universal social insurance, but Canada's is now more clearly redistributive; Canada takes a more collectivist approach to labour legislation and health policies; and Canada had both higher unemployment and higher unionisation in the 1980s. Blank and Hanratty show (in Card and Freeman 1993a) that the poverty rate of US single-parent families would fall from 43 to 16 per cent if the Canadian universal-eligibility safety-net programme were substituted for the means-tested programme of the USA.

The point of this comparison was that small differences in social policies, over time, have profound cumulative effects. The scale of changes required to institute the full-blown Canadian system is considerable: government takes about 5 per cent more of GNP in Canada than in the USA; and Canada's transfer programmes constituted, in 1990, about 4.7 per cent of GNP, versus 1.7 per cent in the USA.[27]

To shift the US economy to a different path, however, does not require the wholesale substitution of one national system for another. Incremental institutional changes, at two levels, can have substantial cumulative effects.

The provision of health care and daycare support for all households – or at least poor or single-parent households – would fundamentally alter work incentives. Many women on welfare now face an onerous trade-off: if they make the transition to full-time work, they lose health care coverage and must pay child-care costs; otherwise, they do not generate enough income to become independent economic units (Spalter-Roth, Hartmann and Andrews 1992). Another national priority is more imaginative, better-funded education, training and work-experience programmes. These programmes' design must recognise the reality of the spatial separation and social polarisation faced by most impoverished adults. It must *also* recognise that these programmes' purpose is, in part, precisely to serve as a fiscal stimulus – a Keynesian injection – for areas badly in need of more spending flows. These programmes might be 'costly', if the Treasury accounts for them on a cash basis. By other methods of accounting – for example, the accrual, present-value, or even human-value methods – they might reap significant surpluses.

Meanwhile, stronger efforts are needed to build capacity and resources in lower-income and minority communities. Such efforts can shift communities from spillover losses to spillover gains. These must emphasise the renewal of mechanisms of economic opportunity: that is, enhanced access to jobs, to human capital and to financial capital. Job opportunities need not be 'busy work', they can be developmental if they are linked to training and education programmes. Access to human capital, in turn, can be made more universal if training programmes are sensitive to the peculiar circumstances of the long-term unemployed. It might also be useful to experiment with credit-market programmes that facilitate borrowing to finance education.

Access to financial capital can be increased in part by substantive enforcement of the CRA, and in part by constructing a network of community development (small-scale, non-profit) banks. An isolated network of this sort, which swims against the tides of financial transformation, could be made more effective if a community development secondary loan market were created to service it. A secondary-market maker for community development loans could underwrite and purchase loans made in lower-income areas (see Dymski and Veitch 1995a). Measures of this sort might generate the resource flows to turn spillover losses into gains in selected lower-income areas.

Two cautionary notes should be sounded. First, in efforts like those suggested here, a spirit of experimentation and learning-by-doing is crucial. The very notion of path-dependence implies that no universal model can work equally well in all circumstances. Second, this two-level programme can avoid the polarisation constraint *only* if the map of US political discourse and coalitions is drawn very differently from its present state. This second Kaleckian constraint illuminates a disturbing feature of the USA in the wake of globalisation: the hard choices have costs whose victims are politically invisible. Unless this political constraint is changed, the Keynesian welfare state – and perhaps the idea of using government policy to protect and enhance mechanisms for economic opportunity – will be the decisive casualty of US social polarisation.

Notes

* The author thanks Barbara Weins-Tuers for research assistance, and the organisers of this volume, Jan Toporowski and John Veitch for helpful suggestions on an earlier version. The remaining errors are his own.

1. The use of AD/AS and multiplier analysis allows us to present the main argument in familiar terms. Post-Keynesian economists have pointed out numerous methodological problems with both AD/AS and multiplier analysis, with which this author agrees. The AD and AS 'curves' are valid insofar as they capture the notion of widespread demand and supply effects; the 'multiplier' is a way of describing the behaviours induced by an exogenous shift.
2. Other economists have offered counter-arguments to these views, which we will not revisit here. Blecker (1994) summarises the 'twin deficits' debate. Cunningham and Vilasuso (1994–95) summarise the arguments for policy ineffectiveness; several papers in the same journal rebut their arguments.
3. Wegner (1983) first used the term 'employment miracle' to characterise US experience.
4. Jackman (1995) observes that increases in US and European unemployment cannot be attributed to restrictive fiscal/monetary policies, since these have been in effect for a long time; or to hysteresis, because labour turnover has been higher than that hypothesis allows (an average of 2 % a month in the OECD). Hence technical change must be the cause.
5. The exception is Great Britain, which has no minimum wage. In 1992 the USA, whose minimum wage was already less than half the average wage, passed an 85 per cent subminimum wage for teenager workers.
6. See Albelda (1985) and Arestis and Paliginis (1995). This section draws heavily on Appelbaum (1981) and Folbre (1994).
7. On the history of US racial minorities, see Takaki (1993). This chapter uses the term 'minority' to refer to ethnic minorities. The terms black and Hispanic are used for brevity.
8. In the 1979–89 period, wives' overall hourly wages climbed by \$1.39, while husbands' hourly wages declined \$0.21 (Mishel and Bernstein 1994: 65). Couples with non-working wives have experienced declining median income since 1973; those with working wives experienced median income growth until 1989.
9. Cutler and Katz (1991) found a structural break in the US poverty rate in 1983, with actual poverty rates after 1983 exceeding predicted rates by 10–20 per cent.
10. In a recent study, Spalter-Roth, Hartmann and Andrews (1992) found that 40 per cent of women on welfare have significant ongoing labour-force involvement.

11. 'Young workers' are defined as those with less than nine years' experience. The racial wage differential has remained constant in the 1973–89 period for high-school drop-outs, at approximately 16.5 per cent; but it has worsened for high-school graduates, from 10.3 per cent to 16.7 per cent, and for college graduates from 3.7 per cent to 15.5 per cent.
12. In South Los Angeles, just after the 1965 Watts riots, the unemployment rate for all males aged 25–44 was 13 per cent; but another 17.7 per cent of this group were out of the labour force (US Bureau of the Census, 1966).
13. Soja, Morales and Wolf (1983) and Johnson and Oliver (1992) provide evidence of these trends for Los Angeles.
14. The paper by Donohue and Heckman (1991) on black economic progress illustrates this explanatory tendency nicely. In these authors' view, civil rights enforcement was responsible for gains in black earnings in the 1960–75 period; before this, black gains were associated with movement out of the South; after 1975, black gains eroded due to technical change/skills mismatch. In effect, these authors are looking for exogenous factors that might shift black earnings and labour-force participation up or down.
15. Since urban areas account for most of the US labour force (see Table 5.1), we assume urban externalities affect US macroeconomic outcomes. Kaldor (1970: 340) recognised that regional and national growth will not necessarily be urban growth, and that connections between urbanity and economic growth are dense.
16. We refer to 'potential' fiscal policy effectiveness because, as Galbraith (1994–95) has warned, expansionary fiscal policy has seldom been tried.
17. See Clark and Summers (1990) for black/white differentials in the period 1954–76; DeFreitas (1991) updates these authors' results for the period 1973–84, and shows that patterns for Hispanic workers are similar to, if less pronounced than, those of blacks.
18. Folbre (1994: 191) shows that Depression-era public works programmes discriminated against women and minorities.
19. Cutler and Katz (1991) object that unemployment rates in inner-city areas have become less sensitive to macro-policy shifts, but labour-force participation by black men and women is extremely sensitive to business-cycle fluctuations; so economic expansion induces discouraged workers into the labour force, and affect black employment more than is indicated by shifts in the unemployment rate.
20. Galster and Mincy (1993) and Kasarda (1993) provide evidence that neighbourhoods have become more dissimiliar in the extent of impoverishment, access to jobs and amenities.
21. The material in this section draws heavily on Dymski and Veitch (1995b).
22. For example, transaction fees are routinely waived in exchange for hefty minimum account balances.
23. Caskey (1994: 89) reports that whereas 35 per cent of all banks offered no-fee cheque accounts in 1977, only 5 per cent did in 1991; and he presents evidence that fees and minimum balances have skyrocketed.
24. To illustrate: in 1992, much of Los Angeles burst into flame in the midst of the largest urban upheaval since the 1960s; and three years later, the federal response – apart from some funds for emergency assistance, relocation, and small-business credit – was still awaited.

25. Caskey (1994) argues that, for the poor, the informal financial sector is a functional replacement for the formal sector. This may be true for transaction services. But Caskey's suggestion that pawnshops are short-term credit markets for poor people rings false. Pawnshop loans are used to defray emergency expenses, but not for capacity-building expenses (such as school fees or working capital for business). Pawnshops are mechanisms of asset decumulation, not accumulation.
26. Or for that matter, how many prostitutes in San Diego would be farm labourers in the Philippines? See Rosca (1995). Borjas ignores the elements of force accompanying much of the international flow of labour (the extent to which the internationalisation of capital has internationalised the exploitation of women).
27. Blank and Hanratty (1993) show that installing the Canadian programme on a pay-as-you-go basis, with no supply-side effects, would increase after-tax income in the lowest income quintile (for example) by $1912 per family, while decreasing it in the highest income quintile by $1957 per family.

References

Albelda, R. (1985) 'Nice work if you can get it: segmentation of white and black women workers in the post-war period', *Review of Radical Political Economics*, 17(3), pp. 72–85.

Amin, A. (1994) 'Post-Fordism: models, fantasies and phantoms of transition', in A. Amin (ed.), *Post-Fordism: A Reader* (Oxford: Basil Blackwell), pp. 1–39.

Appelbaum, E. (1981) *Back to work: Determinants of Women's Successful Re-entry* (Boston, MA: Auburn House).

Appelbaum, E. and Schettkat, R. (1994) 'The employment problem in the industrialized countries', International Labour Organization, Geneva, 26 September, Mimeo.

Appelbaum, E. and Schettkat, R. (1995) 'Employment development in the industrialized countries and the prospects for full employment', in P. Arestis and M. Marshall (eds), *The Political Economy of Full Employment* (Aldershot: Edward Elgar).

Arestis, P., and Paliginis, E. (1995) 'Fordism, post-Fordism, and gender', *Economie Appliquée*, 48(1), pp. 89–108.

Arthur, W. B. (1994) *Increasing Returns and Path Dependence in the Economy* (Ann Arbor, MI: University of Michigan).

Bean, C. R. (1994) 'European unemployment: a survey', *Journal of Economic Literature*, 32(2), pp. 573–619.

Beshouri, C. and Nigro, P. (1994) 'Securitization of small business loans', E&PA Working Paper 94–8, Office of the Comptroller of the Currency, Washington.

Blank, R. and Hanratty, T. (1993) 'Responding to need: a comparison of social safety nets in Canada and the US', in D. Card and R. B. Freeman (1993a) *Small Differences that Matter* (Chicago: University of Chicago Press), pp. 191–231.

Blecker, R. A. (1994) 'The new economic stagnation and the contradictions of economic policy making'. in M. Bernstein and D. Adler (eds), *Understanding American Economic Decline* (Cambridge: Cambridge University Press), pp. 276–309.

Borjas, G. J. (1993) 'Immigration policy, national origin, and immigrant skills: a comparison of Canada and the United States', in D. Card and R. B. Freeman (1993a), *Small Differences that Matter* (Chicago University of Chicago Press) pp. 21–44.

Borjas, G. J. (1994) 'The economics of immigration', *Journal of Economic Literature* 32(4), pp. 1667–717.

Boston, T. D. (1988) *Race, Class, and Conservatism* (London: Unwin Hyman).

Bound, J. and Freeman, R. B. (1991) 'What went wrong? the erosion of relative earnings and employment among young black men in the 1980s', mimeo, Harvard University.

Brinkley, A. (1995) 'Liberalism's third crisis', *The American Prospect*, 21 (Spring), pp. 28–34.

Card, D. and Freeman, R. B. (eds) (1993a) *Small Differences that Matter* (Chicago: University of Chicago Press).

Card, D. and Freeman, R. B. (1993b) 'Introduction', in Card and Freeman (1993a), *Small Differences that Matter* (Chicago: University of Chicago Press) 1–19.

Caskey, J. (1994) *Fringe Banking: Check-Cashing Outlets, Pawnshops, and the Poor* (New York: Russell Sage Foundation).

Caskey, J. and Peterson, A. (1994) 'Who has a bank account and who doesn't: 1977 and 1989', *Eastern Economic Journal*, 20(1), pp. 61–74.

Chesler, P. and Goodman, E. J. (1976) *Women, Money, and Power* (New York: William Morrow).

Clark, K. and Summers, L. H. (1990) 'Labor market dynamics and unemployment: a reconsideration', in L. H. Summers, *Understanding Unemployment* (Cambridge, MA: MIT Press), pp. 4–47.

Cunningham, S. R. and Vilasuso, J. (1994–95) 'Is Keynesian demand management still viable?' *Journal of Post Keynesian Economics*, 17(2), pp. 187–210.

Cutler, D. M. and Katz, L. F. (1991) 'Macroeconomic performance and the disadvantaged', *Brookings Papers on Economic Activity*, 2, pp. 3–74.

DeFreitas, G. (1991) *Inequality at Work* (Oxford: Oxford University Press).

Denton, N. (1994) 'Are African Americans still hypersegregated?', in R. Bullard J. E. Grigsby and C. Lee (eds), *Residential Apartheid: the American Legacy* (Los Angeles: Center for Afro-American Studies, UCLA), pp. 49–81.

Donohue, J. J. and Heckman, J. (1991) 'Continuous versus episodic change: the impact of civil rights policy on the economic status of blacks', *Journal of Economic Literature* 29(4), pp. 1603–43.

Dymski, G. A. (1995a) 'The theory of credit-market discrimination and redlining: an exploration', *Review of Black Political Economy*, Winter, pp. 37–74.

Dymski, G. A. (1995b) 'Why does race matter in housing and credit markets?', in P. L. Mason (ed.), *The Frontiers of Research on Discrimination* (Boston, MA: Kluwer Academic Press).

Dymski, G. A., Epstein, G. and Pollin, R. (eds) (1993) *Transforming the US financial System: An Equitable and Efficient Structure for the 21st Century* (Armonk, NY: M. E. Sharpe).

Dymski, G. A. and Veitch, J. M. (1995a) 'A proposal for financing inner-city renewal', in J. Faux, and T. Schafer (eds), *Foundations for a New Century* (Armonk, NY: M. E. Sharpe).

Dymski, G. A. and Veitch, J. M. (1995b) 'Financial transformation and the metropolis: booms, busts, and banking in Los Angeles', *Environment and Planning A*, 28, pp. 1233–60.

England, K. V. L. (1991) 'Gender relations and the spatial structure of the city', *Geoforum*, 22(2), pp. 135–47.

Farley, Reynolds (1991) 'Residential segregation of social and economic groups among blacks, 1970–80', in C. Jencks and P. E. Peterson (eds), *The Urban Underclass* (Washington, DC: Brookings Institution), pp. 274–98.

Federal Reserve Bank of Kansas City (1994) *Reducing Unemployment: Current Issues and Policy Options* (Kansas City: Federal Reserve Bank of Kansas City).

Federal Reserve Bank of New York (1995) 'Colloquium on US wage trends in the 1980's', *Economic Policy Review*, Federal Reserve Bank of New York, 1(1), pp. 1–76.

Feldstein, M. (1976) 'Temporary layoffs in the theory of unemployment', *Journal of Political Economy*, 84(5), pp. 937–58.

Folbre, N. (1994) *Who Pays for the Kids? Gender and the Structures of Constraint* (London: Routledge).

Freeman, R. B. (1991) 'Employment and earnings of disadvantaged young men in a labor shortage economy', in C. Jencks and P. E. Peterson (eds), *The Urban Underclass* (Washington, DC: Brookings Institution), pp. 103–21.

Galbraith, J. K. (1994–95) 'John Maynard Nosferatu', *Journal of Post Keynesian Economics*, 17(2), pp. 249–60.

Galster, G. C. and Mincy, R. B. (1993) 'Understanding the changing fortunes of metropolitan neighborhoods: 1980 to 1990', *Housing Policy Debate*, 4(3), pp. 303–52.

Gordon, P. and Richardson, H. (1991) 'L.A. lost and found', mimeo, University of Southern California.

Hanratty, M. and Blank, R. (1991) 'Down and out in North America: recent trends in poverty rates in the United States and Canada', *Quarterly Journal of Economics*, 107(1), pp. 233–4.

Jackman, R. (1995) 'Unemployment and wage inequality in advanced industrial (OECD) countries', in A. R. Khan, and M. Muqtada (eds), *Employment Expansion and Macroeconomic Stability* (Geneva: International Labour Organization).

Jaynes, G. D. (1990) 'The labor market status of black Americans, 1939–1985', *Journal of Economic Perspectives*, 4(4), pp. 9–24.

Johnson, J. and Oliver, M. (1992) 'Structural changes in the US economy and black male joblessness: a reassessment', in G. E. Peterson and W. Vroman (eds), *Urban Labor Markets and Job Opportunity* (Washington, DC: The Urban Institute Press), pp. 113–49.

Kaldor, N. (1967) *Strategic Factors in Economic Development* (Ithaca: New York State School of Industrial and Labor Relations, Cornell University).

Kaldor, N. (1970) 'The case for regional policies', *Scottish Journal of Political Economy*, 17, pp. 337–48.

Kalecki, M. (1943) 'Political aspects of full employment', *Political Quarterly*, 14(4). pp. 322–31

Kasarda, J. D. (1993) 'Inner-city concentrated poverty and neighborhood distress: 1970 to 1990', *Housing Policy Debate*, 4(3), pp. 253–302.

Katz, M. B. (1989) *The Undeserving Poor: From the War on Poverty to the War on Welfare* (New York: Pantheon Books).

Li, W. (1995) 'Los Angeles' Chinese ethnoburb: evolution of ethnic community and economy', mimeo, Department of Geography, University of Southern California.

Massey, D. and Denton, N. (1993) *American Apartheid: Segregation and the Making of the Underclass*. (Cambridge, MA: Harvard University Press).

Mishel, L. and Bernstein, J. (1994) *The State of Working America, 1994–95* (Armonk, NY: M. E. Sharpe).

Myrdal, Gunnar (1957) *Economic Theory and Underdeveloped Regions* (London: Gerald Duckworth).

Piore, M. J. (1995) *Beyond Individualism* (Cambridge, MA: Harvard University Press).

Pratt, G. and Hanson, S. (1991) 'Time, space, and the occupational segregation of women: a critique of human capital theory', *Geoforum*, 22(2), pp. 149–57.

Rosca, N. (1995) 'Mrs. Contemplacion's sisters: the Philippines' shameful export', *The Nation*, 17 April.

Scott, A J. (1993) *Technopolis: High-Technology Industry and Regional Development in Southern California* (Berkeley, CA: University of California Press).

Shaw, L. B., Champlin, D. P., Hartmann, H. I. and Spalter-Roth, R. M. (1993) *The impact of the glass ceiling and structural change on minorities and women* (Washington, DC: Institute for Women's Policy Research), 15 December.

Sheets, R. G., Nord, S. and Phelps J. J. (1987) *The Impact of Service Industries on Underemployment in Metropolitan Economies* (Lexington, MA: D. C. Heath).

Soja, E., Morales R. and Wolff, G. (1983) 'Urban restructuring: an analysis of social and spatial change in Los Angeles', *Economic Geography*, 58(2), pp. 221–35.

Spalter-Roth, R. M., Hartmann, H. I. and Andrews, L. (1992) *Combining Work and Welfare: An Alternative Anti-Poverty Strategy* (Washington, DC: Institute for Women's Policy Research).

Takaki, R. (1993) *A Different Mirror* (Boston, MA: Little, Brown).

US Bureau of the Census (1966) 'Characteristics of the South and East Los Angeles areas, November, 1965', *Current Population Reports, Technical Studies*, Series P-23, no. 18.

Wegner, M. (1983) 'The employment miracle in the US and stagnating employment in the European Community', *Economics Paper* no. 17 (Brussels: EEC Commission).

Wheelock, J. (1990) *Husbands at Home: The Domestic Economy in a Post Industrial Society* (London: Routledge).

Wolff, E. N. (1995) *Top Heavy: A Study of the Increasing Inequality of Wealth in America* (New York: Twentieth Century Fund).

6 Differences in Economic Performance: Some Comments on Pollin and Dymski

Harald Hagemann

INTRODUCTION

The growth, employment and distribution experiences made in OECD countries after the first oil price shock reveal some remarkable characteristics as well as differences. Compared with the 1960s the rate of growth of output has been more than halved. The same holds for the rate of growth of labour productivity. The widespread productivity slowdown is all the more puzzling since against the background of the sharp increase in unemployment rates in most countries and the diffusion of new technologies based on the microelectronics revolution, the spectre of technological unemployment has come to centre-stage again and the old controversy between labour displacement pessimism and compensation optimism has been revived in recent years. At the same time we can watch a rising inequality in income distribution, although the general slowdown in wage increases and rise in profit margins differ among OECD countries.

On the other hand, there have been significant differences in the development of employment and distribution patterns between the various countries. Whereas in the US unemployment in the last two decades had not exceeded its long-term level but inequality in income distribution has become aggravated, in most European countries unemployment rates have gone up enormously but inequality in income distribution has not increased strongly. This may bring about the idea that slowly growing industrialised countries in a globalised world are confronted with a trade-off between inequality in job or income distribution. The differences between a productivity-driven growth strategy in most Western European economies and a more employment-driven one in North America can be shown by a simple comparison between Germany and the USA for the period between 1960 and 1993. For both countries the average rate of growth of GDP has been 2.7 per cent. In the US employment expanded at 2 per cent per year whereas the annual rate of growth of labour productivity of 0.7 per cent was the lowest of all OECD countries. West Germany, on the other hand, faced an annual increase in labour productivity of 2.5 per cent but a fairly poor capacity in job creation of only 0.2 per cent (Erber 1994).

The different employment and real wage performances have led mainstream economists to celebrate the US 'employment miracle' – with 'Eurosclerosis' as its counterpart – and to claim for a greater downward flexibility of wages and for a greater spread of the wage structure. But an unconditional following of these policy recommendations would be as dangerous as the celebration of the US employment wonder is premature. Dymski has shown convincingly in his chapter on the US that short-term benefits from wage flexibility will be exhausted quickly, while the longer-run political economic costs of polarisation mount. A closer inspection of European countries also shows a more differentiated picture. In countries such as Sweden, for example, *real* wage flexibility always has been rather high. For Germany Wolfgang Franz, the new member of the Council of Economic Advisers and labour market expert, has shown in several recent studies that the wage structure is more flexible than most neoclassical economists assert and that, in general, the German model of autonomous wage negotiations stands the test of time and should not be considered as an *Auslaufmodell* (phase-out model) in view of the far more problematical alternatives (Franz 1995: 15). How doubtful these alternatives are is best shown by the case of the UK. Since the late 1970s the UK has had the highest increase in the spreading of the wage structure with regard to qualifications; in particular, relative wages of low qualified workers have gone down considerably. Nevertheless there has been no reduction in unemployment of this group (Gregg and Manning 1994). In a study of the question how the Thatcher reforms have changed the British labour market performance, Blanchflower and Freeman come to a similar result: 'the reforms in fact brought the UK a mixture of the worst of two possible worlds: the massive wage inequality of the US labour market together with high and lengthy spells of unemployment, European-style' (1993).

DISCUSSION

Dymski argues that globalisation has adversely affected not only income distribution, but also the degree of spatial and social polarisation. Focusing on the USA, he emphasises problems of racial and gender inequality. In European countries with their greater ethnical homogeneity racial problems naturally are less severe. Nevertheless the growing labour migration since the 1960s, which has accelerated since the end of the 1980s, has led to similar problems in many countries, notably in France with her high share of Northern African muslims in the *banlieues* of the major cities. This indicates a high correlation of the ethnical and spatial dimension of polarisation. But independently of the additional racial component, the growth process since 1973 shows spatially dispersed patterns ('Silicon Valley not San Francisco') not only in the USA but also in most European countries such as the UK, France, Germany and Italy, where regional differences have become greater than before.

Concerning the participation rate of women there are great differences between European countries. Sweden, for example, has had the highest rate for a long time, without overcoming segregation on a greater scale since the increase in participation rates has been strongly correlated to the expansion of employment in the public sector with its rather high percentage of part-time work. Unified Germany is a special case, since the participation rate in the former GDR was one of the highest in the world: 89.6 per cent in the age group between 16 and 60 compared to the rather low rate of 63.4 per cent in West Germany (Hagemann and Seiter 1993: 149–50). One of the results of German unification is a growing gender inequality in East Germany where the participation rate of women has been 'harmonised' down considerably to the West German level, with the consequence that the unemployment rates of women in East Germany have been significantly higher than those of men over the last five years.

It is a little bit surprising that the authors skip over the role of technological change in the process of globalisation. As is well known, technical progress affects employment and distribution. With the growth of multinational companies its spatial component has been strengthened. The new computer and telecommunication technologies imply that greater parts of the service sector are not sheltered any more but are affected by international learning processes for the first time. Lufthansa's recent shift of her accounting department to India, where wages of equally qualified employees are only about one-tenth of the German level, is only one of many indicators.

Dymski correctly stresses the importance of two path-dependent mechanisms: Verdoorn's Law, and its mirror image; and spatial and credit-market externalities. According to Verdoorn's Law, productivity growth differences are associated with different trend-rates of growth. The empirical significance of the law consists in the fact that a substantial part of productivity growth is endogenous to the growth process of the economy, being determined by the rate of growth of output through the effect of economies of scale. Recent empirical parameter estimates of Verdoorn's Law suggest that the growth requirements to sustain a given level of employment have significantly decreased over the last two decades (Erber 1994). Nevertheless, employment problems have been aggravated in all European countries. This refers to the role of demand in long-run growth which can best be understood in a Keynesian framework. Kaldor, who contributed so much to the development of this approach from his 1966 lecture onwards in which he had emphasised the export-led character of growth, in later writings (such as Kaldor 1985) increasingly emphasised the role of the growth in 'effective demand' rather than factor supplies for long-run growth. Capital accumulation is as much a result as a cause of the growth of output: that is, it cannot be seen as an independent determinant. Dymski's result (that employment growth is demand-led to an increasing extent in Europe) confirms this, as do Erber's findings that the major cause of the European unemployment problems after the first oil price shock is due to a *Wachstumsschwäche* (weak growth process) in almost all sectors of the economy.

The slowdown in growth rates in the 1980s is more pronounced in Europe than in the USA or in Canada where the slow rates of growth seem to come from the late 1960s. In his explanation Dymski refers to Appelbaum and Schettkat who confront the virtuous circle of full employment in the years 1950–73, in which industries with high and rising productivity attracted labour by paying higher wages, with the reversal in the following two decades. 'At the heart of the change in the relationship between productivity growth and employment growth is the change in the price elasticity of demand for consumer durables from elastic to inelastic as most households in the industrialised economies have achieved ownership of these goods' (Appelbaum and Schettkat 1995: 244). Whereas I agree with this interpretation, it has to be added that the analysis could have been enriched by consulting Pasinetti's two important studies in which the author's main aim is to develop a theory of structural change which is a characteristic of every industrial system in the long-run development (Pasinetti 1981, 1993). In Pasinetti's analysis, not only dynamic impulses such as technological change or changes in factor supplies but also changes in consumers' preferences according to Engel's Law play an important role. The factor ultimately responsible for structural change is technical progress as a result of learning. Increases in productivity lead to increases in *per capita* income. With increases in real income consumers do not expand their demand for each existing commodity proportionally. Moreover, with technical progress new products emerge. It certainly is one of Pasinetti's most innovative achievements to have integrated the structural dynamics of demand by a generalisation of Engel's empirical law, and thus shown so clearly the two facets of technological change on the supply side and on the demand side as well as the interaction between the two.

Real phenomena should be linked to monetary ones, as has been done in Arestis and Sawyer's (1996) recent reflections on the consequences of a European central bank for unemployment and growth. It is also at the very centre of Pollin's analysis which is illuminating as it is, from my point of view, a little bit too US-centristic. Despite the discussion of the globalisation of financial markets there is not much on international comparison in his chapter. One might have expected that with all his emphasis on saving as a financial phenomenon, some reflections on important differences in saving ratios (for example, between the USA and Japan) and their impact on capital accumulation and employment would be incorporated. But I agree with the general tendency to focus on financial barriers to US capital accumulation and on the negative impact of higher real rates of interest on investment.

Pollin discusses Summers' argument that the 'channel through which low national saving leads to reduced investment is through increases in the *cost of capital*'. One may question whether increases in the cost of capital and stagnating investment are due to lower saving ratios. For example, in Germany households' savings ratios remained rather constant. Nonetheless real interest rates were significantly higher in the last two decades than from the 1950s to the early 1970s, as in most other European countries from 1978 onwards, and therefore were a major barrier to investment and full employment. I also would have wished to find something more on the increasing ratio of credit creation to saving, which Pollin had discussed earlier, but which is a missing link in this study.

The deflationary monetary policies to achieve low inflation rates which were pursued by the USA in the Volcker era are mirrored by the excessively contractionary monetary policies adopted by the UK, Germany, France, and, in more recent years, even by countries like Sweden, where they have affected real variables in the economy and thus caused lower rates of growth and higher levels of unemployment. They have resulted in what Bob Solow (1994) has termed 'Europe's unnecessary unemployment'. On the other hand, it has to be said that expansionary fiscal and monetary policies are no longer sufficient to achieve full-employment growth.

I agree with Pollin's analysis that there are three financial constraints on full employment policy, namely:

(a) a bias towards speculative take-overs rather than new investments (a bias which is stronger in the US than in many European countries);
(b) a long-term tendency towards increased financial fragility; and
(c) an increased power of financial markets which has caused a deflationary bias in the setting of macro policy;

and with his final conclusions concerning the implementation of full employment policies.

Pollin and Dymski discuss the reasons for the diminished capacities of conventional expansionary fiscal and monetary policies in greater detail. Two arguments I find missing in this context. First, I would have liked a reflection on Sidney Weintraub's proposal for a tax-based income policy as a reaction to the fundamental dilemma that the danger of inflation increases with the success of a Keynesian-type full employment policy. Second, I would have preferred a more offensive discussion of the Lucas critique, emphasising the relative ineffectiveness of Keynesian monetary and fiscal policies, from a post-Keynesian point of view. In particular it should be stressed that the change in the policy regime as the consequence of rational expectations can also imply a positive effect on investment decisions if entrepreneurs can expect government interventions in the case of effective demand failures which will stabilise their long-run proceeds, thus reducing the need for further policy interventions. On the other hand, the expectation that the government will stay absent may increase the risk and uncertainty of investment decisions and thereby contribute to the proneness to crisis of the economy.

Finally, the policy alternative which both authors draw – a purely supply-side approach as an alternative to demand stimulus in Dymski, a central bank policy to adjust both the quantity and price of credit instead of manipulating government spending relative to tax receipts and thereby the level of aggregate demand to achieve growth and employment goals in the economy in Pollin – in my view is too simplistic.

CONCLUSIONS

In order to reach and sustain full employment over time, society might have to choose a strategy which combines the following elements.

1. A Keynesian-type policy which will raise per capita demand for existing goods.
2. The promotion of R&D for new goods. Since technical progress not only leads to an increase in productivity but also to product innovations with a high potential for an increase in demand, investment and employment, a more supply-side oriented policy of this kind aims at strengthening this secondary tendency to compensate the first one (Grossman and Helpman 1991). It should be supplemented by a modern industrial policy, as discussed by Amable and Petit.

3. A policy of shortening the annual working time, not necessarily to enjoy more leisure but also to have more time for qualification and training programmes.
4. A policy of improving the public infrastructure and investment in human capital, two elements which have been stressed from Adam Smith to the new endogenous growth theories. However, there is a certain danger in overemphasising training and transition programmes for the unemployed, if it puts all of the weight on the supply side. The best training programme certainly is training on the job.

References

Appelbaum, E. and Schettkat, R. (1995) 'Economic development in the industrialized countries and the prospects for full employment', in P. Arestis and M. Marshall (eds), *The Political Economy of Full Employment* (Aldershot: Edward Elgar), pp. 238–55.

Arestis, P. and Sawyer, M. (1996) 'The problematic nature of independent central banks', in A. Cohen, H. Hagemann and J. Smithin (eds), *Money, Financial Institutions and Macroeconomics* (Boston, MA: Kluwer Academic Publishers).

Blanchflower, D. and Freeman, R. (1993) 'Did the Thatcher reforms change British labour market performance?', in R. Barrell (ed.), *The UK Labour Market: Comparative Aspects and Institutional Developments* (Cambridge: Cambridge University Press).

Erber, G. (1994) 'Verdoorn's or Okun's law? Employment and growth experiences in OECD countries, 1960–1993', discussion paper no. 98, December (Berlin: Deutsches Institut für Wirtschaftsforschung).

Franz, W. (1995) 'Die Lohnfindung in Deutschland in einer internationalen Perspektive: Ist das deutsche System ein Auslaufmodell?', discussion paper no. 24, April (Konstanz: Centre for International Labour Economies).

Gregg, P. and Manning, A. (1994) 'Labour market regulation and unemployment', CEPR conference paper, September (London).

Grossman, G. M. and Helpman, E. (1991) *Innovation and Growth in the Global Economy* (Cambridge, MA: MIT Press).

Hagemann, H. and Seiter, S. (1993) 'Structural change, productivity and employment: perspectives from a unified Germany', in I. Rima (ed.) *The Political Economy of Global Restructuring. Volume 1: Economic Organization and Production* (Aldershot: Edward Elgar), pp. 140–58.

Kaldor, N. (1966) *Causes of the Slow Rate of Economic Growth of the United Kingdom: An Inaugural Lecture* (Cambridge: Cambridge University Press).

Kaldor, N. (1985) *Economics without Equilibrium* (Armonk, NY: M. E. Sharpe).

Pasinetti, L. L. (1981) *Structural Change and Economic Growth. A Theoretical Essay on the Dynamics of the Wealth of Nations* (Cambridge: Cambridge University Press).

Pasinetti, L. L. (1993) *Structural Economic Dynamics. A Theory of the Economic Consequences of Human Learning* (Cambridge: Cambridge University Press).

Solow, R. (1994) 'Europe's unnecessary unemployment', *International Economic Insights*, March/April, pp. 10–11.

7 The Viability of Keynesian Demand Management in an Open Economy Context

Paul Davidson

INTRODUCTION

When the Old Keynesian analysis of the 1940s and 1950s failed to resolve the stagflation problem of the 1970s, it became fashionable to declare that Keynesian economics was dead. Hi-tech forms of classical economics were resurrected by the younger generation of economists to justify the elimination of governmental responsibility for maintaining full employment. This New Classical economics rationalised the need (i) to free markets from governmental regulation and (ii) to provide an independent Central Bank. New Keynesians accepted the logic of New Classical analysis, but they argued that unemployment was due to some grand market failure caused by wage and/or price rigidities and/or asymmetric information and/or co-ordination failure.

This New Classical counter-revolution and New Keynesian counter-counter-revolution to Keynes's *General Theory* provided the rationale for policies encouraging the complete decontrolling of foreign exchange markets and global financial flows. It provided intellectual prestige to the siren song 'Get the Government off the backs of the people' that became the theme of the Reagan Administration in the USA, the Thatcher government in the UK and the Republican sweep in Congress 1994.

For Keynes (1936: 381) when 'effective demand is deficient ... the public scandal of wasted resources [is] intolerable'. The counter-revolution's belief in NAIRU implies that full employment inevitably means accelerating inflation. Accordingly, the existence of unemployed resources is not a scandal. It is necessary to maintain unemployment at NAIRU. It is the inevitable cost of a free market system that fails to achieve classical money neutrality in the short run.

Keynes's demand-influencing policies are no longer the way to ameliorate the two major faults of an entrepreneurial system: 'the failure to provide for full employment and ... [the] arbitrary and inequitable distribution of wealth and income' (Keynes 1936: 372). Instead, the necessary policy medicine promotes *free market supply conditions*, reduces government spending to a minimal proportion of GDP, and dismantles the welfare state. This policy prescription aims to loosen up product and labour markets. Supply-side purgatives, not demand influences, are the sound bites associated with modern mainstream economic thought.

Mainstream economic theory has become very anti-Keynes in the past 20 years. People in political authority are, to paraphrase Keynes, distilling their frenzy against expansionary demand influences from these academic mainstream scribblers. The conventional wisdom now is that Keynesian demand-influencing policies are neither effective nor needed. An independent central bank monetary policy in tandem with minimum government deficits is the 'only game in town' for achieving economic growth without inflation. In an open-economy context, flexible exchange rates, free trade and the supply side law of comparative advantage is claimed to provide the keys to prosperity.

What has been the effect on global economic performance of this counter-Keynesian revolution into government policy? Two decades after Keynesian demand policies were downgraded by most orthodox economists – whether they label themselves as New Classical or New Keynesians – the market-oriented system of capitalism, while clearly having outperformed the state-planned economies of Eastern Europe, has regressed to economic performance levels that have not been so weak since Keynes's Revolution. In 1994, the International Labour Organization (ILO) reported over 38 million people were unemployed in OECD nations and more than 120 million worldwide. Double-digit unemployment rates persist throughout Europe. The distribution of income within nations as well as globally has become more arbitrary and unequal than in the last quarter-century[1] while substantial numbers of the world's population have experienced declining living standards since the early 1970s.

POLITICALLY CORRECT DEMAND MANAGEMENT IN WESTERN DEMOCRACIES

Between 1947 and 1972, there was a global golden age of full employment and unprecedented economic growth, while the average living standard of the entire free world population increased substantially (see Table 7.1). This required Keynes-type demand-influencing policies. Unfortunately the domination of mainstream theory and its belief in the existence of an empirically elusive NAIRU has made cowards of most economists who call

Table 7.1 Real GDP (annualised growth rate)

	Real GDP per capita (%)		
Years	*OECD nations*		*Developing nations*
1700–1820	0.2		
1820–1913	1.2		
1919–40	1.9		
1950–73	4.9		3.3
1973–81	1.3		
	Total real GDP		
1950–73	5.9		5.5
Additional estimate of real GDP per capita growth rate (annualised)			
Years	*Major industrial nations*	*NICs*	*LDCs*
1973–1990	2.5	3.5	−0.1

Source: Adelman (1991). (Additional estimates provided to author by I. Adelman (1994), private correspondence, 16 November.)

themselves Keynesians, or at least when they get into the corridors of power. For example, the only apparent difference between conservative monetarist Alan Greenspan and liberal New Keynesian Alan Blinder of the Federal Reserve is that Greenspan believes NAIRU is between 6.0 and 6.5 per cent, while Blinder believes it is in the 5.6 per cent to 6.2 per cent range. Thus, demand-expanding interest rate policy must be constrained long before full employment is achieved.

Some forms of aggregate demand management policy are still advocated by politicians, central bankers and economic 'expert' talking heads on television. In an open economy, increasing the demand for exports faster than the growth in imports to obtain export-led growth (and current account surpluses) is perceived to reduce domestic unemployment rates, encourage economic growth, generate more domestic saving and produce fewer inflationary pressures, while old-style Keynesian demand policies reduce domestic savings and fan inflationary tendencies. In the 1980s, 'successful' economies racked up large and growing export surpluses (for example, Japan, Taiwan, Singapore and Germany). Unlike old Keynesian expansionary demand policies involving domestic components of the aggregate demand function, not all countries can pursue this export-faster-than-import growth programme. The global double-entry bookkeeping system does not permit it.

In sum, only two possible domestic demand management policies still exist in mainstream economic circles, including the so-called New Keynesians.

1. A monetary policy to control interest rates to induce a growth of domestic investment spending to keep effective demand at NAIRU. This stimulus of a domestic component of aggregate demand will, however, be constrained by the need to reduce, if not eliminate, the fiscal deficit.
2. A strategy that expands export demand growth.

After the 1992 election, President Clinton was quickly educated by his neoliberal economic advisers to see that the best demand management economic policy was to reduce the deficit through higher taxes and some spending cuts. This would encourage the bond market and make it possible for the Federal Reserve to reduce interest rates to stimulate investment and housing demand in the economy (Woodward 1994). Simultaneously, US trade negotiator Mickey Kaplan could pressure Japan to increase imports from the USA while Treasury Secretary Bentsen would talk down the dollar from its 120 level at the end of 1992 to approximately 95 to expand US exports faster than its imports would expand and thereby achieve the 'soft-landing' balanced trade some Treasury consultants from a Washington think-tank promised.[2]

The proponents of this two-pronged demand-management approach promise a Utopia of a high-saving, productive economy with zero inflation. How can anyone be against such a wonderful policy agenda?

ARE THE TWIN DEFICITS (FISCAL AND EXTERNAL) RESTRICTIVE?

The USA's twin fiscal and external deficits since 1982 are often accused of being the fundamental symptoms of a failure of Reagan's Keynes-type demand-stimulating policies. In reality, these deficits are not the problem.

They are the levers that extricated the industrialised world from the great economic depression of 1979–82.

From November 1982 to July 1990 the USA (followed by most of the industrialised and industrialising free world) experienced the longest peace-time expansion in the post-war era. The 1984 Gramm–Rudman Act and the Budget Reform Act of 1986 slowed this global expansion but the demand expansion of the Reagan deficit fiscal policy was so vigorous that even these legislative constraints were insufficient to end this long peace-time expansion.[3] Only after the Federal Reserve continually raised interest rates between 1987 and 1991 *and* George Bush renounced his 1988 'no new taxes' pledge were sufficient negative demand management forces in place to push the global economy into recession. The 1991–92 recession and the slow growth rebound since have been the legacy of the Bush surrender to the conventional rhetoric in tandem with a Federal Reserve's paranoid fear of rising prices.

IS THERE AN APPLICABLE MESSAGE FROM KEYNES?

Any deliberate attempt by the US government to increase domestic saving by deficit reduction and simultaneous unilateral action to reduce the US trade deficit (as the last two years of the Bush Administration and early Clinton Administration accepted as necessary) tends to reverse, *ceteris paribus*, the global progress made in the 1980s to extricate the global economy from the greatest recession since the Great Depression. Such mindless negative demand management policies can cause the entire free world to suffer from either chronic recession or such sluggish economic growth that the global real income growth will not keep up with global population growth. Consequently, poor nations will find real GDP per capita declining, while even rich nations experience, on average, paltry per capita growth rates compared with the global Golden Age of 1947–73 (see Table 7.1).

The economic problem of industrial economies in the twentieth century is rarely, except in times of war and/or Keynesian full employment prosperity, a real supply-side constraint: that is, a shortage of workers and/or savings, or a Malthusian scarcity of raw materials. Rather, the problem is that every accumulation of wealth creates additional productive capacity and acts as a damper on further private accumulation unless overall aggregate demand can be nurtured to grow vigorously. The need to stimulate global effective demand growth is too important to be left to the vagaries of the free market in the growing global economically interdependent world.[4] We need global demand expansion policies!

Unpublished, preliminary studies by Eileen Appelbaum of the Economic Policy Institute suggest that, in the current global environment, improving productivity of labour in the manufacturing sector of OECD nations will result in fewer high-wage jobs globally because of a lack of growth in global demand for manufacturing products.[5] Consequently, the first priority of any global civilised society must be to develop demand policies that encourage higher consumption for manufacturing output rather than induce greater domestic savings out of any given aggregate income flow.[6] If the *laissez-faire* market-determined consumption plus investment expenditures cannot generate enough effective demand to reach full employment, then it is the responsibility of civilised governments to influence aggregate demand through fiscal policy and a low interest rate policy, even if these policies increase budget deficits. To the extent that full employment sets off intolerable inflationary rent-seeking proclivities, then a civilised society must develop incomes policies to deal with such uncivilised economic behaviour without using the unemployed as cannon fodder.

When post-war demand-influencing policies kept all nations close to full employment, owners of employed resources soon learned that the possibility of persistent slack markets because of a lack of effective demand had been vanquished by government edict. Consequently, these owners tended to increase their relative rent-seeking proclivities. An 'industrial reserve army of the unemployed' (to use Marx's term) was thought necessary to keep rent-seeking workers and capitalists in their place under the nomenclature of NAIRU. If elected politicians pushed for the full employment goal (legislated under the Humphrey–Hawkins Act), this army of unemployed would no longer exist. The absence of a deliberate policy to constrain the rent-seeking proclivities of owners of (close to fully) employed resources in an expansionary Keynesian demand regime led to the myth that only an 'independent central bank' could secure price stability by maintaining NAIRU.

THE SEDUCTION OF MERCANTILIST DEMAND MANAGEMENT

In an open system, nations can be seduced by an uncivilised mercantilist mechanism where increased effective demand and employment growth occurs by expanding export sales faster than import demand. The 'economic miracle' of Germany, Japan and the Pacific Rim NICs (newly industrialised countries) depend on this mercantile approach. When successful, it increases the wealth of the individual country by exporting its unemployment problem to other nations.

In a flexible exchange rate regime, moreover, this mercantilist policy can be simultaneously an anti-inflationary policy. Any nation that runs a persistent export surplus can, by exchange rate appreciation, also export inflation (see the Appendix for an analytical proof). This mercantilist induced state of bliss lasts only as long as the other nations are willing – and able – to finance both their persistent trade deficits and the resulting increasing international debt service obligations.

In the context of the 1980s, this mercantilist policy was effectively pursued by some of the major trading partners of the USA when that great Keynesian in the White House, Ronald Reagan, acted as the engine of growth, pulling the industrialised free world from the second greatest Depression of the twentieth century. Mercantilist demand management by Japan, Germany and the Pacific Rim NICs in the 1980s had the effect of diluting the growth impact on the US economy of Reagan's Keynesianism.[7] The resulting US trade deficits meant that the USA continued to be the world's engine for growth only so long as the USA acquiesced in absorbing its prosperous trading partners' persistent tendency to oversave.[8] This willingness of America to accommodate foreigners' propensity to oversave since 1982 has been the global solution to the second great economic depression of 1979–81. The US current account deficit is not the problem, as long as its major trading partners refuse to live up to their means.

Yet the conventional wisdom is that the USA's current economic problems and future economic woes are the result of the USA living beyond *its* means, spending more than its export earnings and maintaining a persistent internal government deficit. Worldly wisdom suggests the USA adopt restrictive policies that substantially reduce the budget deficit (ultimately a balanced-budget) and end the US external deficit.

Those who fail to study history are destined to repeat its errors! After the 1988 election, a group headed by Presidents Ford and Carter provided such conventional advice to President-elect Bush by urging him to raise taxes. These two former Presidents, who followed conventional wisdom during their terms of office, presided over the 1970s precipitous decline of the US economy. Their economic policies (remember Ford's WIN – whip inflation now – buttons, and Carter's oil policy MEOW, the moral equivalent of war) did nothing to ease the economic problems of their day. When in 1990 Bush bowed to this conventional wisdom and raised taxes to reduce the twin deficits, he not only lost the Presidency but he exacerbated the domestic economic problems.

When, in the first days of the Clinton Administration, this history was ignored and Clinton bowed to the deficit hawks at the beginning of his term of office he almost ensured the Republican landslide of 1994, just as Bush raising taxes to reduce the deficit ensured his place as a one-term President.[9]

A POST-KEYNESIAN VIEW OF RECENT ECONOMIC HISTORY

The 'hard-core' post-Keynesian truth is that without the big-spending, tax reduction policies plus a benign attitude to the resulting growth in imports over exports exhibited by Ronald Reagan, the economies of Europe, Asia and America would have been hopelessly mired in the depression and financial crisis that began in 1979. The 1982 forced reversal (because of the Mexican default) of Chairman Volker's high interest policy would not, by itself, have provided an engine of growth for the free world; it merely provided the liquidity lubricant that allowed Reagan's Keynesianism to promote the industrial world's economic growth.

The twin deficit 'problem' of the 1980s was, largely, due to the fact that the prosperity initiated by Ronald Reagan was not sufficiently promulgated by West Germany, Japan and the NICs who did not even come close to living up to their means. These nations steadfastly refuse to spend much of their export earnings on the products of foreign industries. Instead they have a propensity to hoard international reserves in a 'Silas Marner' fashion. For example, in the 12 months ending in October 1994, Japan's foreign reserves rose by 26 per cent to $123.7 billion. (By comparison, the USA's total foreign reserves were only half as much: $67 billion.) Once the Bush recession and a soaring yen put pressure on Japanese exports from its domestically located industries, the Japanese GDP lost its propensity for vigorous growth although Japan still behaved as an oversaving economy. The Japanese apparently can never possess too many foreign reserves, especially since conventional economic theory does not suggest how much is enough.

Occasionally, as the dollar depreciates, the Governor of the Bank of Japan and the Japanese Finance Minister buy US dollars to support the dollar. They apparently prefer to buy and hold US dollars and dollar-denominated liquid assets rather than encourage their citizens to buy and consume US beef, pharmaceuticals, grain and other imports. Japanese policies to encourage the purchases of US products would strengthen the dollar and reduce the USA's twin trade and budget deficits. The consumption by Japanese citizens would be substantially improved. There would be an overall increase in global real income without any new US taxes or US government spending cuts.

The major problem facing the developed and developing world is a lack of sufficient global effective demand, not a shortage of global saving,[10] due to the persistent underconsumption (oversaving) tendencies of modern mercantilist nations. If they would consume more of their export surplus, the world's international debtors would earn more. This would allow these debtors to invest more and to improve further the standard of consumption of their citizens. What is needed is a co-ordinated global demand policy geared to belt loosening, if the free world is to continue to prosper in the twenty-first century.

If the marginal propensities of Japan, Germany and the NICs to consume and to import had not been so low in the 1980s, then more of the Keynesian multiplier effect of the expansionary demand factors of Reagan budget deficits would have been fed back to the USA. Instead, the effect was to permit the multiplier expansion to leak out into foreign GDP growth and lower unemployment rates. Moreover, in an era of flexible exchange rates, those nations where exports increase faster than imports found their currency appreciates on the exchange market. This provides domestic workers more purchasing power per unit of local currency, providing higher real wages without having to demand higher money wages. Accordingly, domestic inflationary pressures are reduced. Simultaneously, currency appreciation provides a mercantilistic real wealth effect that encourages the 'bargain' transference of ownership of national treasures such as Old Masters, real estate and domestic enterprises from the trade deficit nations.[11] These real wage and real wealth effects could not have occurred under a fixed exchange rate system. Hence the incentives to pursue mercantilist export-led growth policies were much lower under the Bretton Woods system.

The 1993–94 expansion in America's GDP is often credited to the new policies of the Clinton Administration. In reality, expansion began in the waning Bush days of 1992 as the Federal Reserve began its demand-expansion policy of reducing interest rates. Clinton was willing to sign a Faustian pact with Greenspan where, if the Administration reduced the deficit, the Federal Reserve would grant a 100 basis point reduction in the interest rate. As a result, monetary policy demand management was expansive until the California Earthquake Relief Act of February 1994. This act permitted an increase in federal government spending of almost $8 billion during 1994. That signalled to the Federal Reserve that the Administration and Congress had broken its Faustian deficit reduction promise. Hoping to keep the US economy from falling below a 6 per cent NAIRU, Greenspan began a series of interest rate increases to offset the demand expansion set in motion by the California Earthquake Relief deficit spending to rebuild public and private infrastructure.[12] The stimulating demand-management effect of the earthquake relief spending on California (and the export-led growth of other states who exported products to help in the California rebuilding) had (at least until the beginning of 1995) tended to more than offset any reduction in demand due to higher interest rates.

WHO WANTS TO BE THE ENGINE OF GROWTH?

In the current flexible exchange rate system and the resulting universal desire for export-led demand-management growth, global economic prosperity requires one or more nations to act as the 'engine of growth' by running significantly large trade deficits and increasing its/their demand for imports significantly. This effort creates a trail of foreign and domestic debts that leaves the benefactor 'engine' between a rock and a hard place. Financial prudence (in the guise of financial market opinion) will not permit debtors to continue forever to contribute to the well-being of the global community. Since the latter years of the Reagan Administration, the talking heads of economists interviewed on television have espoused the conventional wisdom that the financial market knows the future and the market, and have told the USA that it cannot continue to spend itself poor and its trading partners rich. When, however, the 'wisdom'[13] of the market is followed, the result will be that by 'tightening our belt' the entire world will be, on average, worse off. Nevertheless, as the Woodward volume clearly documents, the Clinton Administration is as much intimidated by this conventional wisdom as was the Bush team. As Keynes noted, 'Worldly wisdom teaches us that it is better for reputation to fail conventionally than to succeed unconventionally' (Keynes 1936: 158).

Hard-core post-Keynesians recognise, as Keynes did, that financial markets have no godly gift for foretelling the future; instead, market 'valuation is established as the outcome of the mass psychology of a large number of ignorant individuals' (Keynes 1936: 154). To permit such mass psychological ignorance to dictate our economic policies can only be the height of foolishness.

The conventional wisdom is that the solution for the spending 'binge' of the Reagan Administration (which was responsible for generating whatever prosperity the world has experienced after the dreadful decade of the 1970s) is for the USA to cut federal spending and raise taxes merely to reduce the budget deficit. For the USA to adopt this stringent fiscal policy is a mug's game, a negative sum game where if the engine acts in a 'fiscally responsible' manner, the entire globe will suffer a loss of real income. The effect in 1990 of President Bush reversing his 'read my lips' pledge and raising taxes while the Federal Reserve tightened up on monetary policy was to slow significantly, if not almost completely to stop, the growth of the Japanese and the Pacific Rim NICs while pushing the USA and many European countries into recession.

THE FLEXIBLE EXCHANGE RATE MARKET

On 7 March 1995, the *New York Times* noted that in international financial markets 'where image is often more important than reality ... the dollar is being dragged down by the peso' while the German mark and Japanese yen appear to be the only 'safe harbours' to portfolio fund managers. By 11 April, the dollar's plunge against the yen had become so severe that the Japanese Finance Minister, Takemura, was quoted as questioning whether the system of free-floating exchange rates adopted in 1973 should be reconsidered so that governments had more influence over their currency.

Under the floating exchange rate system adopted in 1973, foreign currencies have become objects of speculation. Any significant change in the exchange rate can create enormous profits (or losses). Any whiff of currency weakness can become a conflagration spread along the 'information highway' as fund managers and multinational controllers, in search of speculative yields and 'safe harbours', can move funds from one country to another in nanoseconds with a few clicks on a computer keyboard.

Federal Reserve Chairman Alan Greenspan was quoted in the *New York Times* (11 April 1995) as having testified to Congress that 'Mexico became the first casualty ... of the new international financial system' that permits hot portfolio money to slosh around the world 'much more quickly'. Fund managers in plush offices have made Mexico the first casualty by slashing the real income of the Mexican population almost in half.

The North American Free Trade Agreement (NAFTA) (and to a lesser extent the General Agreement on Tariffs and Trade (GATT) was promoted to the American people on the promise that it would deliver an expansion of high paying jobs in export industries without inflation. With the plunge of the peso, America's trade surplus to Mexico has already turned to a deficit and the promised export industry jobs have vanished in a puff of exchange rate smoke.

With US export industries unlikely to improve their penetration into Japanese and German markets despite the dollar's plunge, and with the loss of the promised NAFTA export expansion in Mexico, the US economy's lacklustre two-decade performance will continue even if an economic downturn does not occur. The last two decades have produced a decline in the real median income, while creating greater inequalities in the distribution of income. Since 1973, fewer Americans are becoming significantly richer while most of the middle class and the poor are becoming worse off.

If the Federal Reserve raises interest rates to encourage fund managers in search of yield to move money back into US securities in order to stem the dollar's plunge against the yen and the German mark, then it is quite possible that the US economy will be plunged into recession or depression by the current instability of the currency markets. Then surely the Japanese economy, which relies on the US market for export-led growth, will follow. Like lemmings, other nations will then also follow.

FIGHTING CURRENCY FIRES IN INTERNATIONAL CAPITAL MARKETS

The recent machinations of international financial markets and the potential for a US economic recession spreading via our interconnected global economy should suggest, even to advocates of free international capital markets, that 'hot money' portfolio flows can have massive disruptive economic effects. What is therefore required in this global economy with computer linked financial markets is not a system of *ad hoc* central bank interventions while what Greenspan calls the 'new international financial system' burns the real economy. What is necessary is to build into this international system permanent fireproofing rules and structures that prevent imagery-induced currency fires. Crisis prevention rather than crisis rescues must be our primary long-term objective. If the developed nations do not hang together on a currency fire prevention system, then we will all hang separately in a replay of the international financial market crisis of the Great Depression.

It is not a violation of civil liberties to prohibit people from boarding an airplane with a gun. Moreover, no-one would think we are impinging on individual rights if society prohibits someone entering a cinema with a Molotov cocktail in one hand and a book of matches in the other, even if the person indicates they have no desire to burn down the theatre. Yet, in the name of free markets, we permit fund managers to imagine an exploding Molotov cocktail and then yell 'fire' in the crowded international financial markets any time the 'image' of a possible profitable fire moves them. Fifty years ago, Keynes (1980: 86) recognised that 'there is not a country which can ... safely allow the flight of funds [hot money] ... Equally there is no country that can safely receive ... [these portfolio] funds which cannot be used for fixed investment.'

REFORMING THE WORLD'S MONEY TO PREVENT FIRES AND RESTORE GLOBAL PROSPERITY

There is an urgent need to reform the international payments system to prevent future liquidity crises breaking out in the many currency markets (such as the dollar) that are 'too big to fail'. If we do not, the global economy might easily collapse into another Great Depression.

Moreover, if we are not to perpetuate the poor global economic performance of the post-1973 floating rate era, but instead to restore the golden age of global economic growth experienced in the years 1947–73, international monetary reform is needed. The only question is what to replace the current system with.

Even advocates of the current international monetary system, such as *The Economist* (6 January 1990) and the *Financial Times* (17 February 1987), have admitted that the current system 'was sold under a false prospectus' and that it has 'failed' to promote balanced trade and global prosperity. The system fails whenever some nations tenaciously export more than they import (that is run an export surplus) while others persistently import more than they export (that is experience a trade deficit).

Under the current international system, nations that can achieve export growth are rewarded by being able to maintain substantial job growth in their domestic industries as long as their export markets are growing, while their domestic industries are assured of dominant positions in the market at home.

If export surplus nations have no incentive to increase their purchase of imports, then nations with trade deficits must either buy fewer imports (thereby causing a loss of profits and unemployment abroad) or become indebted to foreigners to finance their excess of imports over exports. Under the current international payments system, the IMF insists that the prudent thing to do is to reduce import spending.

In sum, the current international system fails to produce a prosperous global environment because it resolves any persistent trade deficit problem by following the conventional wisdom of forcing a deficit nation to depress its economy (euphemistically called 'belt tightening') in order to lower its citizens' income so that they cannot afford to buy as many goods (including imports) as before. The resulting lowering of import demand spreads contractionary forces globally by lowering employment and income in other nations' export industries.

What is the solution to the trap whereby the political economic conventional wisdom of the last decades of the twentieth century resurrects nineteenth-century classical homilies and seventeenth-century mercantilism? Those nations currently pursuing persistent mercantilist export-led growth must reverse these actions by spending more to save their own prosperity, as well as that of the world. Moreover, the accumulated reserves from the persistent trade surpluses of these nations provide them with the wherewithal to pursue global *belt loosening* policies that will lighten the debt burden of their trading partners. I have suggested a global institutional revision of the international payments system to create incentives for all nations simultaneously to adopt expansionary demand management policies (see Davidson 1992–93: ch. 16). Unless progress is made on this issue, the dismal science of economics will be condemning the global capitalist economy of the twenty-first century to a bleak future, just at the time when it has won the war against the Communistic economic system.

APPENDIX: WHY THE PREFERENCE FOR EXPORT-LED GROWTH?

In a flexible exchange rate world, governments can have an incentive to pursue export policies rather than stimulating internal components of aggregate demand if growth without inflation is an objective. To demonstrate the existence of this incentive, let us, for simplicity, assume labour is the only variable factor of production. The money wage (w) divided by the marginal product of labour (MPL) is equal to the marginal cost of domestic industry (MC). Accordingly, in a purely competitive economy,

$$[w/MPL] = MC = P_d \tag{7.1a}$$

where P_d is the price level associated with domestic output. If there is a given degree of monopoly (m) at any level of employment, where $0 < m < 1$, then $P_d > MC$, and

$$(w/MPL) = MC = (P_d)(g) \tag{7.1b}$$

or

$$P_d = w/[(MPL)(g)] \tag{7.1c}$$

where g equals one minus the average degree of monopoly in the system (see Davidson and Smolensky 1964: 128–39). Thus, in a purely competitive system where $m = 0$, $g = 1$, the more general Equation (7.1b) is reduced to the specific case of equation (7.1a)

Equation (7.1b) can be rewritten as

$$(w/P_d) = (MPL)(g) \tag{7.2}$$

Neoclassical economists claim that the aggregate marginal productivity of the labour curve is the demand curve for labour when $g = 1$. Post-Keynesians, on the other hand, have argued that the marginal productivity of the labour curve (multiplied by any value for the scalar g) can be envisioned as a real wage determining curve or, in Patinkin's terms, a 'market equilibrium curve', rather than a demand curve for labour (see Brothwell 1984; Davidson 1984). This is not the place to revive this analytical dispute. In either case, it appears that the real wage at each level of employment is related to the MPL schedule.[14]

A downward sloping *MPL* curve merely means that industry 'is subject to decreasing returns ... so that the marginal product ... necessarily diminishes as employment increases' (Keynes 1936: 17). In other words, marginal costs for domestic industries are rising as domestic employment increases. Figure 7.1 presents a downward sloping marginal product curve (multiplied by g) for domestic output. If production occurs instead under constant returns, then the marginal product and the *MPL* (g) curves will be horizontal (as shown in Figure 7.2).

As far as labour is concerned, its real wage is determined by its money wage divided by the price level (P^c) of the consumer products (wage goods) bought by labour. In other words, the equation for the real wage, whether the economy is open or closed is

Figure 7.1 Diminishing marginal labour productivity and labour supply schedules

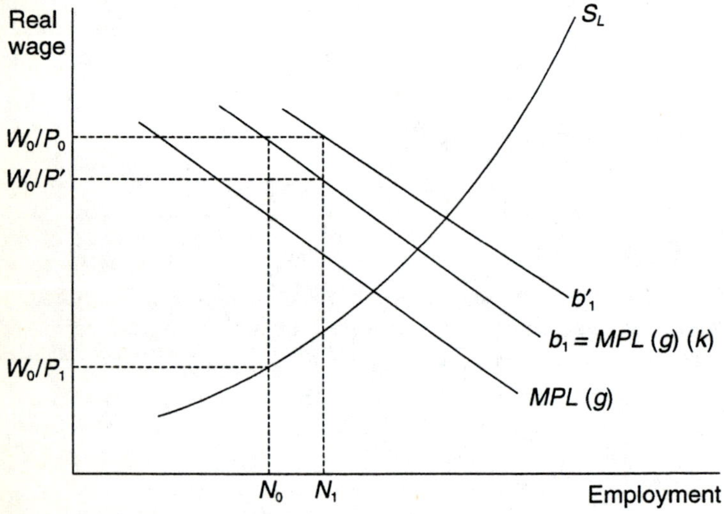

Figure 7.2 Constant marginal labour productivity and labour supply schedules

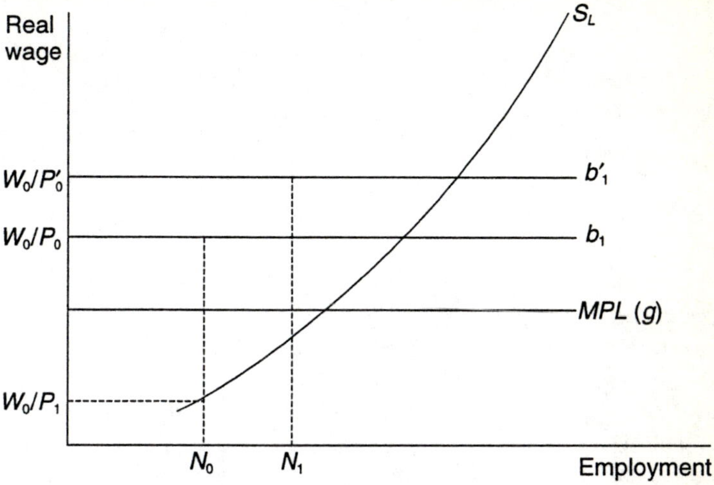

$$w_r = (w/P^c) \tag{7.3}$$

where w_r is the real wage. As a first approximation, one may assume that the price level of domestically produced consumer goods (P^c_d) is equal to (P_d), the price level associated with all the domestically produced goods (that is the GNP price deflator). Hence, for a closed economy, equation (7.3) can be written as

$$w_r = (w/P^c) = (w/P^c_d) = (w/P_d) = (MPL)(g) \tag{7.4}$$

In an open economy, on the other hand, the price level associated with domestic consumption expenditures (P^c) is given by

$$P^c = (P^c_d)(1 - \phi) + (P^c_m)(\phi) \tag{7.5}$$

where P^c_m is the price of consumer good imports in terms of domestic currency and ϕ is the proportion of aggregate domestic consumption expenditures spent on imports. Assuming $P^c_d = P_d$, substituting (7.5) into (7.3), then the real wage in an open economy is

$$w_r = w/P^c = \frac{w}{P_d(1 - \phi) + P^c_m(\phi)} \tag{7.6}$$

$$= \frac{w}{(P_d)(1/k)} \tag{7.7}$$

where

$$(1/k) = [(1-\phi) + (P^c_m/P_d)(\phi)] \tag{7.8}$$

Since the price of imported goods is necessarily lower than the price of the domestic goods that they replace in domestic markets, then P^c_m/P_d is necessarily less than one, and hence according to (7.8), $1/k$ must be less than unity.

Substituting the right-hand side of (7.1c) for P_d in (7.7) gives the real wage rate in an open economy as

$$w_r = MPL(g)(k) \tag{7.9}$$

where $k > 1$. Thus, in Figure 7.1, S_L is the aggregate supply curve of labour while the real wage determining Equation (2) in a closed economy is drawn as the *MPL* (*g*). Comparing (7.9) with (7.2) it is obvious that the real wage determining curve in an open economy (b_1 in Figure 7.1) will be some multiple (*k*) of (*MPL*)(*g*). This b_1 curve lies above the *MPL*(*g*) curve as the price level of imported goods is lower than the price level of domestic goods at any employment level and $\phi > 0$. Moreover, the more open the economy (the greater ϕ), *ceteris paribus*, the greater the vertical distance between *MPL(g)* and *MPL* (*g*)(*k*). If the exchange rate should appreciate, and imported products become even cheaper, *k* will then be even larger and the real wage determining curve will shift upwards to b'_1, even if the proportion of imports purchased (ϕ) is unchanged.

Consequently, for any given proportion of imports in total domestic expenditure, there will be a higher real wage determining curve for each employment level, the more the exchange rate appreciates. In Figure 7.1, at N_0, the real wage W_0/P_0 exceeds the minimum real wage required to bring N_0 workers[15] into the labour market W_0/P_1. Given the existence of involuntary unemployment in the system, if the government (or the central bank) initiates a policy of domestic expenditure expansion so that employment expands to N_1 in Figure 7.1, then the real wage would fall to W_0/P' as the average price level rose (inflation) due to the law of diminishing returns. As drawn in, Figure 7.1 N_1 is still less than the full employment level, but the economy is experiencing rising prices with every increase in employment because of diminishing returns. If, moreover, workers insist on cost of living adjustments (COLAs) as prices rise, then the resulting money wage inflation will exacerbate the inflationary problem induced by domestic demand expansion.

If, on the other hand, the government were to wait for export-led growth (due to an initial expansion in one's trading partner's economy) then the real wage determining curve would shift upwards from b_1 to b'_1 as the improved export-import relationship of the domestic economy leads to an appreciation of the exchange rate.[16] In Figure 7.1; the real wage remains at W_0/P_0 (by construction) as employment rises from N_0 to N_1. Thus, even though domestic output prices rise due to diminishing returns, the domestic consumer does not experience inflation in the price level of the market basket of goods purchased as the cost of living is modified by lower import prices.

Accordingly, there would be less pressure for higher money wages for COLAs as the domestic economy expands. Moreover, the appreciating exchange rate improves the competition of foreign firms with domestic producers while making potentially cheaper foreign workers available to multinationals currently operating factories domestically. These competitive factors threaten domestic workers and thereby weaken workers' bargaining power for higher money wages. Simultaneously, it strengthens any anti-labour resolve of the government and consumers to resist giving into strikers' demands for higher money wages. Finally, previously employed workers (N_0) do not experience any decline in their real wage as additional workers are employed. Hence they are not likely to become restive.

Export-led growth can, therefore, lead to expansion without inducing any inflationary pressures that might otherwise arise if a domestic component of demand was exogenously increased. Simultaneously, export-led growth weakens labour unions' ability (and the rank and file's desire) to raise money wages.[17] Internally stimulated growth in aggregate demand, on the other hand, would lead to expansion with inflation due initially to diminishing returns which lower real wages and may then induce wage-price inflation as workers vainly attempt to re-establish the original real wage via COLAs.[18]

In sum, in a flexible exchange rate system, export-led growth can permit policy makers in any one nation to achieve higher employment without inflation, provided some trading partner is willing and able to take on the task of acting as an initial engine of economic growth. In a world of fixed exchange rates, on the other hand, there can be no exchange appreciation and hence the price of imports will not fall when the nation experiences a trade surplus. In Figure 7.1; under a fixed exchange-rate regime employment expands only via a movement down the b_1 curve. Consequently, there would be no significant difference in the rate of inflation experienced in the nation whether growth was due to being export-led or whether growth was driven by some increase in an internal component of domestic demand.[19]

The story does not change significantly if domestic industries operate under constant returns rather than diminishing returns. If, in a flexible exchange rate system, the economy's *MPL* curve is horizontal as in Figure 7.2, then export-led growth, which results in exchange rate appreciation, leads to higher real wages and a falling price level for the consumer's market basket, as long as money wages are unchanged. For example, as the economy moves from N_0 to N_1 under export-led growth in Figure 7.2 the real wage would rise from W_0/P_0 to W_0/P'_0. In this constant returns case, export-led growth leads to simultaneous rising real wages, rising employment and falling prices.[20] This situation may resemble West Germany's experience between 1985 and 1989.

Of course, this delightful situation of rising employment, real wages and little or no inflation, which the export-led growth nation enjoys, does not imply that global inflation and unemployment problems have been resolved. These problems are, as in the card game of Old Maid, merely being passed on as the Black Queen to some other players in the international economy. Inflationary tendencies (and unemployment if the authorities undertake orthodox policies to stop inflation) will appear in those trading partners whose rising trade deficits lead to depreciating exchange rates. This may merely exacerbate inflationary tendencies if the deficit nation tries to maintain employment and workers demand real wage protection either via cost-of-living adjustments, or catching-up negotiations in new labour contracts.

From a global perspective, the existence of flexible exchange rates can encourage each nation to try to resolve problems of unemployment and inflation by merely pushing it off, in a most uncivilised way, to others! If all act this way, then the result can be a global recession and stagnation (or even global stagflation). If, however, one nation acts as the engine of growth, as long as it continues to expand – even as it runs a balance of payment deficit – the trading partners who pursue export-led growth will experience an economic miracle that they may attribute to their virtuous ways and even to their superior central bank that would willingly accept a recession rather than permit any wage inflation!

Under a fixed exchange rate system, on the other hand, there is no advantage in pursuing export-led expansion and hoping for a trading partner to act as an engine of growth. Accordingly, the fixed exchange-rate circumstances will focus the public's eye, and the minds of policy makers, on how to avoid painful recessions and stagnation. No longer will the pursuit of deflationary domestic employment and wage policies be seen as a virtue that gains the economic miracle of growth without inflation. The trading partner who puts a drive for higher real output above the need for planned recessions will be seen as the virtuous one. Planned recessions and unemployment due to tight monetary and fiscal policies will be clearly revealed as an Emperor without clothes. Then positive policies for expanding domestic demand and utilising an incomes policy to fight inflation can again be raised for discussion in public policy forums.

Notes

1. In three decades the USA, once the mecca of opportunity and equality, has regressed from one of the less unequal distribution nations (when Keynesian demand-management policies were in vogue) to become the industrial nation with the most inequitable distribution of income and wealth.
2. A one-time $17.5 billion infrastructure spending stimulus was briefly advocated until the lower interest rate and higher export growth demand management policies could bite. This one-shot small stimulus was quickly abandoned in the face of some Congressional opposition and some unpleasant signals from bond market participants.
3. Many would have preferred the Reagan fiscal deficits to have been spent on improving infrastructure and productive facilities, but if conventional political wisdom prefers less productive forms of government stimulus, then 'wasteful' expenditures on military and tax reductions to stimulate consumption are preferable to no expansionary demand management at all.
4. Neoclassical economists including eclectic Keynesians merely assume that, in a free-market economy, in the long run, real economic growth will track along a full employment growth path. Keynes and hard-core post-Keynesians believe that the historical record demonstrates that entrepreneurial economies do not automatically achieve full employment economic growth, even in the long run.
5. This growth is determined by a weighted average income elasticity of demand for manufactured goods where the weights involved the global distribution of income.
6. This will increase the magnitude of the multiplier for autonomous spending as well as help deliver the fruits of economic growth to society.
7. Between 1982 and September 1985, Germany, Japan and other surplus nations experiencing export-led growth induced by US trade deficits were also experiencing inflation as the costs of their imports rose as the dollar appreciated due to speculative capital flows swamping net trade payments. Accordingly, in those years, conservative governments in West Germany and Japan would not stimulate domestic demand for fear of further exacerbating inflationary pressures. After 1985, as the dollar declined, these nations continued to enjoy export-led growth but now were doubly-blessed by the absence of inflation as they continued to expand. Consequently, there was no pressure to change orthodox policies limiting domestic demand growth.
8. Oversaving in an open economy context can be defined when a nation's spending on imports and direct foreign equity investment is less than its income earned from exports plus income from foreign investments plus net unilateral transfer payments (see Davidson 1994: ch. 16).
9. I need not remind the reader that despite Reagan's rhetorical support of the balanced budget amendment and his willingness to cast a few crumbs to Phil Gramm and Warren Rudman, his has been the only successful two-term Presidency since the Kennedy–Johnson years.
10. Inflation is a symptom of a fight over the distribution of income. Orthodox anti-inflation policies that emphasise NAIRU are barbaric in that they attempt to stop this fight by weakening most participants through reducing aggregate real income.

11. Unfortunately for these surplus nations, many of the national treasures of the USA were bought before the dollar bottomed out. As long as the dollar keeps falling, yesterday's bargain appears to be overpriced today.
12. This $8 billion in government spending in California was approximately half of the one-shot demand stimulus package Clinton proposed to spend in 1993 to stimulate the economy temporarily until he could get lower interest rates and export-led growth to stimulate the economy permanently.
13. How wise can 'the market' be when it eagerly snaps up things that are advertised as 'junk' bonds or 'derivatives' of the real thing?
14. Nothing of substance would be lost if less than perfect competition was analysed; all that would be required is that the *MPL* curve be multiplied by a scalar whose magnitude was less than unity.
15. This situation is consistent with Keynes's (1936: 128) definition of involuntary unemployment.
16. If there is some substitutability of imports for exports, the higher exchange rate would increase the openness of the domestic economy as the proportion of spending on foreign products increased at each level of employment. This would increase the magnitude of ϕ, thereby shifting the real wage determining curve further upwards. For simplicity we will ignore this *further* factor, increasing the real wage with export-led growth, since this would only increase the force of our argument as developed here.
17. As the domestic currency appreciates, the cheaper imports yield higher real wages without labour having to demand higher money wages at the bargaining table.
18. If some other nations are tied to this nation via a common market which maintains fixed exchange rates, then these common market partners can share in the benefits of an appreciating exchange rate that raises real wages in the common market at the expense of the rest of the world.
19. There might be some small *ceteris paribus* differences, if the rate of diminishing returns differs in the foreigners' export industry compared with the diminishing returns experienced in the domestic industries.
20. Or if money wage rates are rising, there is less inflationary pressure.

References

Adelman, I. (1991) 'Long term economic development', Working Paper No. 589, Giannini Foundation of Agricultural Economics.

Brothwell, J. (1984) 'Wages and employment', *Journal of Post Keynesian Economics*, 6 (1), pp. 101–4

Davidson, P. (1984) 'The marginal product is not the demand curve for labor', *Journal of Post Keynesian Economics*, 6 (1), pp. 105–17.

Davidson, P. (1992–93) 'Reforming the world's money', *Journal of Post Keynesian Economics*, 15 (2), pp. 153–79.

Davidson, P. (1994) *Post Keynesian Macroeconomic Theory: A Foundation for Successful Economic Policies in the Twenty-First Century* (Vermont: Edward Elgar).

Davidson, P. and E. Smolensky (1964) *Aggregate Supply and Demand Analysis* (New York: Harper & Row).

Keynes, J. M. (1936) *The General Theory of Employment Interest and Money* (New York: Harcourt).
Keynes, J. M. (1980) *The Collected Writings of John Maynard Keynes*, 25, ed. D. Moggridge (London: Macmillan).
Woodward, R. (1994) *The Agenda* (New York: Simon & Schuster).

8 Uneven Development and the Destabilisation of the North: A Keynesian view*

James K. Galbraith

INTRODUCTION

The work of Hymer (1972) and Emmanuel (1972) inspired the literature on uneven development, unequal exchange, the transnational corporation and North-South trade in general. But most of the literature is devoted to the consequences of such phenomena for developing countries, and is couched in the distinctive idioms of dependency theory. Our insular Northern economics has scarcely been touched by these ideas.[1] Explorations of faltering performance in the developed countries continue along lines unrelated to North-South trade, and efforts to establish linkages have been hotly disputed. To take two early examples, Krugman (1986) emphasised the role of dynamic scale economies in inducing hysteresis in the US trade balance, while Baldwin (1988) modelled the effects of sunk costs of entry in generating hysteresis in import prices. Both models are aimed at trade in general and can be applied to model economies on the same technological and income levels. Neither is geared to the special conditions of the North-South relationship.

Recently, the North-South issue has surfaced in the debate over rising wage inequality in the USA and persistent unemployment in Europe. Bound and Johnson (1992) and Lawrence and Slaughter (1993) have articulated the mainstream perspective: these matters are internal to the developed countries and stem from peculiarities in the evolution of technology. Adrian Wood (1994) has offered an authoritative challenge to these views, but one that is nevertheless rooted in mainstream trade theory and not in macroeconomics.

What the literature is missing, so far, is a distinctively Keynesian perspective, something that can tie historical developments in the patterns of trade and industrial development to actions of policy. To provide such a perspective, we need merely marry a Weintraub–Davidson *Z-D* analysis to an underlying putty-clay, vintage capital structure, and embed the whole in an open-economy model with North-South wage differentials. This chapter constitutes a start – only a start – on such a project.

UNEQUAL EXCHANGE AND REDEPLOYMENT

The special features of North-South trade are defined by Raffer (1987) as consisting first and foremost of unequal exchange, defined as double factoral terms of trade not equal to one, or unequal wages after adjustment for productivity. To this one might add other cost differentials: taxes, regulation, land. North-South relations might also be characterised as including a large share of trade within manufacturing processes (specifically, of advanced capital goods and intermediates in one direction and of finished products in the other), and even within individual firms.[2]

If these are the correct features, then the question of *why* industrial redeployment should occur does not seem very hard. Industries manufacturing finished products for mass markets move because it is profitable to do so. Industries generating new technologies and tied to particular groups of people or infrastructures do not face unequal exchange and do not have a temptation to move. The world is not in steady-state equilibrium.

The more interesting issues concern the speed and scope of redeployment, and the consequences of the ensuing structural reorganisation of production for the national economies in the two regions. 'Pull' factors for Southern investment are well-known, and include political stability, adequate infrastructure, the availability of skilled labour and the reduction of trade barriers in the North. But surely, given sufficient supply of these requirements, 'push' factors become important? Indeed, the actual pace of expansion of North-South trade will turn on two structural features of the Northern economy: (i) the putty-clay nature of fixed capital investment; and (ii) the implicit co-ordination of investment decisions by large producers of consumer goods in the Northern economy. This second feature is influenced, in turn, in a fundamental way by the Northern business cycle, and by policies that manipulate aggregate demand. The role of recessions in forcing structural changes on the Northern economy and in regulating their pace over time is a critical, often neglected, element of the story.

Normatively, there is a subtle blend of necessity and danger in this process, as far as the Northern economy is concerned: necessity, because Southern redeployment, once undertaken by any one major firm or some branch of consumer goods production of the North, becomes a competitive necessity for all direct competitors of that firm. Meanwhile, the fixed factors of production must remain, and even expand, in the North: advanced design and manufacture of capital goods and intermediates. Yet in this the seeds of crisis are present, for competition in the capital goods sphere is a risky, problematic, unstable business.

AN ANALYTICAL FRAMEWORK

I shall describe a Northern system, specify certain rules of behaviour for it, and then indicate what may happen when such a system is opened up to the conditions of North-South trade. The treatment of production follows Robinson (1969) and Salter (1969), within a macroeconomic accounting framework like that of Kalecki (1971/1933).[3] The structural description attempts to capture a key feature of advanced economies, namely the role of the large corporation in the manufacture of consumer goods (Galbraith 1967). While the model is substantially abstract, its implications do in fact correspond to some of the major problems Northern economies have experienced in episodes of the recent past.

It is useful to distinguish three productive sectors within the Northern economy: a K-sector producing capital goods with labour (and dated labour); a C-sector producing consumer goods with capital goods and labour; and an S-sector producing services with labour alone. Differences of form and behaviour between these sectors will drive the evolution of performances in the Northern economy as the relationships between these sectors change.[4]

Capital Goods

The capital goods sector is described by a vast diversity of products, but also by technological homogeneity in the special sense that each product is always produced in the most efficient known way. The sector is science-based, heavily dependent on human capital, and rapidly evolving with respect to choice of technique. Thus, old techniques (and associated products) pass quickly out of use when superior ones appear,[5] and the whole industry moves forward at the pace of applied technological advance.

Total output in the sector at any time is limited by capacity, which means (since the K-sector is skill-intensive) by the sheer number of skilled workers trained and available to work in each product line. When technological revolutions occur the immediate result is extreme (and profitable) scarcity, as old techniques become unacceptable and customers line up for limited supplies of the new.

Capital goods prices at sectoral full employment are thus determined by demand in an environment of dynamic price discrimination. The position *off* the demand curve depends on macroeconomic conditions (see Figure 8.1); while the position *on* it depends on the stage of the product cycle. Firms

Figure 8.1 Transient price discrimination in capital goods

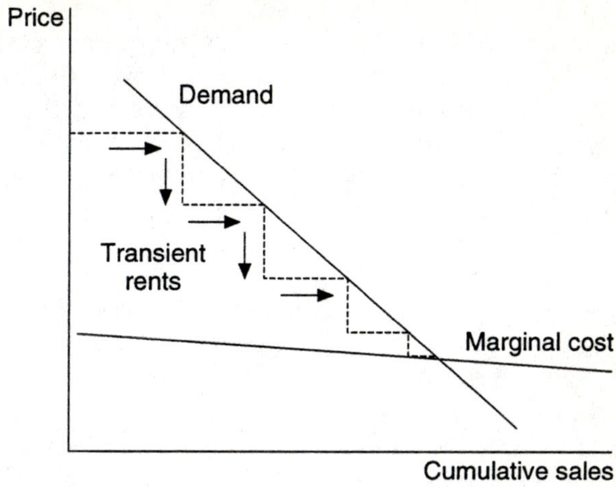

introducing new products pick demanders off their demand curves at their reservation prices, and move down those curves as new output becomes available.

Each product line within the sector is therefore a lottery, a competitive struggle to produce a superior version of the product, with the winner clearing all prizes and the losers accepting the scraps. Winning the first time provides the resources for further technological advances, so the process mimics dynamic increasing returns, but there is no necessary reason that costs or input requirements for any particular product should fall with increased (static or cumulative) scale of output. Thus there is always the risk of being brutally undercut from an unexpected technological quarter. The lottery has a cumulative but unstable character.

When the capital goods sector is at (well-defined) full employment and/or in a period of rapid technological advance, wage rates tend to rise rapidly as firms compete for the best workers. When demand slackens, on the other hand, output slumps and wage rates fall only slowly, if at all. This may be modelled as an asymmetric adjustment of wage rates, which rise with prices (effectively, a share system) at full employment in the sector but remain constant otherwise.

Since output and labour requirements are determined by capacity and technology, respectively, and the sharing ratio for wages is an institutional constant, this implies a proportionate relationship between prices and profits in the sector.

Consumer Goods

In the consumer goods sector, plants of widely differing vintages must co-exist if market volumes necessary to meet demand are to be supplied. The sector is therefore technologically diverse (in the same sense that homogeneity prevails in capital goods production). Its plants will have widely differing cost structures, with the newest only exhibiting minimum costs (to simplify, a minimum labour/output ratio). Older plants suffer from the disadvantages of outdated technology, factor combinations rendered suboptimal by subsequent relative price changes, and rising maintenance costs. The putty-clay nature of fixed capital investment ensures that these problems only get worse with time: they cannot be remedied once plant design is complete. Yet plants will continue in production as long as prices justify unit costs, with producers that, in general, the consumer cannot distinguish from those produced by more modern plant. Arraying capital stock by unit costs, as in Figure 8.2, we have a version, or a transformation, of the Weintraub Z-function.

The profile of plant vintages poses a problem of long-term corporate stability for firms in the consumer goods sector. (Companies are marked A, B, C in Figures 8.2 and 8.3.) Any firm with just one plant is doomed to a fast start and a slow but inevitable decline. Corporate immortality and stability of market share requires at a minimum that each corporation hold a portfolio of plants, whose unit cost structure mimics the profile of the industry as a whole. It is for this reason that large corporations exist, that the minimum scale of the

Figure 8.2 Costs and prices in mass production

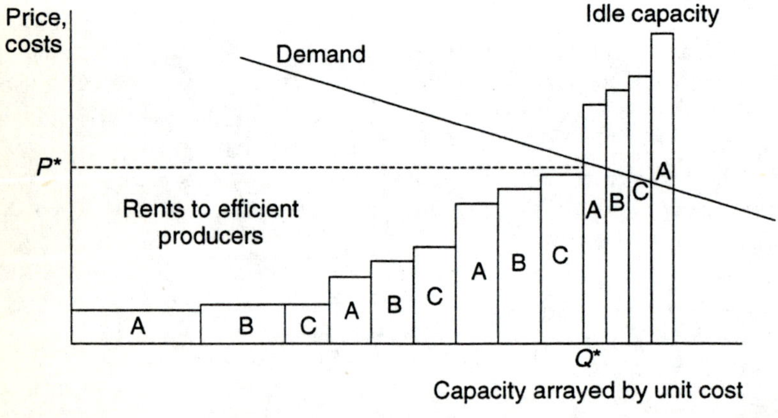

Figure 8.3 Effect of new investment

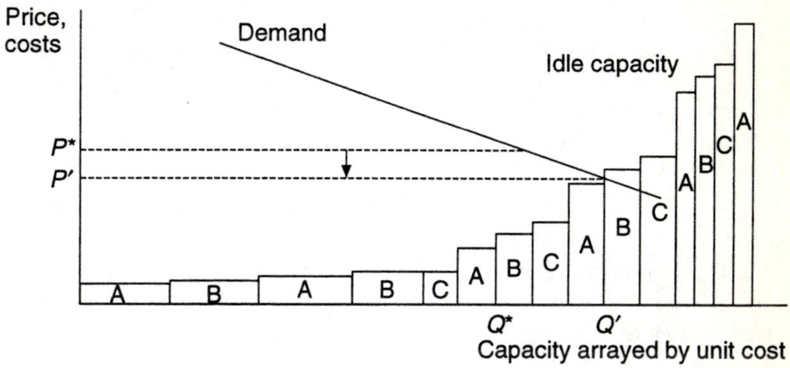

firm so far exceeds the minimum efficient scale of the plant. In turn, it suggests an interest by such corporations in implicit co-ordination with their rivals of investment decisions, and this will be dealt with later. The means of co-ordination and the corporations that use it may be described as a Planning System, to use the term introduced in *The New Industrial State* (Galbraith 1967).

Wage rates in the consumer goods sector are again an institutional matter, and are determined in part with reference to the wage changes in the leading sector, capital goods. Wage contours transmit impulses from the capital to the consumer goods sector; however, long-term contracts (which exist for efficiency reasons, in part because bidding for labour is less critical to success in consumer goods than in capital goods production) ensure that consumer goods wages respond with some lag. The wage bill in this sector is the common wage rate times employment, noting that labour requirements per unit of output vary by plant.

Production in the consumer goods sector is limited, not by trained labour as in capital goods, but by the capacity of the capital stock, which is a function of the history of past investments and past scrapping. One may think of a supply curve that tends to be cut off, or truncated, at output rates just above those prevailing in normal times. Furthermore it is a curve that drifts upward with time, and which changes shape, flattening at the bottom and shifting to the right when new plant and equipment are added to the stream of productive capacity.

Irreversibilities in the evolution of the C-sector arise particularly in technical progress and in the abandonment of older plant and equipment.

It turns out that technological developments and price adjustments are linked together. That is, prices must cover the costs of the plant on the Ricardian margin, which is the plant with the highest labour/output ratio, yielding no profit. From this it follows that average profits per unit in the industry must be a mark-up on wages, with the mark-up coefficient given by the difference between the average and the highest labour/output ratio, between average and worst-practice technique. When a plant is scrapped, the Ricardian margin falls and with it, price.

Since new techniques lower the average cost only gradually, the rate of scrapping and not the rate of technological advance governs movements of the average rate of profit in the short run. The potential for instability in the investment decision is large: aggressive campaigns by technical innovators to expand plant and equipment can result in rapid forced abandonment of older plant, flattening the supply curve, forcing down prices in the industry as a whole and eliminating profits (a shake-out). There is no market, moreover, within which the investment decisions of individual firms are co-ordinated, so as to ensure that just enough new capacity is built to meet demand while preserving acceptable levels of profitability in the industry as a whole. On the contrary, there is a prisoners' dilemma: in the face of aggression the only defence of position and market share consists of investment on the same scale as that of the aggressor, even if that results in further flattening the technical profile and loss of profits for the industry as a whole. In the shake-out, both profits and the stability of inter-firm relations are threatened.

The potential threat of an unco-ordinated investment explosion, like an arms race, can be handled through mutual restraint. All firms in an industry may react with extreme conservatism towards investment decisions. Better to refrain altogether from greenfield plant construction lest war break out, particularly if any one firm's adoption of new technology would increase the efficient scale of the plant beyond the growth of the market and so threaten to alter market share. As long as entry, substitution of alternative products and foreign imports can be staved off, corporate strategy may consist of no investment and no technological upgrading at all. The result of such behaviour could then be arteriosclerosis of the industrial system: the Soviet Union in two words.

THE NEW POLITICAL BUSINESS CYCLE

The above gives us the basic mechanism of the business cycle, or more precisely what Darity and I (Galbraith and Darity 1994) have termed the 'new political business cycle'.

Downturns can occur for any reason affecting expected profitability of future output: the marginal efficiency of capital (MEC). The model, however, suggests that an economy of the kind described, which is characterised by cycles, will perform differently, and indeed perhaps better, over the long run than an identical economy whose macroeconomic stability is preserved by policy action.

The reason is that recessions provide a solution to the investment co-ordination problem. They are a common signal to firms that large-scale scrapping, to be followed by new investment, is in order. If the industry is stable to begin with in the sense described earlier (all major firms have technical profiles approximating that of the industry as a whole), then common scrapping does not affect the relative position of firms. Now, a gap between productive capacity and potential demand emerges, so that new investment by all firms is possible without disturbing market share. The question of how to settle on a next generation of techniques is decided in common: the whole industry picks the best technique available at that moment. Because scrapping occurs on a large scale, the subsequent installation of new capacity occurs on a larger scale than would have been the case without the recession. There is a temporary sacrifice of output and profits, but industrial stability and technological progressiveness are reconciled. Not surprisingly, a political constituency favouring periodic recessions for this purpose can develop (Figure 8.4).

In the slump the path of capacity growth flattens as new investment falls to levels of normal scrapping, and may dip downward if scrapping exceeds investment. In the recovery that follows, the rise in production reflects the

Figure 8.4 Effect of recession

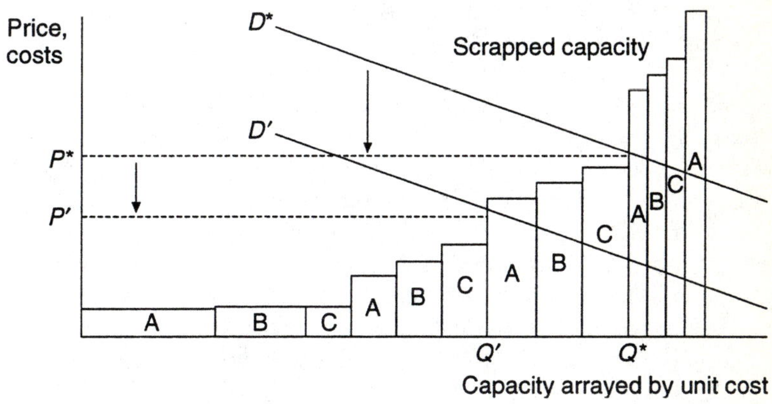

Figure 8.5 Investment in the recovery phase

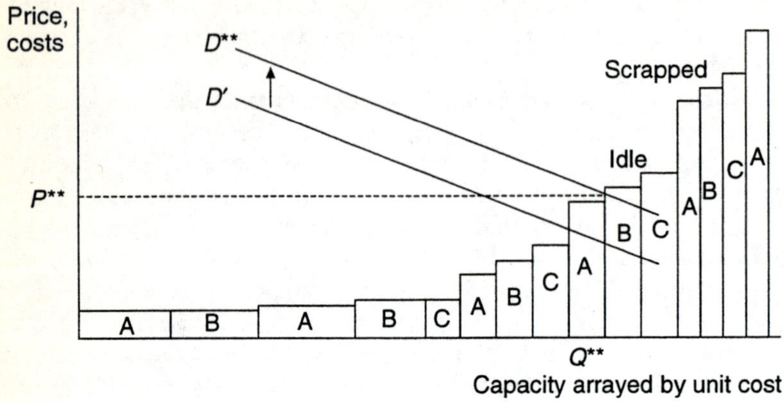

productivity of new investment; thus, production of consumer goods rises more rapidly in the recovery, once new investment comes on line, than would have been the case had the recession not occurred.

One crucial question is whether the supply of consumer goods in the recovery will tend to exceed or fall behind the demand for such goods. This turns on the performance of wages in each goods producing sector, which is the sum of (i) growth of capital goods production at existing wage rates; (ii) the change in wage rates in the capital goods sector; and (iii) the change in the wages bill in the relatively wage-rigid consumer goods sector. Equivalently, subtracting the change in the consumer sector wages bill from both demand (expenditure) and supply (revenue), one may ask whether wages in the capital goods sector outstrip the growth of profits in the consumer goods sector (thus, creating excess demand for consumer goods).

By hypothesis, K-sector prices and wages float rapidly upward, in response to vigorous competition for the best available labour, as soon as the K-sector has been restored to full employment. Now all depends on whether the scrapping in the recession has been temporary or permanent (Figure 8.5).

The immediate effect of irreversible scrapping is to drive prices and capacity in the C-sector downwards, while the gap in demand for new goods quickly pushes the K-sector towards full employment (of the existing skilled-labour pool). Only if this effect is offset by large decreases in average labour requirements in the C-sector can the risk of a squeeze on C-sector supply be avoided. However, this is unlikely to have occurred in time: the K-sector is going full blast well before the additional, advanced consumer good capacity comes on line. Thus, compression of the cost profile in the C-sector leads to unbalanced demand pressures in the ensuing expansion; not when full employment is reached overall, but soon after it is reached in the K-sector.

What then? Possibilities in the closed economy include (i) increased saving ('forced saving') out of K-sector wages until the goods come on line, for which unfortunately no mechanism exists; (ii) temporary inflation of C-sector prices and profits, for which no reliable mechanism (the Walrasian auctioneer) exists either. That leaves (iii) a combination of back-ordering and displacement of demand to the services sector, and either rising service sector prices and wages (pure income inflation) or increasing supply of labour to that sector.[6] The shift to services, if it occurs, ultimately implies movement of consumer demand down Engel curves to less income-elastically supplied goods, something that is not good for C-sector profits.[7]

On the other hand, if plants have been mothballed but not scrapped, the effects of the recession are quickly undone: high-cost plant is brought back into production, C-sector prices and profits rise, and the expansion washes out the effects of the recession. But this, of course, means less incentive to invest. Thus, there is a tension in the closed economy between the co-ordinating function of recessions and the desire to be prepared to meet the ensuing boom in demand for goods. C-sector firms in the closed economy will be tempted to hoard obsolete plant through the recession, so as to have it available to meet rising demands for goods afterwards.

The question appears to be a matter of the degree of difference between worst- and best-practice technique. Companies will be more willing to scrap and invest the larger are the gains from so doing. In addition, customers will be more willing to wait for back-ordered goods, rather than switch to services, if the promised prices are lower, which is a matter of the amount of older plant eliminated in the downturn. In general, the larger the gains to renewal of plant and equipment, the more firms will take the opportunity the recession provides to indulge in permanent elimination of old plant.

The opening of a Southern alternative may tend to resolve this question in favour of irreversible scrapping, almost irrespective of the degree of pure technological advance that may have occurred. The reason is the simple one featured at the beginning of this chapter: unequal exchange.

NORTH-SOUTH TRADE OVER THE CYCLE

The special features of North-South trade are easily interjected into this scheme: they lie in the fact that Northern exports consist of capital goods, while imports consist of consumer manufacturing, and in the fact that

Southern wages are below Northern wages for equivalent productivity (unequal exchange). Further, advanced capital goods production is tied to a competitive market for superior workers and research goods, and so is immobile. Consumer goods production may well require skilled labour, but the skills are standard ones and can be taught anywhere; thus consumer goods production is highly mobile.

From this, several propositions are apparent. First, in the expansion following the slump, there is a large advantage to locating new C-sector capacity in the South. And not just to one firm: whole industries will migrate at the same time, impelled by considerations of relative position as much as by the absolute size of the additional cost reduction.

Second, anticipating the above, firms take advantage of the slump to make permanent what might otherwise be merely a temporary shutdown of older Northern plant. Thus, each recession is characterised by dislocation, and each expansion is characterised by a rising propensity to import. There is now a Northern C-sector profit squeeze, because while scrapping has reduced the high-cost margin, the diminution and displacement overseas of advanced C-sector investment is slowing the downward movement at home of the average domestic labour requirements. Thus, internationalisation implies an increasingly flat C-sector cost profile in the home country. The profits are now overseas, out of the Northern tax base and perhaps effectively exempt from taxation altogether.

Third, in the expansion, the best-practice technique (reducing average labour requirements) comes on line. But now there is the additional factor of low wages (and other costs) in the new plant. To the firm, average wage rates in the expansion now include wage rates in the Southern country.[8] Low Southern wages compound the effects of technological changes that have taken place. But low Southern wages also mean that technical improvement need not be so extensive for the same profitability, and the goods gap can be filled more quickly with smaller technical changes than would otherwise be the case.[9] The effects of low Southern wages on Northern prices, which continue to be set at the Ricardian margin, run indirectly through two channels: if more scrapping has occurred in anticipation of higher profit from Southern operations and, importantly, if Southern wages come to influence the rise of Northern wages directly.[10] Thus, the initial disinflationary effect of the recession is greater and/or more sustained than would otherwise be the case.

Fourth, combining the above, a sustained rise in the Northern exchange rate has multiple disinflationary effects through distinct channels: the rise in imports it induces may suppress wages in the C-sector, while the fall in exports suppresses wages via the channel of the K-sector. This fall in exports also has grave effects on the development and diffusion of technology, and on the competitive position of the affected Northern economy if there exist in the world multiple North-South Planning Systems that compete with each other on technological grounds.[11]

Fifth, to the extent that the import boom occurs within the Southern operations of Northern firms, the rise in Northern company profits due to lower Southern wages helps preserve the international macroeconomic balance. That is, there is now a services export (repatriated profits on overseas operations) to help pay in part for the higher imported goods consumption of K-sector workers. Only the Southern wages bill is a net outflow. But if the Southern firms are foreign (and foreign-financed), then no profits repatriation occurs and, without a prodigious performance of K-sector exports, difficulties of both company and national finance cannot be far behind. Each Northern country thus has an interest in the Southern success of its own firms.

Sixth, to restore trade balance (and maintain competitiveness) requires the growth of K-sector exports, to the extent of the net outflow. This is *ipso facto* inflationary over the medium run. Exports of capital goods lead to wage-led inflation in the home country, followed by wage rate increases and a wage-price spiral in consumer goods (as long as the latter cannot be held off by yet another increase in C-sector imports). If there is reserve capacity overseas but not at home after the recession, so that an import boom comes first and the export recovery follows, we have the typical pattern of the US economy in the 1980s: a non-inflationary recovery with a large trade deficit followed by increasing inflationary pressures as exports finally recovered. Only if the patterns of wage solidarity that normally flow from the K-sector to the C-sector are broken does the inflationary pressure disappear. There is strong evidence that this is, in fact, happening in the USA (Galbraith and du Pin Calmon 1994, 1996).

Finally, one may consider the permanent effects of expanded North-South trade on the structure of the Northern economy. One of the simpler effects is a rise in the ratio of capital to consumer goods output, at market prices, and of services relative to goods. Increasingly, the Northern country will come to specialise in the unstable business of the K-sector, while the intermediate operations of the C-sector migrate as quickly as the co-ordinating mechanism of the business cycle permits.

One might ask, will a change in these ratios affect productivity growth in the Northern country? In principle, productivity growth in the goods-sectors should increase. But we note that export booms in Northern countries (the USA in 1977–80) are in fact accompanied by falling rates of measured productivity growth. Why? One part of the answer presumably lies in the shift to services, which exhibit no change in productivity due to the way in which output is measured. The other may well lie in the notorious inability of national income accountants to measure P_k as well as P_c (Block 1985). One price of a rising share of technically-advanced production may be a declining ability to capture costless quality change and so the real volume of output, with the result that measured productivity growth may appear to decline even when technical progressivity is at its peak.

CONCLUSIONS

In the model presented above, a Planning System employs the political instruments of macroeconomic management to co-ordinate decisions on plant scrapping, new investment and choice of technique that would otherwise threaten to provoke destabilising intercorporate warfare. The putty-clay nature of fixed capital investment, corporate diversification over plants of differing vintages, and effective political control over the timing of business cycle recessions are the essential features of this schema.

Expansion of North-South trade extends the Planning System across national frontiers. It changes nothing with respect to the co-ordinating role of recessions in investment planning. But it does widen the gap between the cost of production *ex ante* and *ex post*, by introducing wage differentials into the picture in addition to the closed economy's mechanisms of technical change. Such differentials, unequal exchange in two words, are both necesary and sufficient to provoke transnational redeployment. The pace of this redeployment, however, is not indefinite; rather it is governed by the pace of the business cycle in the Northern country. Redeployment occurs in the expansion to the extent of secular market growth plus scrapping in the previous recession. For redeployment beyond that point another recession is needed.

One might therefore expect that a rising capacity to install advanced consumer goods producing plant and equipment in low-wage countries would increase pressures for policy-induced recessions in the Northern country. Such pressures will indeed recur (irrespective, for example, of inflationary pressures or lack thereof) as long as the transition to low-wage production can continue.

Allowing this conjecture, one could go so far as to speculate on a preferred frequency of policy-induced recessions, from the standpoint of Northern C-sector firms. Recessions raise the obsolescence rate and so (for a given pool of available techniques) the pace of cost reduction. But too-frequent recessions can also slow the expected average growth rate of demand, depressing the expected profitability of new investment. The trick of policy must be therefore to create an environment in which each succeeding recession is regarded for practical purposes as a one-time-only event, to be followed by a prolonged expansion in which all new capital investments (up to the full capacity of the capital goods sector for a sustained period) will be rewarded. Thus deep recessions, clearing the way for large redeployments at one swoop, will be preferred to frequent ones, which might endanger the subsequent climate of effective demand and expected profitability.

At the same time, the world of North-South trade wipes out the traditional vision of the policy-induced recession as a permanent curative for inflationary pressures and inflationary expectations. In this world, recessions end inflations quickly and effectively in the short run. But they also lay the groundwork for a resurgence of inflation when the initial import boom has been absorbed and export expansion takes over. The vision of a stable, sustained non-inflationary growth path all the way to full employment seems beyond reach, without wage control in the advanced sectors. Instead, governments face the choice between engineering slow expansions, or running a stronger but high-currency expansion with stable prices but an unsustainable accretion of external debt.

For the North, it is certain that redeployment causes major problems. The Northern country is now less secure on two counts: its enlarged K-sector is inherently unstable, and it relies on the unstable vagaries of external demand. The ambit of the Planning System is weaker in the North as it becomes extended transnationally. The Northern distribution of jobs is more unequal too: there is a decline in the solid C-sector middle, while below-middle S-sector jobs may increase to offset the increasing unreliability of manufacturing incomes. Inflationary wage pressures may be stronger, due to the larger weight of the inflation-prone K-sector in the labour mix, or weaker, due to the loss of bargaining power in the C- and S-sectors.

Is the Northern country worse off, in some Hicks–Kaldor sense, as a result of redeployment? Not necessarily; much depends on whether the climate of expectations for growth and development remains favourable long enough. The K-sector must grow to supply the world with capital goods, implying accelerated technological development, and the terms of trade between K-goods and C-goods can be favourable enough to support the Northern country's standard of life (particularly if Southern profits are coming home). Indeed, the K-sector of the Northern country may expand to provide the bulk of its manufacturing employment, so long as the development process is sufficiently large and sufficiently sustained, and so long as mechanisms to spread the wealth are in place and politically protected. With the expansion of the pool of trained Southern workers, along with the relaxation as a result of technical progress of other 'constraints of nature' on production, the concept of a full employment barrier to expanded production all but disappears. The effective limit to growth becomes merely the maximum sustainable output rate of the K-sector in the Northern economy, which rules the dissemination of the only scarce physical factors of production, knowledge-intensive capital goods.

Whether the limit can be reached depends on the course of world-wide effective demand, and this is the critical problem. The Northern national institutions that subsidise consumption and sustain demand do not extend to the low-wage economies of the South. The Northern companies that produce in the South do not benefit from a reduction of wage differentials. Meanwhile, trade deficits resulting from the unbalanced application of consumption subsidies generate incessant political pressure to cut back on consumption subsidies in the North.

For these reasons, global Keynesian policies to support the growth of investment possibilities in the Southern economies and of Southern consumption *pari passu* with productive capacity are necessary, if markets for the expanded production of consumer goods are to exist. Suppression of demand growth and investment in the South – the key result of periodic debt crises – returns to haunt the North in the form of gravely diminished prospects for sustained technological transformation.

Notes

* A version of this chapter was first presented at a conference on 'North–South Trade and Development' at the University of North Carolina in September 1988. I thank Lance Taylor, William Darity, Philip Arestis and Malcolm Sawyer for comments. Figures are adapted from James K. Galbraith and William Darity, Jr (1994) *Macroeconomics* (Boston, MA: Houghton Mifflin).

1. The hypothesis of Northern de-industrialisation through trade, presented in Europe as the *New International Division of Labor* (Frobel, Heinrichs and Kreye, 1980), met with early, determined and effective opposition (at least in the USA; for a survey, see Norton 1986). Krugman's (1981) North-South model, a peculiarly perverse case, relies on increasing returns in a manufacturing North and constant returns in an agricultural South to show causes for the specialisation in manufacturing of the Northern economy, and so runs counter to the redeployment hypothesis. Pasinetti (1981) is, on the other hand, an indispensable guide to basic theory in these matters.
2. I published a book in 1989 making this point about the composition of North-South trade, which seemed obvious to me at the time. A short article by Andrew Warner (1994) finally called these patterns to the attention of the mainstream. I suppose my earlier work would be called pathbreaking if the jungle had not closed over it so completely.

3. The motivation (or lack of it) attributed to the firm follows Galbraith (1967) as elucidated in an earlier article of mine (Galbraith 1984). The notions of historical process follow Veblen (1898) as reprised in Kaldor (1985). These connections are explained in Galbraith (1988). The paper also owes debts to Darity and Fitzgerald (1982) and to a survey by Dutt (1988).
4. The distinction between sectors requires us to stipulate a national income and product identity that distinguishes types of production as well as expenditures and incomes. We have

$$CE + I + G + X - M = P_c C + P_k K + P_s S = W_c + W_k + W_s + \Pi_c + \Pi_k$$

where *CE, I, G, X, M* are (nominal) consumption expenditures, investment, government, exports and imports, *C, K, S* are physical volumes of output of wage goods, capital goods and services, the P_s are prices for those goods, and the W_s and Π_s are wages and profits earned in each sector. Note that as no capital is used, no profits are earned in the services sector.
5. Exceptions in the real world, like steel, may perhaps be explained by the presence of subsidies and trade protection. On the other hand, there are many good examples, such as the turnover in generations of aircraft and computers.
6. Such irreversibilities are not matters of dynamic scale economies (natural monopoly), as these do not comport with the observed long-term stability of market share across firms, or of barriers to entry (which surely exist), since there are important irreversibilities that do not require the creation of new firms.
7. Of these, the latter is particularly likely to occur, given (i) displacement of former C-sector workers in the previous recession; and (ii) a high elasticity of supply of household workers into the S-sector (not modelled). Moreover, once the new labour supply in the S-sector is established, it may be permanent: there is hysteresis in labour supply.
8. This happens because the previously high incomes of a few individuals are transferred to a larger number of individuals before returning to the circuit of demand for consumer goods.
9. Moreover, if a slow-down of export trades slows the introduction of new techniques, the need for redeployment is greater than it would otherwise be.
10. Which, in the North-South context, requires an advance of financial capital: yet another story.
11. It might be thought that in a world of rational long-run expectations such an environment is impossible. But rational expectations are not necessarily a problem. If the expansion is expected to be sufficiently long so that the losses from the next expected recession are heavily discounted, rational firms will be motivated to invest at a maximal rate even though they know that a new recession will happen at some time in the future. The key is that actual expansions be sufficiently long, and that actual recessions be sufficiently infrequent.

References

Baldwin, R. (1988) 'Hysteresis in import prices: the beachhead effect', *American Economic Review*, 78, pp. 773–86.

Block, F. (1985) 'Post-industrial development and the obsolescence of economic categories', *Politics and Society*, 14(1), pp. 71–104

Bound, J. and Johnson, G. (1992) 'Changes in the structure of wages in the 1980s: an evaluation of alternative explanations', *American Economic Review*, 82, pp. 371–92.

Darity, W. and FitzGerald, E. V. K. (1982) 'A Keynes-Kalecki model of world trade, finance and economic development', Center for Economic Research Discussion Paper, University of Texas at Austin, September.

Dutt, A. K. (1988) 'North-South models: a critical survey', mimeo, September.

Emmanuel, A. (1972) *Unequal Exchange, A Study of the Imperialism of Trade*: *Monthly Review Press* (New York).

Frobel, F., Heinrichs, J. and Kreye, O. (1980) *The New International Division of Labor* (New York: Cambridge University Press).

Galbraith, J. K. (1967) *The New Industrial State* (Boston, MA: Houghton Mifflin).

Galbraith, J. K. (1984) 'Galbraith and the theory of the corporation', *Journal of Post Keynesian Economics*, VII, pp. 43–60.

Galbraith, J. K. (1988) 'Trade and the planning system', mimeo, forthcoming in S. Bowles R. Edwards, and W. G. Shepherd (eds), *Unconventional Wisdom, Essays in Honor of John Kenneth Galbraith* (Boston, MA: Houghton Mifflin).

Galbraith, J. K. and Darity, W. (1994) *Macroeconomics* (Boston, MA: Houghton Mifflin).

Galbraith, J. K. and du Pin Calmon, P. (1994) 'Industries, trade and wages', in D. Adler and M. Bernstein (eds), *Understanding American Economic Decline* (Cambridge: Cambridge University Press).

Galbraith, J. K. and du Pin Calmon, P. (1996) 'Wage change and trade performance in U. S. manufacturing industries', *Cambridge Journal of Economics*, 20, pp. 433–50.

Hymer, S. (1972) 'The multinational corporation and the law of uneven development', in J. Bhagwati (ed.), *Economics and World Order* (New York: The Free Press).

Kaldor, N. (1985) *Economics without Equilibrium* (Armonk, NY: M. E. Sharpe).

Kalecki, M. (1971/1933) 'The determinants of profits', reprinted in *Selected Essays in the Dynamics of the Capitalist Economy* (Cambridge: Cambridge University Press).

Krugman, P. (1981) 'Trade, accumulation and uneven development', *Journal of Development Economics*, 8, pp. 149–61.

Krugman, P. (1986) 'Pricing to market when the exchange rate changes', NBER Working Paper no. 1926, May.

Lawrence, R. Z. and Slaughter, M. (1993) 'Trade and U.S. wages: great sucking sound or small hiccup?', Harvard University, mimeo, June.

Norton, R. D. (1986) 'Industrial policy and American renewal', *Journal of Economic Literature*, 24, pp. 1–41.

Pasinetti, L. L. (1981) *Structural Change and Economic Growth: A Theoretical Essay on the Dynamics of the Wealth of Nations* (New York: Cambridge University Press).

Raffer, K. (1987) *Unequal Exchange and the Evolution of the World System* (London: Macmillan).

Robinson, J. (1969) *The Accumulation of Capital*, 3rd edn (London: Macmillan, New York: St Martin's Press).

Salter, W. E. G. (1969) *Productivity and Technical Change* (Cambridge: Cambridge University Press).

Veblen, T. (1898) 'Why is economics not an evolutionary science', *Quarterly Journal of Economics*, XII, July, pp. 215–40.

Warner, A. (1994) 'Does world investment demand determine U.S. exports?', *American Economic Review*, 84, pp. 1409–23.

Wood, A. J. B. (1994) *North–South Trade, Employment and Inequality: Changing Fortunes in a Skill-Driven World* (Oxford: Oxford University Press).

9 Creative Destruction or Regressive Stagnation? Comments on Davidson and Galbraith

Jonathan Michie

INTRODUCTION*

In considering the relevance of Keynesian economics in the late twentieth century, there are two questions to be asked: first, to what extent do (what might be termed) 'Keynes's insights' help in analysing the world today; and second, to what extent does the integration of national economies, and what has come to be described generally as the 'globalisation' of the world economy, affect the implementation and efficacy of Keynesian economic policies? The chapters by Galbraith and Davidson tackle these two questions: James Galbraith considers the relevance of Keynesian concepts in analysing the global economy of today, and Paul Davidson discusses Keynesian policies given the changes in the world economy.

NORTH-SOUTH TRADE AND THE DESTABILISATION OF THE NORTH

James Galbraith uses a Keynesian analysis to analyse North-South trade, with global recessions induced by demand-deficiency leading to capacity being scrapped or mothballed in the North; and with the choice between scrapping and mothballing being influenced by the existence of competing low-wage capacity in the South, in favour of scrapping (since in the expansion following the slump, there is a large advantage to locating new capacity in the South); and with this therefore having a relatively dynamic effect on the world economy, since it will lead to more investment in new capacity being required in the North than would otherwise have been the case, and with the capacity being taken up in the subsequent upturn therefore being on average newer and more productive.

So, first, recessions have a function in that they leave capacity idle and some of this will be scrapped and therefore replaced, via increased investment, in the upturn. And second, the existence of a low-wage Southern alternative will encourage a greater proportion of this unutilised capacity to be scrapped (rather than mothballed) so that the dynamic effects will be that much greater, with a greater increase in investment required in the subsequent upturn, and with the resulting capacity therefore being of a newer average vintage.

It is important to avoid the dangers of 'functionalism' in such a discussion; to describe the function played by recessions is not the same as explaining their causes. But this is not to say that recessions do not play this sort of function; indeed, various possible functions were described by Marx (for example, in his discussion of the counteracting tendencies to the falling rate of profit), by Schumpeter with his 'gales of creative destruction', and by Kalecki with his discussion of the political economy of full employment.[1] But the concerns of Keynes (and Keynesians) is that these recessions could just as well prove to be periods of *un*creative stagnation and of economic and social destruction and regression:

> The Great Depression, lasting for the full decade of the 1930s, gravely impaired the accepted commitment to the concept of a full employment norm at stable prices. Clearly, unemployment, underproduction and severe price deflation were more than a current and even curative episode, as was held by Joseph Schumpeter and his acolytes, who believed the depression to be a temporary, self-corrective and ultimately benign occurrence in the broad course of economic development. (Galbraith 1991: 23)

This contrasting of the positive functions of recessions, on the one hand, and negative dangers on the other, should not be interpreted as a call to passivity, explaining away the negative consequences as a necessary concomitant to the positive benefits along the lines of 'if it's not hurting it's not working' and that unemployment 'is a price well worth paying'.[2] On the contrary, it should lead to the question of whether there is no alternative, such as 'Social Corporatism', with wage-pressure forcing the pace of economic scrapping and modernisation?

Thus, Galbraith's chapter argues that the pace of technical advance is limited by the rate of physical obsolescence of existing capital equipment. But scrapping is economic rather than physical, and can be brought about by either reduced demand or increased wages; the latter course was chosen for decades in Sweden, with a deliberate use of high wage growth to force the pace of development (a more Keynesian way of forcing scrapping than enduring demand-deficient recessions).[3]

THE VIABILITY OF KEYNESIAN DEMAND MANAGEMENT IN AN OPEN ECONOMY

In Paul Davidson's chapter there are a number of points on the USA which ring true for a British reader, such as Reaganism having seen a Keynesian demand-expansion, much like the UK's Lawson boom, fuelled by tax cuts and consumer spending. On the central message of his chapter – that we need globally-managed demand-expansion policies – the question is how to get them, and here the British government has taken the lead in attempting to obstruct progress at every international meeting. Some of the passing remarks in Davidson's chapter about export-led growth, devaluation and fixed exchange rates have, though, a rather different connotation in the UK than they may have elsewhere. In the UK such statements are often used to justify policy inactivity.

On the issue of export-led growth, Davidson states that not all countries can pursue an export-led growth programme simultaneously, and while the point being made is clear and unobjectionable, it does need more elaboration and justification than to simply assert that the global double-entry bookkeeping system just does not permit it. Certainly, export-promotion strategies, devaluations and so on are often portrayed as zero-sum, beggar-thy-neighbour style policies, but this is not an acceptable accusation unless it is compared with an alternative approach which would be less bad. To be specific, if there is a world recession with governments generally pursuing restrictive monetary policies, then if several countries attempt to expand by cutting interest rates in order to devalue their currencies this may well have an expansionary effect overall.[4]

Conversely, those who argue in such situations *against* devaluation are all-too-often prepared to *countenance* a restrictive macroeconomic policy instead, often with an eye, actually, on the balance of payments effects, either to directly restrict the demand for imports by restricting domestic demand, or else to put downward pressure on domestic prices and hence to gain competitive advantage over other countries' goods in both home and export markets. In both cases the result is, in effect, 'beggar-thy-neighbour' deflation, which is very probably a *negative* sum game. This is what happened, for example, following Mitterrand's 'U-turn' in the early 1980s, with a rejection of devaluation leading to years of tight monetary policy which in effect exports unemployment just as surely as might a devaluation –

or an export-led growth strategy – while at the same time creating unemployment domestically (see Halimi, Michie and Milne 1994).

The key question is whether the countries concerned are pursuing expansionary or contractionary economic policies *alongside* their export-promotion ones. Potentially, export promotion may expand both exports and imports in tandem, *and also* the level of domestic national income and employment – by virtue of the export-promotion policies if these include interest rate cuts, direct public investments and so on – thus leading to an overall expansion of global output and employment. Certainly, there are trade policies which can be damaging to other countries, as with the mercantalist policies pursued by the Bundesbank (see Michie and Wilkinson 1995); the point being made here is that this cannot be generalised as being necessarily the case, particularly when those policies are aimed at overcoming balance of payments constraints to expansion. This may be an important point in challenging the line of argument behind policy makers' inactivity.

Similarly, if export-led growth is successful, it will create jobs domestically, and whether an equal number of jobs are lost in the country to which the increased exports are going will depend first of all on whether these are *additional* sales or not; second, on whether the increased exports are matched by simultaneously increased *imports*, whether planned or not; and third, what policy response any trade deficits and surpluses which do occur will have: for example, whether the international trading and financial system is based on deliberately expansionary rules, or whether, on the other hand, they are based on the sort of restrictive ones which Keynes termed 'nonsense'.[5]

The Appendix to Davidson's chapter touches on some of these points, but only in passing since the focus there is on the specific issue of fixed versus floating exchange rates, regarding which there again needs to be a health warning attached to any advocacy of fixed rates, namely that the defence of an overvalued fixed rate can be damaging, and more generally, that any fixed rate system requires first to avoid being based on deficit countries having to deflate; second, the reintroduction of some form of exchange control system; and third, to have some mechanism for realignments (see Kitson and Michie 1995a, 1995b).

CONCLUSION

To step back from the two chapters (by Galbraith and Davidson), and consider the underlying question of what is this 'global' economy, it is important to make two points: first, that there have indeed been major qualitative changes in the degree of globalisation which do require us to respond both in analysing the world and in considering policy; but second, it is important not to allow exaggerated generalisations to subvert such an analysis: it is important that the lessons of history are not lost, via a re-writing of history as if none of these issues of globalisation had arisen before. First, on setting this globalisation in a historical context, the following description of the globalisation of economic activity is apposite:

> All old-established national industries have been destroyed or are daily being destroyed. They are dislodged by new industries, whose introduction becomes a life and death question for all nations, by industries that no longer work up indigenous raw material, but raw material drawn from the remotest zones; industries whose products are consumed, not only at home, but in every quarter of the globe. In place of the old wants, satisfied by the productions of the country, we find new wants, requiring for their satisfaction the products of distant lands. We have universal inter-dependence of nations. And as in material, so also in intellectual production.

True, of course. But new? This characterisation of globalisation was written almost 150 years ago.[6]

In addition, of course, policies for macroeconomic expansion to tackle unemployment would best be pursued internationally. But again this is nothing new; Kalecki's call in 1932 for expansionary policies to tackle unemployment made precisely this 'new realist' point: discussing the possibility of increasing employment by 'major public investment schemes, such as construction of canals or roads', financed by borrowing or increasing the money supply, he stressed the effects on the trade balance of increasing output: 'if it were to be carried out on a large scale, it would have to be co-ordinated by an international agreement of the individual capitalist governments, which, given today's quarrelling imperialisms, is almost out of the question'.[7]

Second, on the extent to which there *have*, of course, been genuinely new developments there has been a continued growth in world trade; the activities of transnational corporations has expanded; and the freeing of global financial markets has led to these increased trade and investment flows being far outstripped by the growth of speculative transactions. This explosion in speculative flows is something qualitatively new but, even here, this is not something that Keynes and others had failed to consider. On the contrary, Keynes was clear on the need to curb such activities, arguing back in 1926 that:

> Many of the greatest economic evils of our time are the fruits of risk, uncertainty, and ignorance. It is because particular individuals, fortunate in situation or in abilities, are able to take advantage of uncertainty and ignorance, and also because for the same reason big business is often a lottery, that great inequalities of wealth come about; and these same factors are also the cause of the unemployment of labour, or the disappointment of reasonable business expectations, and of the impairment of efficiency and production. Yet the cure lies outside the operations of individuals; it may even be to the interest of individuals to aggravate the disease. I believe that the cure for these things is partly to be sought in the deliberate control of the currency and of credit by a central institution ...
>
> I believe that some coordinated act of intelligent judgement is required as to the scale on which it is desirable that the community as a whole should save, the scale on which these savings should go abroad in the form of foreign investments, and whether the present organisation of the investment market distributes savings along the most nationally productive channels. I do not think that these matters should be left entirely to the chances of private judgement and private profits, as they are at present. (Keynes 1984/1926: 291–2)

The logic behind these arguments is as valid now as ever; the issue is a *political* one of how the sort of policy measures advocated successfully by Keynes could be implemented today. Certainly the power of national governments to pursue policies is limited, although even here it is important not to re-write history; thus, for example, the British Prime Minister, Harold Wilson, described how in November 1964:

> That night we had our most desperate meeting with the Governor of the Bank. Claiming that our failure to act in accordance with his advice had precipitated the crisis, he was now demanding all-round cuts in expenditure, regardless of social or even economic priorities, and fundamental changes in some of the Chancellor's economic announcements. Not for the first time, I said that we had now reached the situation where a newly-elected Government with a mandate from the people was being told, not so much by the Governor of the Bank of England but by international speculators, that the policies on which we had fought the election could not be implemented; that the Government was to be forced into the adoption of Tory policies to which it was fundamentally

> opposed. The Governor ... had to admit that was what his argument meant, because of the sheer compulsion of the economic dictation of those who exercised decisive economic power. (Wilson 1971: 37, cited in Glyn 1986: 37–8)

It is also important to remember the political dimension to political economy, as pointed out in the well-known passage from Kalecki when in 1943 he was arguing that, if the sort of policies which both he and Keynes had developed for the maintenance of full employment were actually implemented:

> a strong opposition of 'business leaders' is likely to be encountered. Lasting full employment is not at all to their liking. The workers would 'get out of hand' and the 'captains of industry' would be anxious to 'teach them a lesson'. In this situation a powerful block is likely to be formed between big business and the *rentier* interests, and they would probably find more than one economist to declare that the situation was manifestly unsound. The pressure of all these forces, and in particular of big business would most probably induce the Government to return to the orthodox policy of cutting down the budget deficit. A slump would follow. (Kalecki 1971/1943: 144)

Whether the timescale Kalecki had in mind for this reaction was the generation or so which it actually took is open to question, but the process has no doubt occurred, and the 'more than one' economist willing to play the role cast by Kalecki have in fact proved too many to enumerate. This process depicted by Kalecki is most often thought of in domestic economic terms: giving managers 'the right to manage'. But similar forces are at work on a global scale, with Third World countries being weakened by recession. This political economy of slow growth on a world scale, with powerful interests opposing any return to economic development and full employment, has been highlighted before by Ajit Singh (1992). Thus, in a global economy, such processes may be acted out on a global stage, with the advanced capitalist economies having an interest in the weakened power of raw material suppliers which follows from slow growth.

The real question, then, is not whether it is best to act at the national or international level; it is how best to secure international action. For all to remain frozen until such time as everyone else moves is inadequate, however eloquent the calls for movement being made might be. Action at the local, regional, national or bloc level, far from being a utopian alternative to the real international stage, might in reality prove a prerequisite to co-operation.

Why, finally, should the world be stuck in such an impasse when there was by contrast such a more active policy agenda pursued in the mid- to late-1940s, from Bretton Woods to the Marshall Plan? One clue is to look at what was pushing the ruling powers in that previous era, as compared to the lack of any such push today. When in 1948 the West European countries were struggling to recover from the devastation of war, Marshall Aid was introduced against a background of significant Communist support in many of the countries of Europe and beyond, including Communist Party participation in the governments of France and Italy. Whether the Bretton Woods system would have been constructed without the Cold War is open to question; the lack of any such external pressure helps to explain today's general failure to act.

Notes

* I have benefited from discussions with James Galbraith and Paul Davidson as well as with Bob Pollin, to all of whom I am grateful although none actually saw the text of these comments and so cannot be held responsible.

1. And have also been considered by Ajit Singh: see below.
2. One of ex-Chancellor Norman Lamont's phrases as he talked himself out of his job.
3. None of these comments is meant to be critical of James Galbraith's chapter which is describing rather than advocating how the effects of recessions might work themselves through both the Northern and Southern economies.
4. This is argued in detail by Kitson and Michie (1994).
5. In, 'so because they won't listen to sense, you propose to talk nonsense', on hearing that the British delegation to Bretton Woods was to accept the US view that deficit countries should deflate rather than having surplus countries reflate.
6. Written in 1847 (published 1848) by Marx and Engels, *The Communist Manifesto*.
7. Kalecki (1990/1932): see particularly pp. 53 and 61; cited by Glyn and Rowthorn (1994: 198, note 13).

References

Galbraith, J. K. (1991) 'The modern dialectic: ideology and economic reality', in J. Michie (ed.), *The Economics of Restructuring and Intervention* (Aldershot: Edward Elgar), ch. 1.

Glyn, A. (1986) 'Capital flight and exchange controls', *New Left Review*, 155 (January/February), pp. 37–49.

Glyn, A. and Rowthorn, B. (1994) 'European employment policies', in J. Michie and J. Grieve Smith (eds), *Unemployment in Europe* (London: Academic Press).

Halimi, S., Michie, J. and Milne, S. (1994) 'The Mitterrand experience', in J. Michie and J. Grieve Smith (eds), *Unemployment in Europe* (London: Academic Press).

Kalecki, M. (1990/1932) 'Is a capitalist overcoming of the crisis possible', and 'On the Papen plan', in J. Osiatynski (ed.), *Collected Words of Michał Kalecki* (Oxford: Oxford University Press), 1990.

Kalecki, M. (1971/1943) 'Political aspects of full employment', in *Selected Essays on the Dynamics of the Capitalist Economy* (Cambridge: Cambridge University Press).

Keynes, J. M. (1984/1926) 'The end of *laissez faire*', in *The Collected Writings of John Maynard Keynes, Vol. IX, Essays in Persuasion* (Cambridge: Macmillan and Cambridge University Press for the Royal Economic Society), pp. 272–94.

Kitson, M. and Michie, J. (1994) 'Depression and recovery: lessons from the interwar period', in J. Michie and J. Grieve Smith (eds), *Unemployment in Europe* (London: Academic Press), ch. 5.

Kitson, M. and Michie, J. (1995a) 'Conflict, cooperation and change: the political economy of trade and trade policy', *Review of International Political Economy*, 2(4), 632–57.

Kitson, M. and Michie, J. (1995b) 'Trade and growth: a historical perspective', in J. Michie and J. Grieve Smith (eds), *Managing the Global Economy* (Oxford: Oxford University Press).

Marx, K. and Engels, F. (1848) *The Communist Manifesto*.

Michie, J. and Wilkinson, F. (1995) 'Wages, government policy and unemployment', *Review of Political Economy*, 7(2) (April), pp. 133–49.

Singh, A. (1992) 'The political economy of growth', in J. Michie (ed.), *The Economic Legacy* (London: Academic Press).

Wilson, H. (1971) *The Labour Government 1964–70* (London: Weidenfeld & Nicolson).

10 The Relevance of Keynesian Policies in Semi-Industrialised Countries: Theoretical Issues and an Empirical Illustration

Amitava Krishna Dutt

INTRODUCTION*

In country after country in the developing world the state is being rolled back. At the insistence of the Bretton Woods institutions and with the blessings of most academic economists, government budgets are being slashed, monetary growth is being curbed, state enterprises are being privatised, and government controls on the private sector are being dismantled. This experience of the Third World is no different from that of the first and second worlds and seems to reflect global consensus on the role of the state in the economy. It would appear that, according to this consensus, Keynesian policies featuring the use of government fiscal and monetary instruments for economic expansion, and the 'socialization of investment', have no place in the Third World.

The purpose of this chapter is to contribute to the examination of the relevance of Keynesian policies for LDCs by examining their relevance for a subset of developing countries (given that the structure of all LDCs is not the same), the so-called 'semi-industrialised' countries (henceforth, SICs). It will do so by reviewing the role Keynesian ideas have played in development economics, by examining some theoretical issues to make the case that Keynesian economic policies are relevant for SICs, and by discussing the Indian case to illustrate the empirical relevance of the theoretical issues. Prior to that, however, we will first clarify what is meant in this chapter by Keynesian policies and by SICs.

Since the debate on general theoretical and empirical issues covers too broad a ground, and the main issues in it are well known (though clearly not resolved), this study will be confined to issues specifically relevant to LDCs in general and to SICs in particular.

KEYNESIAN POLICIES AND 'SEMI-INDUSTRIALISED' COUNTRIES

In this chapter Keynesian policies are taken to refer to policies that are suggested by the basic theoretical framework used by Keynes in the *General Theory*: that is, one in which the levels of output and employment in an economy are determined by the aggregate demand for goods, the level of aggregate demand depends in large part on business expectations regarding investment, and business expectations are formed in an uncertain environment and depend largely on the state of confidence of investors and speculators. Keynesian policies will then be interpreted as all those policies which deal with problems of economies suffering low levels of output, employment and growth as explained by this framework, and those that are mentioned by Keynes in the *General Theory*. Included are cheap money policies, deficit financing, increased government spending, government investment, and redistributive policies shifting the distribution of income towards poorer consumers with higher propensities to consume.

This definition of Keynesian policies is both broader and narrower than alternative definitions. It is broader than the definition which equates it to a policy package which exclusively consists of expansionary fiscal and monetary policies because it does not only refer to *expansionary* policies but to any policies which address issues raised in an economy analysed by Keynes, and because it does not imply that the pursuit of *only* fiscal/monetary policies is the panacea to the problem of underdevelopment. It is narrower than other definitions which rely on particular interpretations of Keynes's scattered writings on economic policy in general (see, for instance, the papers by Eatwell, Lekachman, Tobin and Galbraith in Wattel (1985) for some contrasting views), or which draw on Keynes's writings on various aspects of the problems of developing countries including international monetary and buffer stock policies (see Singer 1985; Thirlwall 1987), or which encompass almost all forms of state intervention in less-developed economies (Reddaway 1987).

It is commonplace to observe that LDCs, despite their similarity in having (relatively) low levels of per capita income, are an extremely heterogeneous group of economies, each with its own history and structure.

While this observation could lead us to the view that we can entertain no generalisations regarding them, but study only the economics of particular countries (or, in a more extreme version, of only local economies, thereby questioning the validity of macroeconomics), it appears more reasonable to settle for the compromise of generalising about a group of LDCs. This is the approach we will follow here by focusing on the group of LDCs that has been called SICs.

The term 'semi-industrialised country' has some currency in the literature on LDCs. Chenery and Syrquin (1986) have provided perhaps the most precise definition in terms of a cross-country model and use several measures which they select as benchmarks to mark the dividing line between an earlier, primary, stage and a later, semi-industrial, state. They focus on shifts in 'internal demand, exports, and production from the primary sector to manufacturing' (p. 85). Their main benchmark 'is the point at which the contribution of manufacturing to growth exceeds that of primary production. Supplementary benchmarks are a minimal per capita gross national product, or GNP (as a proxy for domestic demand for manufactures) and a minimal share of manufactures in exports and production' (see p. 86). They are flexible in taking into account differences in timing resulting from variations in size, resource endowments and development strategies, and also in including countries which fit two out of three of their benchmark criteria. Using this method they select 38 economies as having been semi-industrial in 1976, and this list cover a diverse set of countries including Venezuela, South Africa, Argentina, Brazil, Mexico, Turkey, South Korea, Egypt, China, India, Taiwan, Malaysia and Kenya (pp. 88–9). FitzGerald (1993) follows the Chenery–Syrquin definition, but points out that SICs broadly correspond to the group the World Bank categorises as 'middle-income economies'. However, this identification is not quite accurate. The World Bank's definition of middle-income economies includes countries with per capita GNP in 1992 in current dollars from $670 to $8000, which excludes India and China, with per capita incomes of $330 and $370, respectively.

Rather than define such economies in a precise manner, the term 'semi-industrialised country' refers here to an economy which has a large industrial sector (in terms of its share in GNP) with a relatively high degree of sophistication in terms of technology, organisation methods, and ability to find markets abroad, but which co-exists with a primary sector with poor and subsistence producers. The industrial sector relies to a considerable degree on imported capital goods, but the economy can meet most domestic consumption and basic intermediate requirements. Exports are not large enough to meet imports, and the economy depends on foreign capital inflows which are normally sufficient not to cause chronic import compression. I would expect that this imprecise definition roughly coincides with the Chenery–Syrquin definition.

KEYNESIAN ECONOMICS AND DEVELOPMENT ECONOMICS

Despite the fact that the rise of Keynesian economics may have provided some methodological support to the subdiscipline of development economics during its rise following the second World War – by questioning the validity of the notion of mono-economics (see Hirschman 1981), by shifting the focus of inquiry from the *allocation* of resources to their *mobilisation* as well as allocation, and by legitimising the use of activist state policies to cure the ills of free-market economies (see Singer 1985, 1987) – it made little or no substantive contribution to the subject in its early years. Keynesian economics, which was considered to be relevant for the short run, was generally perceived as being inapplicable to the long-run problems of development. Keynes (1936) himself had little to say about LDCs in *The General Theory* other than his reference to the preference for liquidity in India (p. 337) and to land having a high liquidity premium in the minds of owners of wealth in agricultural economies (p. 241).

The dominant theories in development economics in its early days stressed the need for state intervention to correct for market failures due to externalities and increasing returns, the interaction between advanced and backward sectors using a classical approach in which aggregate demand played no role (Lewis 1954), the problems of savings constraints, balance-of-payments constraints, and deteriorating international terms of trade (Furtado, 1964), and the problems caused by surplus transfers from LDCs to advanced economies (Baran, 1957). The so-called Harrod–Domar growth equation, which was used extensively by development planners, and has clear Keynesian roots, was used to justify higher savings rates and lower capital–output ratios rather than measures to stimulate aggregate demand. When demand factors were stressed at all, as by Rosenstein–Rodan (1943) and other balanced growth proponents in their proposals to co-ordinate investment decisions in different firms and industries, the ideas were derived more from intersectoral co-ordination problems due to market failures than from Keynesian aggregate demand considerations. Some planning models, such as open and semi-closed and even some dynamic Leontief models, which were widely used in development planning exercises, had Keynesian features in their analysis of intersectoral linkages in the absence of supply constraints and in their focus on material balance equations. However, the popularity of these models can perhaps be explained more by the inadequacy of computers to deal with non-linear, general equilibrium models than by a recognition of the relevance of Keynesian ideas.

Development economists in fact argued explicitly that Keynesian economics was not applicable to LDCs, which were often portrayed as subsistence economies not fitting the institutional characteristics of capitalist economies in which hired labour was used for production for making profits and in which savers and investors were different people and institutions (see V. K. R. V. Rao 1952; Das-Gupta 1954); thus, for them, the distinction between aggregate demand and aggregate supply was irrelevant. Moreover, it was argued that supply constraints due to shortages of wage-goods (consisting of agricultural products), capital-goods, working capital, skilled labour, and foreign exchange and government controls, rather than demand constraints, limited production and growth in LDCs (see V. K. R. V. Rao 1952). It is interesting to note that Kalecki, who arguably provided an earlier and better (at least for modern capitalist economies) theory of demand-determined output than did Keynes, and who wrote extensively on the economics of developing countries (see Kalecki 1976), stressed supply (such as capacity constraints and the problem of inflation due to wage goods constraints) rather than demand constraints for LDCs. Demand constraints were argued to be irrelevant because of high levels of population in LDCs, and because of low levels of per capita income which implied that most consumption 'needs' were unmet (Das-Gupta 1954). Finally, Das-Gupta (1954) argued that while Keynes's theory took the money wage to be fixed, unemployment in LDCs was due to a fixed real wage which was determined by minimum subsistence, and was hence of a classical, rather than Keynesian, variety.

In the 1970s and 1980s, partly perhaps as a result of changes in the structures of many LDCs (especially SICs), partly because of the perceived failures of earlier development theories to deal with the problems of LDCs which seemed to be facing demand-side problems (see Bagchi 1970; and Chakravarty 1979a, who analysed the Indian situation), and partly because of the growing popularity of formal non-orthodox macroeconomic theories drawing on the work of Marx and Kalecki, in addition to that of Keynes, development economists increasingly began to accept the relevance of Keynesian aggregate demand issues for LDCs (see Bell 1979; Rakshit 1982, 1989; Taylor 1983, 1991; Dutt 1984; FitzGerald 1993). Some in fact argued that the fragmented nature of commodity markets and credit markets (Rakshit 1989), the uncertainty generated by the instability of the growth process caused by the existence of a multiplicity of constraints (Bagchi 1988), and the importance of assets such as land, gold and precious metals (see Taylor 1983; Rakshit 1989) which provide potential investors in LDCs with opportunities to divert their assets to unproductive channels in the face of this uncertainty, arguably made aggregate demand issues highly relevant for LDCs.

The claim that the institutional characteristics of LDCs, especially SICs, made Keynesian economics irrelevant for them is rejected outright in this new approach, given that these economies have developed industrial sectors which produce with hired labour with the objective of making profits, and since firms make investment decisions based on market prospects and profitability, while savers (households as well as firms) save to hold financial and other assets. SICs, as defined above, can also have large subsistence primary sectors, but this merely implies that one should explicitly incorporate such sectors in macro-models for SICs and not simply reject the relevance of the distinction between aggregate demand and aggregate supply.

The third and latest stage in the evolution of the subdiscipline of development economics can be called the stage of neoclassical resurgence. There are two branches of this resurgence, one microeconomic in nature and the other macroeconomic.

The first branch, with precursors in Lal (1985), Little (1982) and others, and which is reflected recently in World Bank (1991), argues that excessive state intervention in LDCs explains the poor performance of LDCs. While this branch takes its aim at many kinds of state intervention in LDCs, and is not specifically directed at Keynesian policies, it does have implications for the relevance of Keynesian policies in LDCs. As Srinivasan (1993) argues, Keynesian demand problems cannot arise for a small economy which can export any amount it wants to at the price given in world markets. He then argues that if LDCs are small economies and if they cannot increase their exports it must be due to the fact that government policy-induced distortions prevent them from increasing exports.

The second branch points out that expansionary fiscal and monetary policies result in inflation (and sometimes even hyperinflation) and in explosive internal government and external debt situations, with drastic implications for growth in LDCs. This branch is reflected repeatedly in the policy advice given to LDC governments by the IMF, advice which makes LDCs cut government spending and subsidies, put curbs on money supply growth, and undergo devaluation. Such contractionary policies, of course, are recommended in periods in which particular LDCs experience balance of payments problems (which is what makes them turn to the IMF in the first place). The general policy advice of the Bretton Woods institutions (see World Bank 1991) is to maintain macroeconomic stability, and not indulge in populist, expansionary policies.

SOME THEORETICAL CONSIDERATIONS

To fix ideas about the Keynesian approach to SICs, and to address some of the issues raised in the previous section, consider a simple model which has become a standard work-horse in post-Keynesian analyses.[1] Take a closed economy with one sector,[2] which produces an industrial good with capital and labour with fixed coefficients of production. There are two classes, capitalists who receive non-wage income and save a constant fraction of their income (firms may also be interpreted as saving for them), and workers who earn wage income and do not save. Industrial firms are assumed to set their price as a fixed mark-up on unit labour costs and normally to hold excess capital. Firms invest, paying attention to profitability, market prospects and interest rates which are fixed by the monetary authorities.

In the short run output varies to equate demand and supply in the goods market. Short-run equilibrium thus implies

$$u = [1/(1+z)]u + (1-s)[z/(1+z)]u + \alpha + \beta[z/(1+z)] + \gamma u \tag{10.1}$$

where u is the rate of capacity utilisation measured as a ratio of output to capital stock, z is the mark-up charged by firms, s is the savings rate of capitalists, and the last three terms denote investment and government expenditure as a ratio of capital stock as a linear function of profitability (measured by the profit share) and markets (measured by the capacity utilisation rate). Autonomous expenditure is measured by α (which depends on the given rate of interest, the state of business confidence not affected by current profitability and capacity utilisation and government expenditure), and β and γ are positive constants. The short-run equilibrium value of the capacity utilisation rate is therefore given by

$$u = \frac{\alpha + \beta[z/(1+z)]}{[z/(1+z)]s - \gamma} \tag{10.2}$$

In the short run capital stock, K, is given, so that the level of output is determined as uK, and the level of employment is determined as $b_n uK$, where b_n is the fixed labour: output ratio in the industrial sector. In the long run capital accumulation is determined by the investment rate. Assuming away depreciation of capital, the rate of growth of the economy is given by

$$g_n = \alpha + \beta[z/(1+z)] + \gamma u \tag{10.3}$$

where u is determined in equation (10.2). This simple framework shows that the rate of growth of capital and output, measured by g_n, can be increased by expansionary fiscal and monetary policies, and by reducing uncertainty; all of these will have a positive effect on u and g_n by increasing α. Redistributive policies may – but need not necessarily – increase the growth rate by reducing z. It is to be noted that long-run growth depends on aggregate demand as in numerous other neo-Keynesian growth models; unlike what early development economists argued, the relevance of demand is not confined only to the short run.[3]

A problem with this model is that it abstracts from all supply constraints which were argued to be relevant for LDCs, because it assumes that excess capacity always persists; that there is only one input, and no skilled labour, working capital or infrastructure; there is only one sector, thereby ruling out agricultural constraints; and that we have assumed a closed economy, which makes foreign exchange constraints irrelevant. However, there is nothing in our definition of SICs which suggests that these assumptions are generally valid; indeed, an important strand of the argument against the relevance of Keynesian policies for LDCs made by early development economists was regarding supply constraints. To evaluate the relevance of the Keynesian model when supply-side factors are taken into account we can modify the model to introduce supply constraints into it. We do so, for simplicity, one at a time, considering in turn capital, agricultural, balance of payments and fiscal constraints, which have been quite extensively dealt with in the literature.

Regarding capital constraints, it is often pointed out that the basic problem of LDCs is the shortage of capital, not effective demand. Although it is no doubt the case that LDCs suffer from a shortage of capital as measured by the stock of capital per capita, it is not clear that this shortage of capital is due to low levels of saving supply or low levels of investment demand; if the latter is the case aggregate demand is obviously of relevance. There is, however, an alternative definition of the shortage of capital that takes the economy to be at full capacity; in terms of our model this implies that the equilibrium level of u determined by equation (10.2) exceeds the technologically possible maximum which we denote by u_k. In this case, since output is capacity constrained, the price level is flexible, and it will increase to clear the goods market. If the money wage is fixed the price level, and hence the mark-up, z, will adjust so that he equilibrium real wage will be given by

$$V^* = \frac{1}{b_n}\,\frac{(s-\gamma)u_K - (\alpha+\beta)}{s\,u_K - \beta} \tag{10.4}$$

and the equilibrium growth rate by

$$g_n = \alpha + \beta(1 - V^* b_n) + \gamma u_K \tag{10.5}$$

Aside from the fact that it is not very clear what is precisely meant by 'full' capacity, one can question whether this model appropriately represents LDCs. First, if one allows for substitution between capital and labour in the relevant range, there is no reason why the 'full' capacity level should be fixed. Second, even if such an equilibrium sometimes prevails, it is an empirical question whether it is always the correct model to use for SICs. If autonomous demand happens to be high, the economy may be driven to some 'full' capacity level, but there is no reason – at least not in the model given in equations (10.1) and (10.3) – why this must necessarily be the case: even if there are population pressures in many such economies and per capita incomes are low (so that there are many unsatisfied consumption 'needs'), as noted by some critics, demand depends on real income and effective demand rather than on numbers of people and their 'needs'. But even if the SIC economy is better described by the model of equations (10.4) and (10.5), when Keynesian policies increase α, equation (10.4) implies that this reduces V^* (as long as the money wage does not rise equiproportionately with the price level) and this increases the rate of growth of K and output.

Regarding the agricultural constraint, critics of Keynesian policies have argued that demand expansion may simply increase the price of agricultural goods since the supply of such goods is constrained by institutional barriers. To examine this issue, following Taylor (1983; see also Rakshit 1982), we add an agricultural sector to our model. Assume that in this non-capitalist sector sharecroppers pay a fraction Θ of their production to landlords. Assume further that the level of agricultural output, X_a, is given in the short run, and that its growth rate is given exogenously by institutional factors. If s also denotes the savings rate out of agricultural rent income and sharecropper farmers do not save, if there is no investment in the agricultural sector, if all consumers spend a fixed fraction, μ, of their consumption expenditure on the industrial good and the rest on the agricultural good, and if we maintain all the other assumptions of our basic model, short-run equilibrium in the economy, where both agricultural and industrial markets clear by price and output changes respectively, implies:

$$- \{1 - \mu[(1 - (1 - s)z)/(1 + z)] - \gamma\}u + \mu(1 - s\Theta)kp + \alpha + \beta z/(1 + z) = 0 \tag{10.6}$$

and

$$(1 - \mu)[(1 - (1 - s)z)/(1 + z)]u - [\mu + s\Theta(1 - \mu)]kp = 0 \tag{10.7}$$

where $p = P_a/P_n$ and $k = X_a/K_n$. In this model with a fix-price industrial sector and a flex-price agricultural sector, equation (10.6) clears due to variations in u and (10.7) due to variations in p. In the short run, given the level of k, the equilibrium level of u is given by:

$$u = \frac{\alpha + \beta z/(1+z)}{1 - \gamma - [1 + (1-s)z]/(1+z)[1 + s\Theta(1-\mu)/\mu]} \tag{10.8}$$

and the equilibrium value of p is given by

$$p = \frac{\alpha+\beta z/(1+z)}{k\{[(1-\gamma)(1+z)[s\Theta+\mu/(1-\mu)]/[1+(1-s)z]]-[\mu/(1-\mu)]\}} \tag{10.9}$$

In the long run k changes according to the equation

$$(dk/dt)/k = g_a - g_n \tag{10.10}$$

where t denotes time and where g_a is the exogenous institutionally given rate of agricultural growth. Since u is independent of k, as shown by equation (10.8), and as equation (10.3) still applies, g_n is also independent of k. Depending on the levels at which the parameters of the model, including α and g_a, are fixed, g_n may exceed or be less than g_a. If g_n exceeds g_a (as is the case with most SICs) so that k falls over time, the terms of trade move in favour of the agricultural sector (that is, p goes up), but by our assumption that the total consumption of agricultural goods remains the same for a given amount of total expenditure (implying a unit price elasticity of demand for both goods), there is no effect on the real demand for the industrial good, so that u and g_n remain unaffected. In this case, when Keynesian policies are used to increase α, as equations (10.8)and (10.9) show, equilibrium u and p both increase in the short run given k so that, by equation (10.3) g_n increases. Over the long run the average rate of growth rises both because g_n rises and because the share of the industrial sector in total output at constant prices rises.

It may be objected that the assumption that the demand for agricultural goods has a unit price elasticity is unrealistic in LDCs; it is more likely that a rise in p will imply that the share of total consumption expenditure spent on agricultural goods will rise implying a price-inelastic demand for agricultural goods. To take this into account we assume that μ depends inversely on p. In this case, provided that the agricultural good is not too price-inelastic, it can be shown that $du/dk > 0$ (since a higher agricultural output depresses p but increases μ, thereby raising the real demand for the industrial good), so from equation (10.3) it follows that g_n now depends positively on k. Now, if we continue assuming that g_a is exogenously given by institutional forces, the long-run equilibrium value of k will be found when $g_n = g_a$, and it can be shown to be stable. Expansionary Keynesian policies which increase α will, in the short run, increase both u and g_n. In the long run this will reduce k, increase p, shift consumption expenditure towards the agricultural sector, thereby reducing u and g_n; in long-run equilibrium, since g_a is unchanged, g_n will return to its initial level, and so will u, as seen from equation (10.3). Thus agriculture does constrain industrial growth, but this is not to say that no industrial gains are being made: there is a short-run rise in industrial growth and the economy is, in the new long-run equilibrium, more industrialised.

We may take the discussion a step further by asking whether g_a is actually given exogenously be institutional factors. Though the determinants of agricultural growth in an SIC are complex, consider two possibilities that have been discussed in the literature. If we assume that more favourable relative prices induce farmers to increase agricultural production more rapidly (due to the quicker adoption of new techniques and labour-based capital accumulation in the form of, say, irrigation), as k increases, since p falls, g_a falls. This implies that a rise in α will have the long-run effect, as before, of reducing k, but since at the new long-run equilibrium g_a will be higher (due to p being higher), g_n will also be higher. Alternatively, assume that agricultural growth is constrained by the provision of infrastructure (in the form of, say, irrigation and technological extension services) by the government. Assume also that government spending on such infrastructure is constrained by government revenues which depend in major part on industrial production (as is the case in India, where there is no agricultural income tax). In this case it can be shown that expansionary Keynesian policies which increase industrial demand, capacity utilisation, tax revenues and hence government infrastructural investment in agriculture, can raise the long-run growth rate of the economy (see Dutt 1991; J. M. Rao 1993).

Balance of payments issues can readily be introduced into our framework by assuming (see Taylor 1983, 1991) that the SIC imports intermediate goods as a fixed proportion of output, capital goods as a fixed proportion of investment, and consumption goods for capitalists and agricultural rent receivers. Furthermore, assume that the SIC exports industrial goods, and exports (as a ratio of capital stock) depend on world demand and on competitiveness: that is, domestic price, the exchange rate and the price of foreign substitutes. It can then be shown that if the economy has a maximum possible level of trade deficit as a proportion of capital stock or output (determined, for instance, by prudent capital inflows) its growth can be constrained in one of three ways: (i) by a demand constraint in which excess capacity prevails and when the maximum trade deficit is not reached; (ii) by a savings constraint in which full capacity utilisation prevails and the maximum trade deficit is not reached; or (iii) by a foreign exchange constraint when there is excess capacity and perhaps excess demand and the maximum trade deficit is reached. This model is a variant of the structuralist two-gap model, but one in which demand factors play a role which they did not in the structuralist framework.

In an economy depicted by this model it is not always the case that the foreign exchange gap will be binding. When it is not, demand factors may be relevant in promoting growth if excess capacity prevails and the economy is demand constraint. If the economy is capacity constrained, expansionary policies may increase growth but be inflationary, and possibly worsen the balance of payments situation by reducing exports and possibly by increasing imports; but this may not be a problem if the economy is not balance of payments constrained. If the economy is balance of payments constrained, demand factors are still relevant in at least two ways. First, it is not as if the economy 'hits' a physically-given balance of payments constraints; various things can be done in the short run which prevent it from 'hitting' it, such as running down reserves, getting access to new sources of financing in an active way and, more relevant for our purposes, contractionary policies. Here again, Keynesian demand management becomes of crucial importance, not only in the obvious sense that contractionary policies have to be pursued to reduce balance of payments deficits, but also in the sense that such policies can be used in ways that can have the lowest cost to the economy in terms of growth potential and social effects. Second, some of the parameters which affect the balance of payments constraints are themselves affected by demand factors. Exports, which can be argued to depend on competitiveness, which in turn depends on productivity growth in a broad sense, can be linked at least partly to Kaldor–Verdoorn type demand effects. Regarding imports, it is arguable that economic growth and higher levels of learning will be associated with lower import coefficients. Foreign capital flows, which depend on business confidence, make Keynesian uncertainty highly relevant. Policies that are credible and stabilising will presumably lead to greater investor confidence and thus to great capital inflows. Direct foreign investment – arguably the most stable kind of foreign capital flow – has been found quite generally to come to economies which have experienced sustained growth which can be achieved, among other things, by demand expansion.

Finally, to incorporate fiscal constraints, the basic model can be extended by introducing government taxes and expenditures including capital expenditures which have crowding-in effects on private investment (see Taylor 1991). If we assume that there is a maximum public sector borrowing requirement (PSBR) which is feasible, the economy can be shown to be constrained by an additional, fiscal constraint: when the maximum PSBR constraint is hit, the government cuts capital expenditures and this reduces private investment and hence the growth rate.

Although it is no doubt the case that some SICs may have unsustainable government deficits, maximum limits to PSBR ratios should be viewed with some scepticism. Expansionary Keynesian policies can make economies grow out of government debt (see Dutt and You 1995) unless the economy is balance of payments constrained, and financial crowding-out can be prevented with the use of financial 'repression' as well.

To summarise our argument so far, the existence of a number of constraints implies that an SIC may sometimes be constrained by demand, but it may sometimes be constrained by other factors such as capital, foreign exchange, agricultural growth or fiscal problems. However, there are reasons to question the existence of these 'binding' constraints, and some of them may bind only as a consequence of government policies which restrict economic expansion fearing their existence. Moreover, some of the long-run parameters which define these other constraints are not immutably given, but arguably determined by demand growth.

The multiplicity of constraints also implies that when exogenous parameters are changed by shocks (say, from the world economy, by weather conditions, or by internal political disturbances), the economy can switch from one constraint to another. As Bagchi (1988: 256–8) has argued, exogenous shocks affect a number of constraints which, directly and indirectly through government policy responses, introduces greater uncertainty into the economy, which in turn can reduce private investor confidence and the confidence of foreign investors, as well as that of the government in its attempt to negotiate the dangerous curves of its desirable growth path. Thus, in the presence of the multiplicity of potential constraints, and of instabilities affecting them, aggregate demand may be more depressed than it would have been in their absence, which may make it likely that the economy will be demand-constrained more often than in the absence of the multiplicity of supply constraints (as, for instance, if only the capital constraint were relevant).

We conclude this section by addressing some issues raised in the context of the recent neoclassical resurgence in development economics.

On the general argument regarding state intervention and microeconomic inefficiency, the argument in its strong form – that in the absence of state intervention all development problems would disappear – can be questioned on a myriad of theoretical and empirical grounds even for relatively advanced economies, let alone LDCs, and there is no need to rehash such well-worn issues here. Even if some validity is given to the argument in its weak form –

that government intervention has some deleterious consequences for economic performance – there is no reason why the implications of such arguments cannot be examined using our Keynesian model. For instance, the relaxation of industrial licensing restrictions can be represented by an increase in α in our model, which will increase capacity utilisation and growth by increasing investment demand. Other industrial liberalisation policies may improve industrial efficiency and speed up technological change, and the consequences will depend on the effects of such changes on profitability, and investment incentives not captured by profitability. While higher rates of growth can occur, that is not a necessary outcome: it is possible that labour-saving technological change can increase open unemployment, reduce the real wage, and slow down growth by reducing aggregate/demand in what has been called a wage-led or stagnationist growth regime.

Concerning the more specific small open economy critique it is not clear that all SICs are small open economies in the sense that they can export any amount they wish to (if there is enough supply) at the going world price. SICs, as mentioned above, may export some primary products but will have diversified into the export of manufactured goods. While there may be supply constraints for primary products, as well as demand constraints if individual SICs export a large share of total world exports, for manufactured goods it is arguably more appropriate to think in terms of models of monopolistic competition and oligopoly than in terms of price-taking competitive behaviour: the problems of breaking into distant foreign markets are well known even in the absence of trade restrictions.

Regarding the macroeconomic branch, it is no doubt the case that if an SIC finds that it is up against a balance of payments crisis, as reflected, for instance, by an inability to repay loans that have to be repaid, it will have to compress its imports and appeal to the IMF to provide some financing and to give it the stamp of approval which will help it to get financing from elsewhere. Both will imply contractionary policies which are unavoidable. While this is not likely to controversial, it is quite a different issue whether in normal situations, when foreign exchange crises do not loom large, governments should follow a policy of containing aggregate/demand growth.

THE CASE OF INDIA

The previous section has argued that there are theoretical grounds on which to argue that Keynesian policies may be relevant for SICs. Whether or not they actually are, however, is an empirical issue, and one that requires us to turn to the actual experience of SICs. This section considers the case of India to suggest that, at least for that country, they are indeed relevant.

Early analyses of Indian development issues focused on the need to increase the savings rate and to shift the composition of investment towards the investment goods sector, and India embarked on a period of planned, state-led development during which the saving rate was raised significantly and a heavy-industry base was developed. However, after a couple of decades of planned development, many observers of the Indian economy came to the conclusion that, despite some progress, India's performance both in terms of growth and social indicators left much to be desired.

After it was noticed that since the mid-1960s there had occurred a deceleration in India's economic – especially industrial – growth, there was wide agreement that India's economic performance was being constrained by a number of factors. A lively and controversial literature developed on this issue (see Bardhan 1984; Ahluwalia 1985; and the contributions in Nayyar 1994). Some analysts laid the blame on the agricultural sector, and argued that it stifled growth both from the demand side by restricting the market for industrial goods, and from the supply side especially through a wage goods constraint. Others focused on cuts in government expenditure, especially government investment expenditure, due to large increases in subsidies necessitated by India's complex political economy. Yet others concentrated on the link between an unequal distribution income and a narrow home market which dampened investment incentives and constrained growth. Finally, some focused on microeconomic inefficiencies resulting from government intervention which led to low productivity, low rates of technological change and low growth in exports.

One important characteristic of this debate was that demand-side factors were being suggested as constraints on growth in addition to supply-side factors, marking a sharp change from the earlier preoccupation with the latter. Many of the contributors explicitly noted the relevance of low levels of consumption, investment and government demand in causing low rates of capacity utilisation, accumulation and growth. Raj (1976) and Chakravarty (1979b) both stressed the importance of demand and the role of the poor performance of the agricultural sector in depressing industrial demand in explaining low rates of industrial growth. Bagchi (1970) and Nayyar (1978) argued that an unequal distribution of income reduced the demand for mass-consumption goods, resulting in excess capacity utilisation, and reduced investment incentives and hence industrial growth. Finally, Srinivasan and Narayana (1977) and Bardhan (1984) argued that a reduction in government investment spending reduced industrial growth. The agrarian, income distribution, and fiscal constraint arguments do not necessarily invoke demand-side factors: agricultural stagnation can depress industrial growth through a profit squeeze along Lewis lines; income inequality can reduce growth by affecting the productivity of labour due to effects similar to efficiency wage effects; and government investment can depress growth by reducing the productivity of industrial capital without affecting demand. However, in the Indian discussion demand did play an important role in all these arguments.

There has been an extensive debate about the relative importance of these different constraints on Indian growth (see, for instance, Bardhan 1984; Ahluwalia 1985). In addition to rather inconclusive debates of an informal nature, there have been some attempts to choose between constraints using more rigorous econometric and other simulation modelling techniques. The evidence suggests that it is best to accept the hypothesis that several of the constraints described above may be relevant for India in the sense that India's growth rate may be improved by relaxing them. For instance, Ray (1991) finds that wage goods, demand, and infrastructure supply are all statistically significant in explaining variations in manufacturing production in India during 1950–51 to 1983–84.

The fact that demand factors are relevant is suggested also by other kinds of empirical work. In the industrial sector there have been periods with a very large amount of excess capacity in several key industries. Theoretically it is possible for excess capacity to be explained by a number of factors, including the shortage of intermediate goods including imported components and power, and due to industrial licensing policies that induce firms to maintain excess capacity to garner a larger share of licences. While both of these explanations have been suggested for the Indian case, detailed industry-level empirical analysis suggests the relevance of supply as well as demand constraints in Indian industry. Moreover, there is much evidence to suggest that industrial prices and mark-up tend to be sticky in the organised sector (Chatterji 1989; Balakrishnan 1991). The shortage of working capital can also be used to explain excess capacity in Indian industry, and at first glance the prevalence of credit controls in a financially-repressed economy may suggest that this in indeed the case. However, a more careful analysis suggests that money supply is determined by demand as in post-Keynesian analyses of endogenous money, if we incorporate selective credit controls as a determinant of desired accumulation by firms (Balakrishnan 1991).

One can also approach this issue by examining what happened in the Indian economy subsequently.[4] India's economic growth, especially industrial growth, picked up significantly in the late 1970s and 1980s. GDP growth in real terms increased from an annual average of 3.4 per cent during 1970–80 to 5.4 per cent for 1980–91. This increase in the growth rate is found for all the major sectors, although not as strikingly in the agricultural sector. Industrial growth increased from 4.5 per cent per annum to 6.3 per cent, while manufacturing growth increased from 4.6 to 6.7 per cent. Using a variety of different series of industrial production, I examined log-linear trends with break years (taken as knot locations so that there are no discontinuities in trend values) at 1965 and 1980. The results show that the growth rate is lower in the middle period (1965–80) than in the earlier or later periods, and that the differences in growth rates are statistically significant at the 95 per cent level of significance.

To ascertain what explains this higher rate of growth, consider, in turn, the determinants of industrial growth as suggested by the earlier debates.

Regarding the agricultural sector, the increase in per capita production in agriculture during the 1980s has been near 1 per cent. Ahluwalia (1991) draws on other studies to show that, adjusted for inflation, there was no real growth in per capita rural income from the 1970s to the mid-1980s. The data on agricultural production show that there has been an increase in the annual average rate of agricultural growth from 1.8 per cent to 3.2 per cent. However, my regression estimates with a knot location in 1978 show that while the growth rate of agriculture between 1950 and 1978 was 2.55 per cent and that between 1979 and 1991 was 3.13 per cent, this difference is not statistically significant at the 95 per cent confidence level (being significant only at the 90 per cent level). This finding corroborates those of similar earlier studies (see Ahluwalia 1991). Thus it is unlikely that the agricultural sector gave a big demand push to the industrial sector in the 1980s. That the sector did not create a wage goods constraint is explained by the food distribution policy of the government, the possibly worsening distribution of income which kept the demand for food low,[5] and the low level of employment growth during the 1980s.

Turning to income distribution, there seems to have occurred no marked improvement, although absolute poverty probably fell in the 1980s due to public programmes. Estimates of the shares of household income or expenditure by percentile groups of households (despite differences in methodology used) reveal a steady increase in the share of the lowest 20 per cent from at least the mid-1960s, and this tendency continues into the 1980s. The earlier tendency of the share of the highest 20 per cent to fall, however, appears to have been reversed in the 1980s. In fact there appear to be some further signs of a recent increase in inequality, especially in urban areas, reflected in rising Gini coefficients and a rising (falling) share of expenditure of the highest (lowest) 20 per cent. Evidence of a rise in the savings rate in the later 1980s, a reduction in the income elasticity of the demand for food, a slowdown in employment growth, especially in the private organised manufacturing sector (which in fact fell annually at 0.6 per cent between 1981 and 1991), and the growing informalisation of employment (the share of employment in the unorganised sector for every major sector increased between 1981 and 1991), also suggest a worsening of income distribution. Thus it is unlikely that distributional changes could have resulted in a change in industrial growth, either by improving it or by worsening it dramatically.

Ahluwalia (1991: 86) argues that during the second half of the 1970s, and more so in the 1980s, there was an acceleration of growth in government infrastructural investment. In fact, during the 1980s the government pursued expansionary fiscal policies. During 1980–91, general government consumption expenditure grew at 7.5 per cent per year in real terms, compared to 4.1 per cent during 1970–80. As a proportion of GDP general government consumption increased from 9 per cent in 1970 to 12 per cent in 1991. There were also increases in interest payments and subsidies. Public administration, defence and other services have grown rapidly in the 1980s: its annual growth at 7.4 per cent during 1985–86 to 1989–90 surpassed all components of GDP except banking, insurance and real estate.

As pointed out earlier, an influential hypothesis explaining low levels of growth, and industrial growth in particular, is the highly autarkic and regulatory policy framework of the government. Since the late 1970s and during the 1980s there has been some amount of liberalisation in India. In particular, there have been relaxations of the industrial licensing apparatus, some liberalisation of import licensing, provision of incentives for exports, and greater support for schemes of modernisation of enterprises through foreign technical collaborations. The 1980s experienced an increase in productivity growth in manufacturing, in addition to increases in the rate of growth of industrial production. Several writers have drawn a connection between liberalisation and higher growth (see Ahluwalia 1991). Relaxation of controls in capacity expansion and in technical collaborations presumably boosted investment demand. Incentives for exports arguably increased export growth and further provided an impetus to demand. Relaxation on imports of inputs also led output growth.

While there certainly has been some connection between liberalisation and growth, this linkage should not be exaggerated. First, as supporters of liberalisation have complained, liberalisation in the 1980s has been half-hearted and slow and it would be difficult to argue at the same time that such policy changes were the major explanation for higher growth. Second, liberalisation is supposed to encourage growth mainly by improving industrial efficiency. In an economy in which industry is constrained by demand, this can happen if there is a sufficient increase in exports, or a sufficient boost in investment; otherwise there is the danger that slower labour absorption (as has happened in India) may reduce income of lower income groups (as may have happened to a limited degree) and thus cause industrial stagnation. That this has not happened is primarily due to the fact that there has been an increase in government spending, which has maintained effective demand. Third, it is not obvious that all the growth in productivity can be attributed to liberalisation. Ahluwalia (1991) finds that cross-industry differences in total factor productivity growth can be largely attributed to value added growth, revealing the importance of increasing returns to scale and learning effects of the Kaldor–Verdoorn type. The regression results show that this effect has become stronger in the 1980s. Thus higher growth may have led to higher productivity growth rather than the other way around.

Thus expansionary fiscal policy seems to be the main factor explaining the growth spurt. This was not due to a containment of subsidies and transfer payments by overcoming political pressures, but was in fact made possible by a rapid expansion of government internal and foreign debt. The abandonment of earlier caution in fact reflected the growing pressures on the state, which became more populist as political uncertainty increased, especially in the later years of the decade (see Kohli 1990). It has been argued that this increase in the public debt may be unsustainable, especially in view of the fact that the economy could not grow itself out of the problem because of foreign exchange constraints on expansion. Moreover, growth was not accompanied by a breakthrough on the export front. Thus economic expansion, which increased imports at a time when remittance inflows and concessional foreign aid were falling, implied a rapid increase in foreign borrowing on commercial terms. This increase in international indebtedness placed the economy in a precarious situation, in which exogenous shocks could quickly bring about an international liquidity crisis and require quick economic stabilisation programmes which imply a reduction in growth rate and also, because of cuts in social spending, distributional problems as well. This is precisely what brought the growth spurt to an end, when the Gulf crisis of 1990 increased the value of oil imports and reduced remittances, and domestic political instability had an adverse impact on international confidence, leading to the downgrading of India's credit rating and to non-resident Indian capital flight (see Joshi and Little 1994). It thus appears that although demand growth due to increasing government spending was the major factor, it is probably not sustainable in the long run. However, this suggests that demand growth by itself is not the answer to development problems. It has to be accompanied by improvements in efficiency, by greater resource mobilisation efforts, and more rapid agricultural growth.

Returning to Srinivasan's (1993) argument, even if one accepts the claim that all distortions are the result of government interventions, one cannot simply wish away the distortions! The pace and nature of economic reform, as any observer of India's political economy knows, is dictated by a variety of political economic constraints (see Kohli 1990). Moreover, after economic reforms are undertaken, changes in the relevant elasticities and prices cannot be expected to be immediate! At least before such changes abolish demand problems it is surely wise to acknowledge the existence of demand-constraints on output and growth, and to try to influence growth through Keynesian policies.

CONCLUSION

This chapter has argued, using theoretical arguments and an empirical illustration from India, that Keynesian policies are far from irrelevant for semi-industrialised economies.

Under general conditions a careful but not overly cautious Keynesian expansionary stance is good for growth, if accompanied by complementary policies such as those which deal with industrial efficiency at the microeconomic level, especially for increasing exports, and land reforms for increasing agricultural productivity and growth. While the pursuit of Keynesian policies of effective demand management by themselves cannot be an answer to the development problems of SICs, in overcoming them Keynesian insights and policies must play a major role.

Supply constraints to growth in SICs should not be ignored. In some cases exogenous shocks may and do disrupt growth processes by adversely affecting the supply side, through agricultural and balance of payments shocks, for instance. When such shocks occur, careful Keynesian demand-management policies may also be called for to impose a brake on the growth process while minimising the damage to long-run growth prospects. However, many of the supply constraints over the long run can be relaxed through the use of expansionary demand policies, and the failure to take this into account can make the economy more susceptible to them.

Notes

* I am grateful to Gaurav Anand, Philip Arestis, Laurence Harris, Jaime Ros, Malcolm Sawyer, Ajit Singh and Anthony Thirlwall for comments and discussions.

1. It cannot be claimed that this model is faithful to Keynes's analysis in the *General Theory*. Indeed, it is closer to the framework developed by Kalecki (1971), since it assumes imperfect competition, fixed coefficients of production, and class-specific consumption patterns. Nevertheless, the framework is Keynesian in the sense that it takes output and employment to be determined by aggregate demand, and it makes investment depend on expectational factors.
2. A self-contained informal sector may be present as well, containing some of the workers not employed by the formal industrial sector considered explicitly in the model. We assume, for simplicity, that there are no other links between this informal sector and the formal sector.
3. It may also be noted that in this model the real wage is given at the level $1/b_n(1+z)$. This undermines Das-Gupta's (1954) argument about the incompatibility of unemployment due to insufficient aggregate demand and a fixed real wage referred to above.
4. The following discussion draws on Dutt (1994).
5. Income distributional changes that have occurred in the 1970s has shifted consumption towards non-food products, and the aggregate income elasticity of demand for food was reduced from 0.5 to 0.29 (Sen 1991).

References

Ahluwalia, I. J. (1985). *Industrial Growth in India. Stagnation since the Mid-Sixties* (Delhi: Oxford University Press).

Ahluwalia, I. J. (1991) *Productivity and Growth in Indian Manufacturing* (Delhi: Oxford University Press).

Bagchi, A. K. (1970) 'Long-term constraints on India's industrial growth', in E. A. G. Robinson and M. Kidron (eds), *Economic Development in South Asia* (London: Macmillan).

Bagchi, A. K. (1988) 'Problems of effective demand and contradictions of planning in India', in A. K. Bagchi (ed.), *The Economy, Society and Polity. Essays in the Political Economy of Indian Planning* (Calcutta: Oxford University Press).

Balakrishnan, P. (1991) *Pricing and Inflation in India* (Delhi: Oxford University Press).

Baran, P. (1957) *The Political Economy of Growth*, 2nd ed (New York: Monthly Review Press).

Bardhan, P. K. (1984) *The Political Economy of Development in India* (Oxford: Oxford University Press).

Bell, C. (1979) 'The behavior of a dual economy under different "closing rules"', *Journal of Development Economics*, 6, pp. 47–72.

Chakravarty, S. (1979a) 'Keynes, "Classics", and the Developing Economies', in C. H. Hanumantha Rao and P. C. Joshi (eds), *Reflections on Economic Development and Social Change. Essays in Honour of V. K. R. V. Rao* (New Delhi: Allied Publishers).

Chakravarty, S. (1979b) 'On the question of home market and prospects for Indian growth', *Economic and Political Weekly*, XIV. (30, 31 and 32) pp. 1229–42, reprinted in D. Nayyar (ed.) (1994), *Industrial Growth and Stagnation* (Bombay: Oxford University Press).

Chatterji, R. (1989) *The Behaviour of Industrial Prices in India* (Delhi: Oxford University Press).

Chenery, H. and M. Syrquin (1986) 'Semi-industrial countries', in H. Chenery, S. Robinson and M. Syrquin, *Industrialization and Growth. A Comparative Study* (New York: Oxford University Press, for the World Bank).

Das-Gupta, A. K. (1954) 'Keynesian economics and under-developed countries', *Economic Weekly*, 26 January, reprinted in A. K. Das-Gupta, *Planning and Economic Growth* (London: George Allen & Unwin).

Dutt, A. K. (1984) 'Stagnation, income distribution and monopoly power', *Cambridge Journal of Economics*, 8(1) (March), pp. 25–40.

Dutt, A. K. (1991) 'Stagnation, income distribution and the agrarian constraint', *Cambridge Journal of Economics*, 15(3) (September), pp. 343–51.

Dutt, A. K. (1994) 'Growth, distribution and the role of the state: the Indian case', unpublished, Helsinki: World Institute of Development Economics Research.

Dutt, A. K. and You, J.-I. (1995) 'The dynamics of government debt and deficits: a post Keynesian view', unpublished, Notre Dame: University of Notre Dame.

FitzGerald, E. V. K. (1993) *The Macroeconomics of Development Finance. A Kaleckian Analysis of the Semi-Industrialized Economy* (London: Macmillan).

Furtado, C. (1964) *Development and Underdevelopment* (Berkeley: University of California Press).

Hirschman, A. O. (1981) 'The rise and decline of development economics', in A. O. Hirschman, *Essays in Trespassing: Economics to Politics and Beyond* (Cambridge: Cambridge University Press).

Joshi, V. and Little, I. M. D. (1994) *India. Macroeconomics and Political Economy, 1964–1991* (Washington, DC: The World Bank).

Kalecki, M. (1971) *Selected Essays on the Dynamics of the Capitalist Economy, 1933–1970* (Cambridge: Cambridge University Press).

Kalecki, M. (1976) *Essays on Development Economics* (Brighton: Harvester).

Keynes, J. M. (1936) *The General Theory of Employment, Interest and Money* (London: Macmillan).

Kohli, A. (1990) *Democracy and Discontent. India's Growing Crisis of Governability* (Cambridge: Cambridge University Press).

Lal, D. (1985) *The Poverty of Development Economics* (Cambridge, MA: Harvard University Press).

Lewis, W. A. (1954) 'Economic development with unlimited supplies of labour', *The Manchester School*, 22(2), pp. 139–91.

Little, I. M. D. (1982) *Economic Development, Theory, Policy and International Relations* (New York: Basic Books).

Nayyar, D. (1978) 'Industrial development in India: some reflections on growth and stagnation', *Economic and Political Weekly*, Special Number, August, reprinted in D. Nayyar (ed.) (1994), *Industrial Growth and Stagnation* (Bombay: Oxford University Press).

Nayyar, D. (ed.) (1994) *Industrial Growth and Stagnation. The Debate in India* (Bombay: Oxford University Press).

Raj, K. N. (1976) 'Growth and stagnation in Indian industrial development', *Economic and Political Weekly*, XI (5, 6 and 7), pp. 223–36, reprinted in D. Nayyar (ed.) (1994), *Industrial Growth and Stagnation* (Bombay: Oxford University Press).

Rakshit, M. K. (1982) *The Labour Surplus Economy* (Delhi: Macmillan).

Rakshit, M. K. (ed.) (1989) *Studies in the Macroeconomics of Developing Countries* (Delhi: Oxford University Press).

Rao, J. M. (1993) 'Distribution and growth with an infrastructure constraint', *Cambridge Journal of Economics*, 17(4), pp. 369–89.

Rao, V. K. R. V. (1952) 'Investment, income and the multiplier in an underdeveloped economy', *Indian Economic Review*, February, reprinted in A. N. Agarwala and S. P. Singh (eds), *The Economics of Underdevelopment* (Bombay: Oxford University Press, 1958).

Ray, S. C. (1991) 'Growth of manufacturing production in India: a time-series analysis', *Journal of Quantitative Analysis*, 7(1), pp. 23–42.

Reddaway, W. B. (1987) 'Some reflections by a Keynesian economist on the problems of developing countries', in A. P. Thirlwall (ed.), *Keynes and Economic Development* (New York: St Martin's Press).

Rosenstein-Rodan, P. N. (1943) 'Problems of industrialisation of Eastern and South-Eastern Europe', *Economic Journal* June–September, pp. 202–11.

Sen, A. (1991) 'Shocks and instabilities in an agriculture-constrained economy: India 1964–85', in J. Breman and S. Mundle (eds), *Rural Transformation in India* (Delhi: Oxford University Press).

Singer, H. W. (1985) 'Relevance of Keynes for developing countries', in H. L. Wattel (ed.), *The Policy Consequences of John Maynard Keynes* (Armonk, NY: M. E. Sharpe).

Singer, H. W. (1987) 'What Keynes and Keynesianism can teach us about less developed countries', in A. P. Thirlwall (ed.), *Keynes and Economic Development* (New York: St Martin's Press).

Srinivasan, T. N. (1993) 'Demand deficiency and Indian industrial development', in P. Bardhan, M. Datta-Chaudhuri and T. N. Krishnan (eds), *Development and Change, Essays in Honour of K. N. Raj* (Bombay: Oxford University Press).

Srinivasan, T. N. and N. S. S. Narayana (1977) 'Economic performance since the third plan and its implications for policy', *Economic and Political Weekly*, Annual Number, February, reprinted in D. Nayyar (ed.) (1994), *Industrial Growth and Stagnation* (Bombay: Oxford University Press).

Taylor, L. (1983) *Structuralist Macroeconomics* (New York: Basic Books).

Taylor, L. (1991) *Income Distribution, Inflation and Growth. Lectures on Structuralist Macroeconomic Theory* (Cambridge, MA. MIT Press).

Thirlwall, A. P. (1987) 'Keynes, economic development and the developing countries', in A. P. Thirlwall (ed.), *Keynes and Economic Development* (New York: St Martin's Press).

Wattel, H. L. (ed.) (1985) *The Policy Consequences of John Maynard Keynes* (Armonk, NY: M. E. Sharpe).

World Bank (1991) *World Development Report 1991. The Challenge of Development* (Oxford: Oxford University Press).

11 International Markets and Open Economy Macroeconomics: A Keynesian view

E. V. K. FitzGerald

INTRODUCTION: OPEN ECONOMY MACROECONOMICS IN A GLOBAL MARKETPLACE

In the late 1980s, with the Cold War at an end and the debt crisis apparently resolved, it seemed reasonable to believe the developing countries would be the main beneficiaries of a dynamic world economy. The extension of free trade throughout the world and the integration of capital markets implied a truly 'global economy' of the kind anticipated by Keynes and his colleagues at Bretton Woods some 50 years ago, allowing rising incomes in non-industrial economies from rapid export growth and massive foreign investment. Moreover, during the 1980s a remarkable degree of agreement had emerged as to the principles of sound economic policy that should guide policy makers in developing countries. The model of economic development established in the immediate post-war years – which had focused on problems of agrarian transformation, forced industrialisation and income redistribution – was replaced by a new paradigm (sometimes referred to as the 'Washington consensus') of trade liberalisation, fiscal stabilisation, structural adjustment and privatisation.

During the present decade, however, this optimism and consensus has begun to evaporate once more as the unsatisfactory conclusion of the Uruguay Round and chronic instability in global financial markets have revealed both the limitations of international regulatory institutions and the risks to developing countries of rapid integration to global markets without adequate economic and institutional capacity. This is not just a 'development' issue because the non-industrial countries not only account for three-quarters of humanity but also for 44 per cent of world production, 24 per cent of global trade and 50 per cent of fixed investment (see Table 11.1).

Table 11.1 The structure of the world economy, 1994

	No.	*% of world output*	*% of world trade*	*% of world investment*
Industrial	23	55	71	48
G3	3	35	33	32
Other	20	20	38	16
Non-industrial	161	45	29	52
Africa	50	3	2	2
Asia	30	23	16	32
M. East	18	5	4	5
L. America	34	9	4	8
E. Europe	28	5	3	5

Source: IMF (1994, May 1995). 'World output' refers to share of world GDP in 1994 on a purchasing power parity basis; 'world trade' is share of world exports of goods and services in 1994; 'world investment' is the region's investment to GDP ratio for 1994 applied to its share in 'world output'.

In this chapter, I shall argue that the way in which capital markets actually work at the international and national level, and how saving and investment interact in practice, requires a reappraisal of standard open-economy macroeconomics beyond that suggested by recent 'New Keynesian' models of market failure. Indeed, a return to the original Keynesian approach to investor uncertainty and effective demand has interesting implications even for the reform of the Bretton Woods institutions themselves.

INTERNATIONAL ECONOMICS IN THE GLOBAL ECONOMY

The standard paradigm for the structural adjustment of developing economies identifies the world market as an efficient allocator of global resources. Openness as a development strategy is a self-evident proposition where any problems are *ex hypothesi* due to misguided domestic policy. It:

> constitutes perhaps the most important opportunity for raising the welfare of both developing and industrial countries in the long term ... Globalization comes with liberalization, deregulation, and more mobile and potentially volatile cross-border flows, which means that sound

> macroeconomic management commands an increasingly high premium. Penalties for policy errors rise. Globalization thus requires closer monitoring and quicker policy responses at the country, regional and global levels ... The process of integration will affect countries unevenly and could increase international disparities ... The global outlook is, in general, bright, but masks wide differences across regions and countries – for many, global optimism coexists with local pessimism. Accelerating outward-oriented growth in the poorest countries will be a special challenge. (World Bank 1995: v)

However, despite progress towards the establishment of the World Trade Organisation and the evident success of some newly-industrialised countries in taking advantage of this globalisation, it is widely agreed[1] that in practice: (i) not all poor countries have been able to take advantage of trade liberalisation, particularly those dependent on primary commodities or without competitive industrial capacity; and (ii) international financial instability has slowed growth in the industrial economies and excluded developing countries from global capital markets.

In the opinion of the IMF, which in this case as in others is representative of the academic and policy making orthodoxy as well as of the global bond market, there certainly is a global savings shortage (Aghevli *et al.* 1990):

> Although it is debatable whether the level of private saving in the world economy is inadequate, there is ample evidence to suggest that world growth and economic welfare are adversely affected by the strong pressures on the available level of financial resources. This is mainly due to the persistent absorption of private sector saving to finance fiscal imbalances in the industrial countries, which accounts for the bulk of the decline in world saving rate since the 1970s. (IMF 1995: 11)

This is based on the fact that most empirical work on savings behaviour has been undertaken in the context of the life cycle model where changes in demographics, income growth, interest rates and inflation should be determinant, although the econometric results indicate that differences in age structure and output growth appear to be the only significant variables (Bosworth 1993).

The Keynesian view is diametrically opposed to this essentially Ricardian model, seeing investment demand as ultimately generating the required level of saving if only liquidity problems can be overcome by appropriate extra-market intervention (Asimakopulos 1991). In the *General Theory* the principle of effective demand itself is a radically different view of how the demand for investment and the willingness to save are brought into equilibrium with each other, the equilibrating force being the level of aggregate income and not the rate of interest. This level would not necessarily correspond to full employment and 'savings equals investment', simply because investment induces a like amount of savings. The problem would arise if the propensity to save were too high, rather than too low. In fact, Keynes's own model is not entirely plausible because of the fixed savings coefficients implicit in its consumption function and the need for large aggregate income variations to adjust savings *ex post* to *ex ante* investment decisions. The redefinition by Hicks of saving in terms of changes in net worth allows for wealth effects in the consumption function, as well as reintroducing the Pigovian ambiguity about the net effect of interest rates on saving.[2] Nonetheless, the central point made by Keynes's savings and investment flows are not brought into balance by interest rates because these are related to the desire to hold the existing stock of bonds (in other words, liquidity preference). This concept turns out to be the key to understanding international capital market behaviour.

The standard view is that declining savings rates are 'associated with lower rates of capital accumulation and growth in the world economy', while 'changes in inflation and interest rates seem to have had relatively small effects on saving behaviour' (Aghevli *et al.* 1990: 3). Moreover, it is well established that capital does not flow between industrialised countries and the rest of the world on the scale implied by relative factor endowments as standard theory requires (IMF 1991). This anomaly can be explained theoretically in terms of the externalities captured by foreign investors from human capital and infrastructure provision on the one hand (Lucas 1990), or by asymmetric information and agency problems on the other (Stiglitz 1994). Nonetheless, mainstream analytic models of international capital markets between industrial countries still rely on an implicit model of independently and identically distributed random shocks and a homogeneous population of consumer-investors (differing at most by their risk-aversions and endowments), and thus cannot readily explain the origins of global financial instability, the rationing-out of risk sovereign borrowers and the systemic problems of international fiscal co-ordination, and speculative currency crises (van der Ploeg 1994). Even the more stable behaviour of direct foreign investment flows is best explained by industrial organisation theory (Dunning, 1992).

However, this recent theorisation of imperfect international capital markets has yet to be explicitly adapted to the situation of non-industrial economies. Although some advance has been made on the interaction between new trade theories, capital flows and LDC growth on a global basis in neostructuralist 'North-South' models (Vines and Muscatelli 1989), the capital flows are still treated as exogenous except for borrowing limits imposed by existing debt burdens. Of course, although the standard HOS model does present a full articulation of international capital markets and macroeconomic adjustment in developing countries, it considers the issue to be an essentially unproblematic general equilibrium problem, in sharp contrast to a Keynesian approach to the disequilibria derived from asset holders' expectations.[3]

In principle, the level of investment in an open economy need not be constrained by savings (and neither would savings have to come into line with investment) because the resultant current account balance could be financed by matching international capital flows. Under the Bretton Woods system of fixed exchange rates such flows were relatively small,[4] so that savings and investment moved together in most large economies. However, from the late 1970s onwards, capital became much more mobile and the USA itself suddenly shifted from a net surplus to a net deficit position, its fiscal deficit was voluntarily financed by Japanese householders until the early 1990s, when the Japanese government was obliged to assume this stabilising function.

Interest rates within the OECD became broadly equalised for similar dollar-denominated bonds by the 1980s, while exchange rates were adjusted in response to domestic interest rate differentials, which in turn allowed for a modest risk margin (Turner 1991). Flexible exchange rates had thus been expected to permit some autonomy to domestic demand management, but in practice the bond markets imposed a uniform monetary policy irrespective of the divergent cyclical position of the national economies. Moreover, the close correlation observed between domestic saving and investment in the industrial economies (Frankel 1992) cannot simply be dismissed as spurious (for example, both being functions of GDP) or attributed to regulatory restrictions. It is more likely that the 'home bias' in the acquisition of financial assets arises from factors such as currency risk, agency problems and asymmetric information, and is endemic to market structures themselves (Brainard and Tobin 1992).

In other words, as Keynes had pointed out at the national level, interest rates do not act so as to clear the international capital market and bring savings and investment into line on a global scale (Goldstein 1993), while exchange rates do not appear to affect trade flows sufficiently to adjust current account deficits rapidly enough to avoid asset adjustment. In effect, a systemic rationing system exists based on market perceptions of sovereign risk, expressed as an assessment of the 'quality' of that country's bonds and thus its longer-term growth potential and fiscal solvency.

The leading international macroeconomic policy models surveyed by van der Ploeg (1994) are superficially 'Keynesian' in the sense that they are demand-driven: the GDP of the industrial economies is assumed to rise until some sort of capacity constraint or an employment/inflation corner is reached. Asset positions enter in the consumption (and by implication savings) function, and savings are essentially by households. Investment functions are basically simple accelerator models with various lags and minor relative-price effects. Interest rates derived from monetary policy stances play a key role in determining exchange rates, and have income effects through the debt burden. The basic macroeconomic transmission mechanism from one economy to another is thus trade, with capital flows adjusting, which generates a potential 'locomotive effect' from the G7 (or even G3) economies to the rest of the global economy. By extension, effective co-ordination between economies (for example, in policy stances) can increase the aggregate level of world GDP reached at equilibrium.

However, in the case of flows between the industrial economies (IEs) and the rest of the world (RoW) there is a clear segmentation between portfolio flows, foreign direct investment (FDI), bank credits and official development assistance (World Bank 1995), each of which form of asset acquisition appears to be driven by different institutional behaviour but where country 'quality' seems to be a determinant factor. This is true even when the investment and savings decisions are the same, in the case of FDI, where externalities prevent profitability from reflecting factor scarcity, while infrastructure and skills are central to the choice of location (UNCTC 1992). In bond markets, it is probably perceived fiscal stances and privatisation that determine quality.

There is also a clear segmentation between country groupings. The decline in bank credit flows from the IEs to the RoW since the debt crisis of the early 1980s, and the rise of portfolio flows in the early 1990s, has been confined to a small group of upper middle-income countries: both have been essentially concerned with public sector finance. FDI flows have similarly been confined to relatively few NICs, and are largely financed by the firms concerned. Aid flows are focused on the poorest countries, and determined by non-economic factors.

In consequence, it would seem to be the case that if investment rises autonomously in one country, it is not necessarily possible to tap a savings-investment surplus in another country because of the portfolio preferences of asset holders. This is broadly true within the IEs (at least as between the USA, Japan and the EU) and *a fortiori* between IEs and the RoW. In a sense, of course, this is a global form of liquidity preference because, although real interest rates are broadly equalised between OECD countries and make exchange rates subject to monetary policy, they do not clear the market for savings and investment because access to global capital markets is highly segmented and the 'quality' of financial assets relates to investors' perception of country characteristics. These characteristics would seem to imply that a Keynesian approach would be useful, which would attempt to understand how uncertainty over asset returns (rather than the availability of liquidity in a form such as strategic drawing rights) would affect the reconciliation of desired asset positions between economies.

Table 11.2 Non-industrial countries: sources and uses of funds, 1993 (per cent of GDP)

	Total	*Africa*	*Asia*	*ME*	*LA*	*EE*
Saving	24.1	15.7	29.8	18.3	17.3	17.9
Investment	26.6	18.1	31.7	22.2	20.5	21.2
Net lending	–2.5	–2.4	–1.9	–3.9	–3.3	–3.3
unrequited transfers	1.3	4.4	1.0	1.2	0.9	1.1
factor income	–1.9	–5.0	–1.2	—	–3.1	–0.9
resource balance	–2.1	–2.2	–1.8	–5.1	–1.1	–3.5
Acquisition of foreign assets	1.3	1.1	2.4	–0.8	–0.2	2.8
change in reserves	1.3	0.4	1.7	0.9	1.0	2.2

ME = Middle East
LA = Latin America
E = Eastern Europe
Sources: IMF (1994).

MACROECONOMIC THEORY AND THE SMALL OPEN DEVELOPING ECONOMY

Standard macroeconomic theory as applied to developing countries[5] is based on a model of the small open economy originally set out in terms of trade and non-traded sectors by Meade and domestic absorption by Polack, subsequently developed as a single model by Dornbusch.[6] The analysis of traded and non-traded sectors, excess demand from budget deficits, the role of the real exchange rate as a key policy instrument, and savings (whether domestic or foreign) as the constraint on growth, and the positive effect of trade liberalisation on employment (and thus income distribution) is now the standard approach:

> macroeconomic stabilization and fiscal consolidation are needed to reduce pressure on prices, real exchange rates, and the balance of payments, while increasing domestic savings for more investment. Governments also need to press ahead with outward-oriented structural reforms that maximize competition in goods and labour markets, expand the opportunities for private enterprise, improve efficiency, and raise productivity growth. In this regard rationalization of large public sectors, trade liberalization, deregulation of investment, and reforms to create more flexible labour markets are all important. (World Bank 1995: 22)

Despite some evident success in underpinning stabilisation policy, the much more ambiguous results of structural adjustment policy in terms of either export growth or poverty reduction[7] have brought standard theory under considerable criticism. At the level of macroeconomic theory as applied explicitly to developing countries, the main critique has come from neostructuralists, whose work is essentially an attempt to set out the insights of the founders of development economics, such as Prebish, Kalecki, Lewis and Kaldor, in the formal framework of modern open-economy macroeconomic analysis (Taylor 1983, 1991; Dutt, 1990).[8] However, despite powerful points of dissent on the constraints placed by world markets on investment, growth and employment,[9] this line of inquiry does not lead to a convincing theory of savings and investment behaviour beyond the suggestions that government expenditure can have positive effects on growth through the 'crowding-in' of private investment and that forced savings are generated by the income distribution which results from the macroeconomic resolution of *ex ante* disequilibria in expenditure plans under resource constraints.

The defence of the standard model has led to its sophistication by the successive inclusion of more plausible assumptions about the structure of developing economies without abandoning the core assumptions of neoclassical theory as to maximising behaviour, the power of relative prices to achieve market equilibria and the nature of optimal policy response to external shock.[10] The relationship between adjustment and income distribution has been made explicit (Bourguinon, Branson and de Melo 1989) and some progress has also been made in endogenising governmental behaviour (Rodrik 1989).

However, this defence does not come to terms with the implications of endogenous growth theory, which are such as to undermine the key assumptions of the standard model as to longer-term growth

> Almost all the views on economic growth relate the accumulation of knowledge to externalities, so that private decisions to save and invest are not optimal and growth is from a social point of view too low. Naturally, this implies an active role for the government; depending on the engine of growth the government should try to support R&D, improve the channels of international communication, promote investment, maintain and expand the infrastructure, and/or invest in education. (van der Ploeg 1994: 535)

In marked contrast, modern mainstream macroeconomic theory as applied to industrial economies (Blanchard and Fischer 1989) now takes systemic market failure far more seriously. New-Keynesian theory in particular provides quantity-constrained models of open economies and shows that imperfect markets lead to the need for, and efficacy of, active fiscal and monetary policies (van der Ploeg 1994). Realistic assumptions about the maximising behaviour of representative firms and households in markets characterised by imperfect competition means that both the positive and welfare analyses of government policy differ significantly from those under Walrasian equilibrium. Two very good examples of the application of new-Keynesian theory to problems in development economics are the interpretation of the consequences of price and wage formation rules for the effect of devaluation on production and income distribution (Edwards and van Wijnbergen 1989), and the analysis of the implications of the effect of asymmetric information in credit markets on investment and firm size (Stiglitz 1994), both of which have considerable implications for the design of macroeconomic policy.

Nonetheless, both the structuralist and new-Keynesian approaches to open economy macroeconomics are severely limited by their implicit assumption that the world economy can be taken as a given and stable point of reference, and the propositions about constrained maximising behaviour within known and continuous production functions, under conditions where expectations can be characterised by measurable risk. This approach takes insufficient account of the heterogenous nature of the private sector (ranging from peasant households to multinational corporations), of the complex institutional nature of the interaction of the relationships between state and civil society, and of the increasing globalisation of the productive and financial systems in such countries. The existence of imperfect markets requires, therefore, a macroeconomic theory disaggregated by different types of representative firms – ranging from transnational coporations to peasant households (FitzGerald 1995) – with different relationships to international capital markets.

The idea that greater access to international capital markets (in the form of FDI, bank loans, portfolio flows or official aid) would enhance poor countries' growth is also derived from the extension of the familiar HOS model from trade to factor flows, so that capital moves to take advantage of natural resources and cheaper labour skills. However, there is no reason to believe that this will lead to optimal resource allocation once externalities are taken into account (Lucas 1990), even if rates of return to capital are equalised as appears to be happening in practice (Wood 1994).

In the orthodox view, a fall in public sector savings results in larger private savings due to the increased PSBR driving up interest rates or, if these are constrained in a closed economy, by increasing the money supply and forcing private savings through a real balance effect (IMF 1987). In the small open economy, the effect is felt through an inflow of foreign savings in the monetary approach to the balance of payments. However, when the expectations of the private sector are taken into account, new-Keynesian 'Ricardian equivalence' models also suggest that fiscal deficits will be balanced by increased private savings in order to provide for future tax burdens (Barro 1989), which means that crowding-in can be possible from the financial as well as the real side implied endogenous growth theory.[11]

In practice, the downward trend in savings in developing countries is partly explained by the loss of income to oil-exporting countries (that is, wealth adjustment), while the high rate of private savings in some of the middle-income countries under adjustment during the 1980s was due to the need to finance capital flight, followed by its return in the 1990s raising consumption and depressed savings rates (IMF 1995). Nonetheless it is interesting to note that the reduced budget deficits and enhanced private savings (from higher real interest rates and profit shares) expected from structural adjustment have not been forthcoming. Cross-section studies of private savings behaviour (Aghevli *et al.* 1990; Bosworth 1993) not only indicate that real interest rates are not a significant determinant, which is hardly surprising, but also that the effect of demographic factors on saving varies greatly across countries for no readily explicable reason. In contrast, public savings behaviour is mainly seen as reflecting the fiscal stance of governments, although welfare entitlements do have a demographic dimension, while tax pressures are limited by the international mobility of factors of production, and debt service becomes endogenous in the longer term.

It is well established in modern microeconomics that uncertainty and access to funds, rather than the interest rate as such, acts as the effective constraint on private investment decisions (Fazzari *et al.* 1988; Dixit and Pindyk 1994), while in developing countries the contribution of human capital and infrastructure provision to profitability are similarly undisputed. When combined with the effect of volatility in world commodity and capital markets, an essentially Keynesian picture emerges where liquidity and expectations – and not disposable savings net of the fiscal deficit and long-term capital inflows as in the standard model – determine the level of aggregate investment, output growth and employment.

In fact, developing countries do suffer from international financial volatility in a number of ways, among which the most important are: (i) exchange rate instability, high interest rates and low investment slow down growth in OECD countries, and thus demand for RoW exports; (ii) high interest rates raise the cost of debt service and cause fiscal strain in LDCs, causing macroeconomic instability and reducing private investment; (iii) global market uncertainty excludes many developing countries from access to private capital flows, and subjects others to destabilising volatility in flows; (iv) the inability of capital markets to work out debt burdens in response to insolvency imposes a long-term resource burden on poorer countries and further reduces their attractiveness to foreign investors; and (v) the more vulnerable LDCs become subject to policy conditionality that goes beyond ensuring that international obligations are met, and raises questions of sovereignty.

Finally, these arguments help explain why financial liberalisation has had such perverse consequences in many developing countries. The standard model of financial repression suggested that once real interest rates were raised, private savings would increase sharply, and so in consequence would private income, particularly if budget deficits were simultaneously reduced (IMF 1987). However, if savings do not respond to real interest rates and investment is not savings-constrained, as we have seen, then there is no reason to expect that the standard model will work. What is more, financial liberalisation in practice appears to involve a combination of (i) 'disintermediation' (where banks cease to provide long-term credit to companies) which depresses investment; (ii) consumer credit expansion which depresses private savings (that is, *net* asset acquisition) and raises imports; and (iii) reliance on volatile capital from abroad attracted by high real investment rates, leading to exchange rate overvaluation and balance of payments fragility (Gibson and Tsakalotos 1994).

ARE KEYNESIAN ECONOMIC POLICIES STILL RELEVANT?

I have argued that a Keynesian view of the intersection between domestic macroeconomic adjustment and international capital market instability might be useful. The obvious question then arises as to whether Keynesian *policies* would also be relevant. I shall argue that they are, but not in the commonly understood sense.

Of course, much depends upon what is understood by a 'Keynesian policy' at the national and international level. At the national level, Keynes himself clearly believed that the transmission mechanisms of administered shocks to the economy was to be through an active *ex ante* response to changing business *expectations* rather than just a passive *ex post* response of output to increased government expenditure. This is underpinned by his theory of effective demand, where macroeconomic adjustment is based on changes in the investment and savings decisions of firms, including decisions on stock levels and employment as well as capacity expansion (Asimakopulos 1991).

However, as Kregel (1994) pointed out, there is little in the *General Theory* on policy apart from this positive impact of expenditure on output and employment in conditions of excess capacity. Keynes's own views on inter-War policy focused on changing market expectations, not by direct price intervention, but rather by reduction of the size and cost of excess stocks. On post-war policy, Keynes appears to have believed in a balanced budget in a special sense: a continual current balance for reasons of efficiency and an anti-cyclical capital budget to maintain employment, balanced over time. This public investment would imply considerable socialisation of overall investment expenditure during the reconstruction period (Kregel 1985). His concern, therefore, appears to have centred on private investor confidence which would be stimulated by public investment but undermined by the prospect of fiscal insolvency.

Various apparently 'Keynesian' domestic policy proposals can be found in the development economics literature, all of which are based on induced demand expansion and seem to overlook the problem of expectations and investment.[12] Leaving aside the intrinsic merits of these proposals, they cannot really be called 'Keynesian' in any real sense, and in fact relate more closely to the management of a centrally controlled economy rather than one where business expectations are the main dynamic force. Ironically, one of the main elements of the criticisms of such proposals by the World Bank and the IMF is precisely their perverse effects on private investment, even though their own view of investment is the curiously Ricardian one of savings acting as a funding constraint.

A rather more promising line for Keynesian policy construction would be to look at investment behaviour, with private capital formation being stimulated by public provision of infrastructure and education as suggested by the endogenous growth and 'new' trade theories mentioned above. Differential tax and credit policies would have to be designed to affect the expectations of different types of firm: multinationals, domestic corporations and small enterprise (FitzGerald 1995). This form of 'crowding in' would arise from the shift in the marginal efficiency of capital schedule (that is, expected supply costs) rather than from the increase in aggregate demand as such, and would seem to be compatible with modern growth theory.

Keynes's view of household saving behaviour does not seem very appropriate for non-industrial economies, and he has little to say about corporate saving; here Kalecki provides more insights, which also link into banking activities in a useful way (FitzGerald 1993). It is empirically evident, even if not theoretically agreed, that higher interest rates do not raise saving; so that a Keynesian policy of low real interest rates to stimulate investment in developing countries would have a great deal to recommend it. The motivations for high real rates in LDCs include financial liberalisation and the desire to attract foreign capital (to be discussed below) but the main cause is undoubtedly the finance of large budget deficits by local bond sales. A Keynesian policy would, as we have seen, require positive fiscal saving, while the nearest practical equivalent to a capital tax (or levy) would be the traditional practice of large reserve requirements on domestic banks to be held in government bonds. Another Kaleckian proposal for developing countries, which is not un-Keynesian in its logic, is the heavy taxation of luxury consumption in order to ensure macroeconomic equilibrium as well as improve income distribution (FitzGerald 1993).

Such an approach would have immediate consequences for IMF-type conditionality (without abandoning public sector solvency and appropriate real exchange rates as the basis of sound policy), and might help to avoid the negative consequences of financial liberalisation as undertaken by most LDCs under the tutelage of the Bretton Woods institutions, such as import booms as banks switch credit towards consumer credit, excess borrowing abroad by private corporations to reduce interest charges while ignoring exchange rate risk, and destabilising inflows of portfolio capital.

In sum, a Keynesian policy at the national level designed to raise employment and sustain growth would be concerned with: (i) public investment designed to shift the capital efficiency schedule; (ii) budgetary policy to support long-term stabilisation, with low interest rates maintained by high reserve requirements; (iii) the stimulation of private investment by affecting the differential expectations of firms; (iv) active use of luxury taxation and development finance; and (v) the management of the balance of payments through real exchange rate stability and banking controls.

These have specific consequences for the linkage with international capital markets. On the one hand, an essentially Keynesian 'externally constrained' accelerator model of investment can be constructed, which takes into account exogenous shocks, public capital, fiscal deficits and regime instability: a model that is not only both theoretically plausible and econometrically satisfactory (FitzGerald, Jansen and Vos 1994) but is also compatible with fiscal stability. On the other, because productive employment depends on investment levels and these are very sensitive to international capital flows in developing countries, the combination of a theory of capital market segmentation (distinguishing between direct foreign investment, development assistance and financial asset acquisition) with a macroeconomic theory of aggregate investment, which allows for the interaction of public and private investment decisions, has interesting implications for the income-distribution effects of shocks transmitted from international capital markets (FitzGerald and Mavrotas 1994). What would require modification, therefore, would not be so much IMF views on fiscal prudence and exchange rate management, but rather those on capital market regulation and interest rates.

Keynes's design at Bretton Woods was clearly designed to help developing countries.[13] As we know, the original plans for a global central bank, an international investment fund and a commodity stabilisation system were not implemented in practice; but the central intent was clearly to stabilise the world economy and thus, by improving expectations, raise investment and employment. Keynes's own views on the details of international economic management were heavily conditioned by the immediate post-war circumstances (and the weak position of Britain in these) and there is not a great deal to be gained from trying to replicate these today under very different circumstances. His concerns about a return to unfettered private capital movements, which had caused such instability in the inter-War period (Kindleberger 1988), are highly relevant today but his solution is not. Above all, the assumption that capital flows would be channelled through central banks is no longer true, while the existence of integrated international capital markets also means that, for instance, leading surplus governments are not necessarily in a position to implement expansionary policies even if they so desired.

Expansionary adjustment of the world economy through investment recovery in the surplus-savings countries of the North can be called Keynesian, but the popular type of so-called 'global Keynesianism' associated with the Brandt Commission – where large amounts of aid transferred from North to South would somehow stimulate world trade and recovery – seems to ignore the way the aid is to be financed. Indeed, it may even lead to reduced world growth and terms of trade deterioration if private investment response in the North is perverse (Vos 1994). LDC debt cancellation, a recent variant on the same theme,[14] would only have a positive effect from a Keynesian point of view if it increases investor confidence, and there is little sign that this is so, except insofar as the willingness of the creditor (the US Treasury in the case of Mexico) to act as lender of last resort, thereby creating liquidity, is credibly signalled.

A modern Keynesian approach might seek to influence his three 'psychological factors' – propensity to consume, long-term expectation as to yields on capital assets and attitude to liquidity – by appropriate institutional design in terms of both operational rules and discretionary intervention. The first might be the subject of international tax regulation, while the latter two relate to the functioning of capital markets, which might turn out to be more relevant than ingenious schemes for the role of the IMF and various forms of bancor.[15] A Keynesian policy towards developing country access to international capital markets would thus presumably involve the reduction of such uncertainty by prudential enforcement of capital adequacy rules on lenders and discretionary intervention to provide liquidity and unwind insolvent debtors.

CONCLUSIONS

In sum, a Keynesian global policy of relevance to the developing countries would act on international capital markets, explicitly recognising that they do not clear investment and savings (and thus the current account of the balance of payments) via interest rates, and that expectations depend on partial and imperfect information, which in turn leads to rationing behaviour by institutions. Any scheme for international monetary reform must contain, therefore, appropriate prudential regulations and information systems for such markets as well as discretionary intervention by an international central bank in order to provide liquidity when and where required.

Savings cannot, in the last instance, be a constraint on investment, although finance can be. This implies that the debates on whether capital inflows raise or lower savings may have little meaning: the key question is what effect they have on investment rates. By the same token, the question of why some regions or countries have so much higher savings rates than others is probably the wrong one to ask. Rather, the issue is why investment rates are so much higher, where explanations in terms of stable macroeconomic regimes, high profitability and adequate infrastructure (including labour skilling) may be more powerful than trade openness or financial liberalisation.[16]

The appropriate Keynesian policy to stabilise the linkage between international capital markets and open-economy macroeconomics obviously depends on the circumstances: not only the structure of the economy and its insertion in the world economy, but also the recent macroeconomic events and prospects that determine the attitude of investors. In his evidence to the Macmillan Commission (Kregel 1994), Keynes had already highlighted the problem caused by the divergence between the rate of interest required to attract foreign capital and cover the current account deficit on the one hand, and the rate required to support the recovery of full-employment investment.[17] His post-war proposal for an international clearing union was aimed at overcoming this problem and permitting an autonomous domestic macroeconomic policy; but in practice the problem of the destabilising impact on global demand of asymmetric adjustments to disequilibrium by creditor and debtor nations was never solved under fixed or flexible exchange rate systems (mainly because of the position of the USA under and after the Bretton Woods system).

The usual reading of Keynes is that:

> In the absence of some automatic mechanisms, such as a clearing union, or international policy coordination, to offset the deflationary tendency of asymmetric adjustment, conventional Keynesian policy to ensure full employment cannot be viable in one country. Ironically, in the post-war period it has fallen to the IMF to ensure that any country that attempts an independent expenditure policy will be forced to reverse it in the interests of stability. (Kregel 1994: 275)

Apart from exaggerating the power of the IMF, this ignores the need to create an orderly capital market in the first place. Although saving cannot be a constraint on investment at the national or the international level, liquidity is; but liquidity is not now an issue of money supply, but rather one of uncertainty as to the true value of assets. The lack of an orderly market is of particular concern to vulnerable open economies.[18]

Notes

1. See the Bretton Woods Commission (1994) for an irreproachably 'blue-ribbon' institutional critique of prevailing arrangements, which stresses the negative effect of volatility in international capital markets.

2. Measured savings differ from changes in net worth because changes in asset values are not included in standard definitions of income, and thus are implicitly excluded from savings once consumption is subtracted. The definition in Hicks (1946) of income equates it to the maximum value that a household (or other economic unit) can consume during a given period while remaining as well-off as it was at the beginning of the period. For a discussion of the application of national accounting procedures at the global level, see Vos (1994).
3. In fact, a series of important issues (such as shock transmission; segmentation in international trade and finance; market regulation by discretion versus rules; global economic co-ordination; or aid as a response to global market failure and global social security entitlement) can probably only be tackled by reference to recent work on global hegemony (Walter 1993). This should be combined with legal scholarship on the regulation of banks and other financial intermediaries to provide a clearer picture of the rules within which agents operate and the feasibility of containing systemic risk on a global scale, including the scope for international fiscal and regulatory legislation from which developing countries might benefit.
4. As Keynes, mindful of the experience of the Gold Standard, had intended them to be (Moggridge 1992), as well as assuming that they would take place between central banks.
5. Dornbusch (1993) and IMF (1987) set out the models; see Khan and Haque (1990) for an interesting attempt to synthesise the analytical approaches of the Bank and the Fund.
6. Dornbusch (1980); it is worth noting that Dornbusch chose the 'Australian' version of the model, which has neoclassical microeconomic foundations, as opposed to the 'Scandinavian' version which, having fixed technological coefficients and not requiring full-employment assumptions, is possibly of more relevance to most developing economies.
7. A related, but different, point is why this model has gained such widespread acceptance among policy makers in developing countries. It is clearly insufficient to attribute this to the power of the Bretton Woods institutions, although their role in the formation of economic doctrine should not be underestimated. Rather, the reason should be sought in the lack of a coherent and viable alternative policy model on the one hand and the need to maintain credibility in global capital markets (including aid agencies) on the other.
8. In fact, the neostructuralist theory of development macroeconomics has close parallels with the post-Keynesian critique of macroeconomics as applied to industrial economies (FitzGerald 1993).
9. Bacha (1990) developed the familiar 'two gap' model still used in practice by the World Bank to show that which of three gaps (savings, foreign exchange or budgetary) will bind depends on the burden of external debt, and thus that policies based on a single macroeconomic theory can easily have perverse effects.
10. Bevan, Collier and Gunning (1990) even subtitle their influential text 'a neoclassical approach to structuralism'.
11. Although it is now suggested that the reputational effect of fiscal deficits on private investment may be so strong that there exists in effect a negative multiplier (IMF 1995).

12. Four popular variants are as follows: (i) the expansion of domestic demand by deficit finance in order to use excess capacity and create unemployment, with the foreign exchange (i.e., import) constraint being overcome by import controls or, in a more subtle variant, by ensuring that the increased expenditure is on non-traded goods and services, such as domestic foodstuffs or road maintenance; (ii) the cancelling of external government debt or an increase in official development assistance, which would allow budgetary expenditure to increase – raising output and employment – without a local currency deficit (which would have to be financed by inflationary monetary expansion) or a loss of external reserves; (iii) a sophisticated version of (i) is the redistribution of income downwards – by a policy of wage and price controls, for instance – on the assumption that the consumption pattern of the poor is more labour-intensive and less import-intensive than that of the rich, so that output and employment can rise in the externally constrained economy without increasing aggregate demand; and (v) the justification for deficit-financed public works in terms of the use of surplus skilled labour with no real resource cost to the economy and of output growth that will generate the matching increase in national saving to balance the increased investment.
13. It should be borne in mind, however, that these were seen as what are now termed middle-income countries (e.g., the 'White Dominions', Latin America and Central/Southern Europe) rather than the then colonies, which now constitute LDCs proper, with the possible exception of India.
14. Arguably the equivalent of the reduction of debt by a capital levy in the *Treatise*, as proposed in UNCTAD (1993: 88–92).
15. Including the Tinbergen–Kaldor proposal for a commodity-based currency reserve system, which was put forward at the first UNCTAD in 1964 as an explicit scheme to reduce volatility. I am indebted to Hans Singer for this point.
16. This is the subject of a current two-year research project at the Finance and Trade Policy Research Centre, funded by the ODA (Overseas Development Administration).
17. A problem highly relevant to Latin America today, and also to Southern Europe. Moreover the hope that the UK could escape from this by leaving the Exchange Rate Mechanism was swiftly proved illusory for the simple reason that the bond markets are the one part of the global capital market that is efficiently integrated.
18. I intend to explore this problem in a research project 'Sustainable macro-management in volatile capital markets', which is now funded by the McArthur Foundation.

References

Aghevli, B. B., Boughton, J.M., Montiel, P.J., Villanueva, D. and Woglom, G. (1990) 'The role of national savings in the world economy', *IMF Occasional Paper* 67 (Washington, DC: IMF).

Asimakopulos, A. (1991) *Keynes's General Theory and Accumulation* (Cambridge: Cambridge University Press).

Bacha, E. L. (1990) 'A three-gap model of foreign transfers and the GDP growth rate in developing countries', *Journal of Development Economics*, 32.

Barro, R. J. (1989) 'The Ricardian approach to budget deficits', *Journal of Economic Perspectives*, 3, pp. 37–54.

Bevan, D., Collier, P. and Gunning, J. W. (1990) *Controlled Open Economies: A Neoclassical Approach to Structuralism* (Oxford: Clarendon Press).

Blanchard, O. J. and Fisher, S. (1989) *Lectures on Macroeconomics* (Cambridge, MA: MIT Press).

Bosworth, B. P. (1993) *Saving and Investment in a Global Economy* (Washington, DC: Brookings Institution).

Bourguinon, F., Branson, W. H. and de Melo, J. (1989) 'Macroeconomic adjustment and income distribution: a macro-micro model', *Technical Paper No. 1* (Paris: OECD Development Centre).

Brainard, W. C. and Tobin, J. (1992) 'On the internationalization of portfolios', *Oxford Economic Papers*, 44(4), pp. 533–565.

Bretton Woods Commission (1994) *Bretton Woods: Looking to the Future* (Washington, DC: Bretton Woods Commission).

Dixit, A. and Pindyck, J. (1994) *Investment under Uncertainty* (Princeton, NJ: Princeton University Press).

Dornbusch, R. (1980) *Open Economy Macroeconomics* (New York: Basic Books).

Dornbusch, R. (Ed.) (1993) *Policymaking in the Open Economy: Concepts and Case Studies in Economic Performance* (New York: Oxford University Press for the World Bank).

Dunning, J. H. (1992) *Multinational Enterprises and the Global Economy* (Reading, MA: Addison-Wesley).

Dutt, A. K. (1990) *Growth, Distribution and Uneven Development* (Cambridge: Cambridge University Press).

Edwards, S. and van Wijnbergen, S. (1989) 'Disequilibrium and structural adjustment', in H. Chenery and T. N. Srinivasan (eds), *Handbook of Development Economics* (Amsterdam: Elsevier).

Fazzari, S. M., Hobbard, R. G. and Peterson B. C. (1988) 'Financing constraints and corporate investment', *Brookings Papers on Economic Activity* (Washington, DC: Brookings Institution).

FitzGerald, E. V. K. (1993) *The Macroeconomics of Development Finance: A Kaleckian Approach* (London: Macmillan).

FitzGerald, E. V. K. (1995) 'Hamlet without the prince: structural adjustment, firm behaviour and private investment in semi-industrialised economies,' in V. Chick (ed.), *Money and Credit in Less-Developed Countries* (London: Macmillan).

FitzGerald, E. V. K., Jansen, K. and Vos, R. (1994) 'External constraints on private investment decisions in developing countries', in J. Gunning (ed.), *Trade, Growth and Development: Essays in Honour of Hans Linnemann* (London: Macmillan).

FitzGerald, E. V. K. and Mavrotas, G. (1994) 'The impact of international capital flows on employment and income distribution in LDCs', *ILO Occasional Papers No. 23* (Geneva: International Labour Office).

Frankel, J. (1992) 'Measuring international capital mobility: a review', *American Economic Review*, 82(2), pp. 197–202.

Gibson, H. and Tsakalotos, E. (1994) 'The scope and limits of financial liberalization in developing countries', *Journal of Development Studies*, 30(3), pp. 578–628.

Goldstein, M. and Folkerts-Landaur, D. (1993) *International Capital Markets* (Washington, DC: IMF).

Hicks, J. R. (1946) *Value and Capital: An Inquiry into some Fundamental Principles of Economic Theory* (Oxford: Clarendon Press).

IMF (1987) 'Theoretical aspects of the design of Fund-supported adjustment programs', *IMF Occasional Paper* 55 (Washington, DC: IMF).

IMF (1991) 'Determinants and systemic consequences of international capital flows', *IMF Occasional Paper* 77 (Washington, DC: IMF).

IMF (1995) *World Economic Outlook* (Washington, DC: IMF).

Khan, M. S. and Haque, N. U. (1990) 'Adjustment with growth: relating the analytical approaches of the IMF and the World Bank', *Journal of Development Economics*, 32(1), pp. 155–179.

Kindleberger, C. P. (1988) *The International Economic Order: Essays in Financial Crises and International Public Goods* (New York: Harvester Wheatsheaf).

Kregel, J. A. (1985) 'Budget deficits, stabilization policy and liquidity preference: Keynes's postwar policy proposal', in F. Vicarelli (ed.), *Keynes's Relevance Today* (London: Macmillan).

Kregel, J. A. (1994) 'The viability of economic policy and the priorities of economic policy', *Journal of Post Keynesian Economics*, 17(2), pp. 261–277.

Lucas, R. E. (1990) 'Why doesn't capital flow from rich to poor countries?', *American Economic Review*, 80(2), pp. 92–96

Moggridge, D. E. (1992) *Maynard Keynes: An Economist's Biography* (London: Routledge).

Ploeg, F. van der (ed.) (1994) *The Handbook of International Macroeconomics* (Oxford: Basil Blackwell).

Rodrik, D. (1989) 'The credibility of trade reform – a policymaker's guide', *World Economy*, 12(1), pp. 1–16.

Stiglitz, J. E. (1994) 'Explaining growth: competition and finance', in M. Baldassari, L. Puganetto and E. J. Phelps (eds), *International Differences in Growth Rates: Market Globalization and Economic Areas* (New York: St Martin's Press).

Taylor, L. (1983) *Structuralist Macroeconomics* (New York: Basic Books).

Taylor, L. (1991) *Income Distribution, Inflation and Growth: Lectures on Structuralist Macroeconomic Theory* (Cambridge, MA: MIT Press).

Turner, P. (1991) 'Capital flows in the 1980s: a survey of major trends', *BIS Economic Papers*, No. 30 (Basle: Bank for International Settlements).

UNCTAD (1993) *Trade and development report* (Geneva: UNCTAD).

UNCTC (1992) *The Determinants of Foreign Direct Investment: A Survey of the Evidence* (New York: United Nations Centre on Transnational Corporations).

Vines, D. and Muscatelli, A. (1989) 'Macroeconomic interactions between North and South', in R. Bryant *et al.* (eds), *Macroeconomic Policies in an Interdependent World* (Washington, DC: Brookings Institution).

Vos, R. (1994) *Debt and Adjustment in the World Economy: Structural Asymmetries in North-South Interactions* (London: Macmillan).

Walter, A. (1993) *World Power and World Money: the Role of Hegemony and Monetary Order* (New York: Harvester Wheatsheaf).

Wood, A. (1994) *North-South Trade, Employment and Inequality: Changing Fortunes in a Skill-Oriented World* (Oxford: Oxford University Press).

World Bank (1995) *Global Economic Prospects and the Developing Countries* (Washington, DC: World Bank).

12 Keynesian Policy in Disarticulated Economies

Laurence Harris

INTRODUCTION

The problems of developing countries today are diverse. While poverty and unemployment are experienced widely, the economies in which they occur have different characteristics. A typical sub-Saharan African country experiences the problems of failure to escape from dependence on primary production and the shock of attempting to increase the proportion of tradables (cash crops) in GDP, and its policies revolve around the management of unsustainable levels of official external debt. The SICs of Latin America face the problems of combining industrial growth with employment generation, with trade especially linked to the North American markets, and macroeconomic policy conditioned by strong but volatile private capital flows. The rapidly industrialising countries of Asia face problems of growth different from either of these, and different from each other (sharply illustrated by the differences between, say, India and China, which remain the two greatest peasant economies in the process of industrialisation), and the strength of some such as Singapore and South Korea make it doubtful whether they should be regarded as developing, rather than industrialised economies.

The diversity, which is greater than those broad stylised categories indicate, suggests that it may be futile to seek a universal theoretical framework for development policy, but as development economists we do work with universal paradigms, a number of which are understood as competing for hegemony. Dutt (Chapter 10) and FitzGerald (Chapter 11) summarise well the policy approaches based on a Keynesian paradigm and those that derive from neoclassical principles. Each paradigm includes variants, but the important point is that each has claims to be a suitable basis for a general theory of development policy, 'the' development theory. It is argued that a single type of development policy, the 'Washington consensus', is being applied throughout the world under the auspices of the Washington-based Bretton Woods institutions and supported by the OECD and other agencies, and the theoretical paradigm underlying it is neoclassical; the 'Washington consensus' establishes global neoclassicism, instead of Keynesian principles, as a universally applicable theory for development policy (Banuri and Shor 1992).

In this chapter I discuss reasons for the weakness of Keynesian theory as a basis for development policy, and suggest that the weaknesses present an insuperable obstacle for any theoretical research programme aiming to construct a coherent Keynesian development theory. At one level the obstacle arises from the apparent diversity of developing countries, since diversity creates difficulty for a universally applicable paradigm. But I argue that a more fundamental obstacle is created by two structural features that are widely shared by developing countries, a commonality only masked by the countries' apparent diversity. They are, first, the fact that developing economies are characterised by disarticulation and, second, that their states cannot possess economic sovereignty in the sense necessary for Keynesian policy. Arguably those same factors are obstacles for any theory of policy, including those based on neoclassical principles, but for reasons of space I concentrate on Keynesian policy alone.

I discuss some background issues next. The problems of disarticulation and sovereignty are discussed subsequently.

BACKGROUND ISSUES

Conventionally, Keynesian models are widely presented in terms of three markets: for goods, money and labour. For some purposes, the bond market (instead of the money market), separate markets for consumption and capital goods, and separate markets for internationally traded goods, are added; but construction as a set of markets is maintained. Dutt and Fitzgerald, incorporating elements from both Kalecki and Keynes, offer a different perspective by emphasising the structural characteristics of those markets and the role of agents, especially capitalists, whose investment decisions are potentially the system's driving force (FitzGerald) and whose oligopolistic behaviour is important for the closure of the system (Dutt). I believe a third perspective, in which the economy is seen as three interconnected systems, offers a useful, complementary starting point for understanding Keynesian theory as a policy framework.

A simple economy may be seen as a system of production, a financial system, and a state system of economic governance (which could encompass any form of regulation from liberal market regulation and intervention, to forms of central planning short of the non-market soviet type). The three systems are connected through the operation of markets; non-market power, which interacts with market relations, also includes at least the power of taxation. Keynesian policy can be seen as attempts by the state system to influence the productive system both directly and through the financial system. The textbook case of fiscal policy to reduce unemployment, for example, involves the state system adjusting taxes and expenditure to expand effective demand within the productive system, part of the effect coming through the expansion of state liabilities within the financial system. Similarly, if textbook monetary policy to affect unemployment succeeds, it is initiated within the state system to affect the financial system, and thereby influences the productive system.

That perspective enables us to focus on the character of each of the three systems. For example, what type of productive system is consistent with the assumptions of a Keynesian model? Clearly Keynesian policies were designed to address the problems of capitalist economies, for socialist production systems are incompatible with the model's key assumption that output can be demand determined. But there exist a number of different types of production systems within capitalism and Keynesian assumptions do not apply equally to all of them. The contrast between 'Fordist' and 'post-Fordist' production systems provides one example. Keynes, whether in the *Treatise* or the *General Theory*, was dealing with a 'Fordist' system in which labour was employed in structured labour markets, firms accumulated unplanned inventories whenever the expectations on which production was based failed to materialise, and voluntary scrapping of fixed capital was low. The elasticity of supply in response to increases in effective demand was based on the existence of excess capacity in fixed capital. But do Keynesian relationships apply equally in 'post-Fordist' production systems? Labour is subcontracted and casualised, just-in-time production reduces involuntary inventory accumulation, and rapid scrapping reduces capacity in recessions, thereby shrinking the base on which output can be produced in response to demand expansion.

Similarly, the applicability of Keynesian principles varies according to the character of the financial system and the state system. Using a stylised distinction between 'market-based' and 'bank-based' financial systems, it is arguable that interest rate changes are transmitted to firms more strongly in the former than the latter, for in 'German-type' bank-based systems firms' financing is based on long-term commitments and banks' direct and indirect holdings of equity.

In the following sections I argue that seeing Keynesian models in terms of interconnected subsystems, and considering the varieties of those systems, enables us to identify the difficulties in applying Keynesian principles to developing economies.

PROBLEM OF DISARTICULATION

The overriding feature of most developing economies is their *disarticulation*, which can be seen in the productive system, the financial system and in every aspect of economic life. In contrast, Keynesian models implicitly assume an integrated, articulated economy in which different industries are linked through regular market interaction and articulated financial systems in which firms and the state are continuously refinanced through the circulation of money and credit (notwithstanding the fact that those relations are interrupted in depressions or crises). A simple illustration of those assumptions is provided by the multiplier; an expansionary shock causes firms initially affected to increase demand for other firms' output both directly and indirectly through increases in workers' income and consumption.

In the simplest case of closed economy models, production and finance systems are both fully articulated. In standard open economy models, trade and financial flows with the rest of the world are subordinate to the dynamic of the domestic system. Production systems in actual developing countries, by contrast, are disarticulated in various ways. One form of disarticulation identified in early development literature was 'enclave production'. Similarly, the dual-economy assumption, underlying both Kaleckian and Lewis-type models, distinguished a modern, industrial or capitalist sector that was segmented from a backward, agricultural, or non-capitalist sector. Although neither approach accurately desribed the real disarticulation of developing economies, they readily showed how it can obstruct Keynesian policies for two reasons: if import substitution is ruled out and the modern sector's principal markets are external, it is not responsive to domestic demand management, and an expansionary shock to the modern sector does not generate multiplier-type demand and output increases in a positive feedback with the backward sector because of their segmentation.

Although the actual disarticulation of developing economies' production systems today takes many diverse forms, and simple dual-economy or enclave models are invalid, it has the same effect of undermining basic Keynesian principles. If globalisation of production is the central dynamic today, its result is that in each developing country production is dominated by world market conditions mediated through transnational corporations' decisions on their global operations. The operations of different firms in a country are not articulated within a national system of interrelated activity, and in that calculus national demand management policies are of little account except insofar as they affect currency instability.

The financial systems of developing countries are disarticulated in two senses, both of which result from the fact that the rise of truly global financial markets and financial liberalisation mean that any developing countries' financial system is an output of the global system. One type of resulting disarticulation is the low degree of interconnection between the different financial institutions within the country (weak local interbank markets and fragile links between domestic institutions and domestic markets). The other is the disarticulation between the financial system and the production system, because portfolio decisions are taken with respect to global markets instead of the markets for domestic savings and investment. As a result, interest rates are determined by world market conditions and exchange rate expectations, and in thin local markets are highly volatile in a manner inconsistent with standard Keynesian assumptions. Such disarticulation is an obstacle to Keynesian demand management partly because it magnifies any crowding-out effects of government deficit financing. Deficit expansion is a signal for increased inflationary expectations on the foreign exchange markets which drives up domestic interest rates to levels at which the cost of capital prevents industrial investment. In the opposite direction, tight monetary and fiscal policy also has a magnified effect as foreign capital is drawn into the domestic financial markets, leading to an overvalued exchange rate that undermines production of tradables.

PROBLEM OF SOVEREIGNTY

The economic fragility represented by disarticulation is one reason for the extreme weakness of the state in developing countries. Policy-oriented models, whether Keynesian or not, assume that a state exists with the power and ability to formulate and execute policy; they assume economic sovereignty. Economic sovereignty is a concept designating the state's power to regulate the economy. It is never an absolute but measures the degree to which a state can exercise authority both with respect to external forces and over the operations of domestic agents. Since the states of most developing countries have extremely low degrees of economic sovereignty, Keynesian policy models cannot be applied.

One cause is economic disarticulation, which prevents the state from developing stable, elastic tax bases, thereby generating chronic fiscal crises that prevent the building of an effective civil administration. The tax base of an economy dominated by globalised production and trading systems is weakened by the ease with which profits are ultimately booked abroad and by that economy's fragmented labour force with significant informal sector activity. In a high proportion of developing economies, the same economic fragility causes external indebtedness which, combined with the weakened civil administration's inability to manage economic policy alone, leads to the effective loss of sovereignty to international bodies that devise and monitor the execution of structural adjustment and stabilisation programmes.

CONCLUSIONS

The problems outlined here seem to present insuperable obstacles to the reconstruction of a Keynesian-type model appropriate for developing economies. A difficulty in presenting any such case is that there exist several interpretations of what the defining characteristics of a Keynesian model are. I have used the simplest textbook versions, comparative static models in which Keynesian demand management would be effective, and considered their applicability. But they were chosen only to simplify the exposition, and it is important to recognise that rather better specified Keynesian dynamic models are the issue for development economics. However, the obstacles I have illustrated with the simple model also apply to the dynamic models ably discussed by Dutt and FitzGerald.

Reference

Banuri, T. and Shor, J. B. (1992) *Financial Openness and National Autonomy* (Oxford: Clarendon Press).

Index